Words of Witness

Wisconsin Studies in Autobiography

WILLIAM L. ANDREWS
Series Editor

WORDS OF WITNESS

Black Women's Autobiography
in the Post-*Brown* Era

Angela A. Ards

The University of Wisconsin Press

The University of Wisconsin Press
1930 Monroe Street, 3rd Floor
Madison, Wisconsin 53711-2059
uwpress.wisc.edu

3 Henrietta Street, Covent Garden
London WC2E 8LU, United Kingdom
eurospanbookstore.com

Printed in the United States of America

This book may be available in a digital edition

Library of Congress Cataloging-in-Publication Data

Ards, Angela Ann, 1969–, author.
Words of witness: black women's autobiography in the post-Brown era / Angela A. Ards.
pages   cm. — (Wisconsin studies in autobiography)
Includes bibliographical references and index.
ISBN 978-0-299-30504-8 (pbk.   )
1. African American women—Biography—Political aspects.
2. African American women authors—Biography—Political aspects.
3. African American feminists—Biography.   4. Autobiography—African American authors.
5. Autobiography—Women authors.   6. Beals, Melba. Warriors don't cry.
7. McNatt, Rosemary Bray. Unafraid of the dark.   8. Jordan, June, 1936–2002. Soldier.
9. Danticat, Edwidge, 1969–. Brother, I'm dying.   10. Davis, Eisa. Angela's mixtape.
I. Title.   II. Series: Wisconsin studies in autobiography.
PS153.N5A84   2015
810.9'49207208996073—dc23
2015009297

In memory of

Roslyn Denise Ards

We are the subjects of our own narrative,
witnesses to and participants in our own experience,
and, in no way coincidentally, in the experiences of those
with whom we have come in contact.

TONI MORRISON

Contents

Acknowledgments

This book would never have been completed without the generous support of several institutions and the counsel of many mentors and friends. While serving as oral historian for the youth-leadership organization LISTEN, I had the first glimmers of this project: using story in service of social justice. I am thankful to its visionary founder, the late Lisa Sullivan, and colleagues from that period who remind me still that it is the people in the text who matter most: Kim Davis, Ditra Edwards, Taj James, Sean Joe, Rehva Jones, Toya Lillard, Marian Urquilla, and Marta Urquilla. The early research of this project was funded by the Center for the Study of Religion (CSR) and the Program (now Department) for African American Studies at Princeton University. I am indebted to a dynamic community of scholars who informed, shaped, and enriched my thinking through generative conversation and camaraderie: Steven Adams, Deborah Blanks, John Bugg, Nadia Ellis, Diana Fuss, Bill Gaskins, Eddie Glaude, Briallen Hopper, Rena Jordan, Su'ad Khabeer, Miriam Petty, Noliwe Rooks, Albert Raboteau, Paul Raushenbush, and Keri Walsh. I especially want to acknowledge CSR fellows Rebecca Davis, Jon Pahl, and Melissa Proctor, who were my first readers and provided thoughtful advice.

The Radcliffe Institute for Advanced Study and the W. E. B. Du Bois Research Institute of the Hutchins Center at Harvard University supported my time away from teaching so that I could conduct new research and complete manuscript revisions. During my time there I had the opportunity to engage with accomplished scholars and artists from a variety of disciplines whose utter brilliance inspired me to persevere with this work: Elizabeth Alexander, Paolo Asso, Raymond Atuguba, Donald Berman, Robin Bernstein, David Bindman, Lawrence Bobo, Daphne Brooks, Jenni Case, Radiclani Clytus, Lisa Coleman, Huey Copeland, Taylor Davis, Paul Desenne, Abigail English, Cedric Essi, Marla Frederick, Rosemarie Garland-Thomson, Karlene Griffiths, Joshua

Guild, Lani Guinier, Alicia Hall-Moran, Anna Maria Hong, Evan Horowitz, Dolan Hubbard, Erica James, Gene Jarrett, Ann Jones, Charla Jones, Lynne Jones, Tayari Jones, Florence Ladd, Josslyn Luckett, Carla Martin, Rose McDermott, Jason Moran, Scott Poulson-Bryant, Joan Ruderman, Jacqueline Santos, Osagyefo Sekou, Lorelle Semley, Amy Sillman, Hank Willis Thomas, John Tiffany, Touré, Stephen Tuck, Kate Tuttle, Jonathan Walton, Omar Wasow, and Joycelyn Wilson.

A very special thanks to the staff and research assistants whose guidance and support made this project a reality. The Radcliffe year was truly one of a lifetime because of the vibrant community convened by Marlon Cummings, Barbara Grosz, Sharon Lim-Hing, Melissa Synnot, and Judith Vichniac. At the Schlesinger Library, I am particularly grateful to Nancy Cott and Marilyn Morgan for invaluable research advice and leads. My dependable and thorough research partners, Victoria Wenger, Fallon O'Dowd, and Julia Jeffries, enriched my project beyond my imagining, and my PowerPoint skills improved immensely under their tutelage. I also had the great fortune of being included in the family that is the W. E. B Du Bois Institute. I am grateful to Alvin Carter III, Vera Grant, Krishna Lewis, Tom Wolejko, Abby Wolf, and Donald Yacovone, who made 104 Auburn Street a home away from home.

I had the opportunity to share earlier versions of various chapters with the Literature Section at the Massachusetts Institute of Technology, the Modernism Seminar at Harvard University, the Center for the Study of Race and Democracy at Tufts University, and the Dallas Institute for Humanities and Culture. Deep thanks to Larry Allums, Peniel Joseph, Anita Patterson, Shankar Raman, and John Paul Riquelme for inviting me into conversations that challenged and strengthened this work. I greatly appreciate colleagues who took the time to read chapters and offered helpful critiques: Shari Goldberg, Dan Moss, Walton Muyumba, and Evette Porter. And I am honored that this book found a home at the University of Wisconsin Press. Thanks to series editor William Andrews for his belief in this project; to executive editor Raphael Kadushin and his editorial team, Matthew Cosby and Amber Rose, for guiding it, and me, through the successive stages; and to the fabulous readers for their absolutely invaluable feedback.

The Department of English at Southern Methodist University has been a nurturing environment for my continued growth as a scholar and writer. A University Research Council grant and an English department research leave allowed me invaluable time to revise the manuscript. I am grateful to my colleagues for their support and camaraderie, especially Richard Bozorth, Darryl

Dickson-Carr, Dennis Foster, David Haynes, Bruce Levy, Ross Murfin, Beth Newman, Nina Schwartz, Willard Spiegelman, Rajani Sudan, and Bonnie Wheeler. I owe great thanks to the department's staff, especially Leslie Reid, for their patience and good humor. And I am indebted to the students in the autobiography courses where I worked through my ideas, though none more than the undergraduates of "Literature for Real: The Memoir and the Essay": Ivonne Balli, Amanda Beard, Emmaline Carrick, Olivia Cassidy, Jeremy Clifford, Miranda Hanson, Michelle Marriott, Mehreen Mazhar, Mary Mikule, Roxanne Perez, Gareth Riley-Ayers, and Callie Summer. My current and former graduate students, Summer Hamilton, Anna Hinton, and Anna Nelson, continue to be sources of inspiration.

For creating innumerable opportunities for me and providing critical wisdom at every turn as I imagined, struggled with, and finally wrote this book, I give abundant thanks to Herman Beavers, Jeanne Whitman Bobbitt, Cassandra Clay, Henry Louis Gates Jr., William Gleason, Jennifer Greeson, Darlene Clark Hine, Marcyliena Morgan, and Mark Anthony Neal. I am especially grateful to Valerie Smith and Richard Yarborough for their great generosity and necessary guidance. For almost a quarter century now, I have benefited from their mentorship, friendship, strategic savvy, spiritual fortitude, patience, and perspective. This book simply would not exist without their support, seen and unseen, and their unwavering faith in me.

Returning to Texas after two decades away was an easy transition because of friends and family, colleagues and creative partners, who accompanied me on the journey. Endless thanks to Jeremy Adams, Ed Countryman, Carol Dickson-Carr, Paula Dobbs-Wiggins, Irina Dumitrescu, Pam Elder, Pam Eudaric, Andrew Gillings, Jeff and Maria Dixon Hall, Kenneth Hamilton, Wendy Hanes, Millicent Johnnie, Lori Jones, Candice Lucas-Bledsoe, Owen Lynch, Alexis McCrossen, Diane Miles, LeAndrew and Barbara Hill Moore, Michelle Nawar, Donée Thomas-Patterson, Kim Persley, Diana Riehl, John Scagliotti, Tinsley Silcox and Joe Guzman, Gretchen Smith, Rosalyn Story, Terri Stroud, Karen Thomas, Melvin and Wanola Thomas, Vickie Washington, LaToya Watson, Jessica Dixon Weaver, Anthony Tillman and Lori White, Joel and Terilyn Winful, Leslie Wingard, and JoAnn Wypijewski. I also extend heartfelt thanks to the Southside of Lamar Boot Camp members whose workouts kept me "looking good and feeling better": Mary, Anita and Roger, Red, Pink, Quinn, Liz and T.C., Nick and Ferrell and baby Kingson, Ms. Zenetta, Vicki, Tracey, Stacey, Yemmi, Al, Oscar, Crystal, Josslyn, Jen, Kami, and our wonderful trainer, Melvin Sanders. And while I truly appreciate the friends who did not mention the book when I did not want to talk about it, I am happy for the extended family that did. Thanks to all my aunts, uncles, and cousins who expected and encouraged me to finish what I started.

I must acknowledge the support of three people in particular who labored alongside me as I completed this book. Lisa Thompson, a dear friend of twenty years, insisted that I keep writing through the ugly drafts and brooked no excuses, all the while sharing weekly check-ins and holiday visits. Her tough love and true sisterhood made all the difference. I am deeply indebted to my writing partner Sanderia Faye for the words of encouragement, walks on the Katy Trail, and all the days that I had to step out on her faith. I cannot imagine this book without the impromptu summer writing retreat where we pulled each other through the lonely slog of revisions. And finally, I owe immeasurable gratitude to Judith Tannenbaum, a confidante and mentor and cherished friend, who cheered me on from afar with the most thoughtful cards and the best chocolate chocolate-chip cake ever.

When I graduated from high school, my English teacher Pat "Doc" Saxon gifted me with a stack of books that included Langston Hughes, Zora Neale Hurston, Richard Wright, Toni Morrison, and Alice Walker, sparking an enduring love of literature and writing. I am forever indebted to her and the late Joyce Rainwater for mentoring and mothering me, and hope that I make half the difference in someone's life that they have made in mine.

My family's support has allowed me to pursue many goals, even as they took me far from home. Everlasting thanks to my beloved mother, Edith Frazier, who taught me to love the music and power of words as I listened to her pray. She is a woman of faith whose "words of witness" have inspired and emboldened my engagement with the world, and I am grateful for her example and enduring love. To my late sister, Roslyn, who named me Angela Ann ("messenger of grace"), providing a sense of purpose that I am still striving to meet. And to my big brother, Reginald, and favorite nephew, Koby, whose abiding love and pride sustain me always.

Words of Witness

Introduction
The Ethics of Self-Fashioning

Before entering graduate studies in English, I was a journalist for more than a decade at the *Village Voice*, the *Nation*, and *Ms.* magazine, where, among other issues, I covered the ways black communities were creating new vocabularies and strategies to address the political and moral dilemmas of the contemporary era. Not coincidentally, many key concerns of my reporting are at stake in the autobiographies featured here: black feminist organizing to bring women's concerns and sensibilities into the public sphere, the meaning of blackness and agency in an age of immigration, the rise of hip-hop culture. With the structural changes in the political economy after the fall of Jim Crow, from the rightward ideological shift after the so-called Reagan revolution to the diversifying interests among black America, scholars have noted the need for "a shift in the political lexicon," a recalibration in vocabularies and strategies of struggle.[1] I witnessed and experienced that reality firsthand as the historian for Local Initiative Support Training and Education Network (LISTEN), a youth-development organization founded by the late Lisa Y. Sullivan, one of the most dynamic black activists of the 1990s. In the spirit of Ella Baker and Septima Clark, LISTEN developed youth leadership from the ground up, providing infrastructure support for varying models of community activism. Sullivan often noted that, across the political spectrum—whether engaged in "hip-hop activism," modes of black nationalism, or pragmatic, policy-oriented approaches—an emerging generation lacked the language and values, an ethical discourse, that might give their politics meaning and context. Her insight echoes Cornel West, who has argued that without an emotive, spiritual language that engenders *metanoia*, a radical change in how one perceives herself in the world and consequently responds to its challenges, it is impossible to revitalize black civil society.[2]

Thinking about this relationship between language and action prompted me to consider the role of narrative—sheer storytelling—in developing a progressive politic. I imagined writing a memoir that documented the various activist strategies in relation to each other, thinking that, through the juxtaposed narratives, the evolving ethics embedded in each might be more evident by contrast and, thus, *useable* for fashioning a contemporary progressive politic. However, I found myself stalled. First, I needed distance, temporal and psychic, from the reporting. Second, I needed to work through some methodological questions: How to bring lived experience to bear on communal questions of identity and agency without falling into the navel-gazing trap of solipsism so characteristic of the "neoconfessional" trend in contemporary memoir? How to create a linked-fate narrative when black communities, never monolithic, reflect an even greater multiplicity of identities that complicate old paradigms based solely on race? I examined the works of contemporary black women autobiographers to see how they approached these questions. *Words of Witness* is the result.

The book's critical approach of examining the intersection of personal narrative and political discourse builds on critical frameworks that bring scholarship on black autobiography into conversation with the broader field of autobiography studies.[3] In the last generation, mainstream criticism has focused on the discursive nature of identity construction, the processes and strategies of life writing.[4] Critics of African American autobiography have focused less on deconstructing narrative selves than on proving them capable of participating in the broader public sphere.[5] In attending to language, its performance and structures, while also considering how those structures relate to the larger political economy, the autobiographies featured here seek to place black feminist thought in conversation with modern political theory. Autobiography is often called the founding motif of the black literary tradition, but it is arguably the foundation of black political thought as well.[6] Since its eighteenth-century origins with the slave narratives, black American autobiography has been a platform for political argument and ideological commentary, from Olaudah Equiano's genre-defining *Interesting Narrative* and Frederick Douglass's three autobiographical volumes, to Angela Davis's self-titled political autobiography and Barack Obama's two presidential memoirs. *Words of Witness* situates itself within this longstanding literary and political history as it examines the ways contemporary black women autobiographers craft their life stories to engage modern political and social thought.

Interrogating the intersections of personal narrative and political discourse, or what I call here "the ethics of self-fashioning," has increasingly been the focus of conferences, journals, and books as Obama's historic presidency and memoirs have piqued academic and popular interest in the relationship between black subjectivity and politics.[7] For instance, James Kloppenberg's *Reading*

Obama examines the narrative technique and structure of both *Dreams from My Father* and *The Audacity of Hope* for how they engage American democratic thought, from the Constitution to philosophical pragmatism, through characterization, scene reconstruction, and narrative. And Robert Gooding-Williams's *In the Shadow of Du Bois* uses Du Bois's *The Souls of Black Folk* as a lens to reevaluate the history of black American political thought, building upon Eric Sundquist's seminal readings of Douglass's *My Bondage and My Freedom*. The current trend, however, reinforces the "great men" paradigm that has long characterized most accounts of black intellectual activity. In focusing on autobiographies of black women writers, *Words of Witness* is part of a renewed effort in African American studies to recover the history of black women as intellectual subjects.[8] An earlier study, Margo Perkins's *Autobiography as Activism: Three Black Women of the Sixties*, examines how the Black Power memoirs of Angela Davis, Assata Shakur, and Elaine Brown chronicle the formation of "radical black female subjectivity" and the ways those texts seek to inspire readers to oppositional politics. Here, the focus is not on charting the process of political radicalization— even though that is central to some of the narratives discussed, as is the idea of how these texts engage readers in political discourse and practice—but on placing these writers within contemporary political thought.

Building the burgeoning field of black women's intellectual history requires that scholars consider not only geographies, that is, how place and history contextualize ideas, but also intellectual genealogies, the social discourses and various interlocutors subjects engage.[9] The five texts featured here were published between 1994 and 2009, five decades after the passage of *Brown v. Board of Education*, the landmark legislation that established the precedent for ending racial segregation in the United States. They reflect a range of feminist responses to the civil rights and Black Power movements, two and three generations removed, with each using terms and concepts that are in dialogue with particular legacies, such as the Little Rock Nine campaign (Melba Beals's *Warriors Don't Cry*) and the Free Angela campaign (Eisa Davis's *Angela's Mixtape*); microhistories, such as the 1960s welfare rights movement (Rosemary Bray's *Unafraid of the Dark: A Memoir*); and social issues, such as immigration (June Jordan's *Soldier: A Poet's Childhood* and Edwidge Danticat's *Brother, I'm Dying*). All are revisionist, alternate histories rooted in the familial and social experiences of these activist-writers whose narratives reflect, from different vantage points, their own relationships and conversations with the social movements of the 1960s and '70s.

Black women's autobiographies represent, to borrow a phrase from Joanne Braxton, "a tradition within a tradition" for the ways that they deconstruct male-centered notions of black identity, progress, and freedom, as first championed in Douglass's 1845 *Narrative*, reified in *The Autobiography of Malcolm X*, and arguably revived in Obama's *Dreams from My Father*.[10] Contemporary scholarship on black women's autobiography often follows Braxton's approach of considering the relationship between gender and genre, the ways black women's writing differs in theme and style from that of black men.[11] Gender politics has been and remains an important area of critical inquiry. However, rather than the gender-genre nexus, *Words of Witness* examines these autobiographies as part of an intellectual history that stretches back at least to Jacobs. The point is not to show how black women's autobiographical discourse is inherently different from men's but to give it voice as a body of feminist thought in conversation with modern political theory. Melissa Harris-Perry's *Sister Citizen: Shame, Stereotypes, and Black Women in America* has a similar aim as it explores the impact of stereotypes, or "the politics of misrecognition," on black women's citizenship practices and possibilities. Using lived experience as a source for research is a central methodology in black feminist thought. Harris-Perry relies on focus groups, alongside contemporary fiction and social science research. *Words of Witness* approaches this project through autobiography, for embedded within personal narratives are inherent theories of identity formation that can be read for their relationship to political concepts such as citizenship rights and responsibilities, affect and agency. Just as Douglass's *Narrative* engaged the Emersonian notion of "representative men" and as Harriet Jacobs's *Incidents in the Life of a Slave Girl* deconstructed the nineteenth-century "cult of true womanhood," *Words of Witness* argues that the narrative personas embedded within these texts are reflective of post-*Brown* political aesthetics.

Although the book is invested in how autobiographers use rhetorical strategies and cultural idioms to create a persona, it is less interested in how language characterizes the writer than in how it illuminates the times, how narrative identities underwrite contemporary political discourse. Understanding the relationship between aesthetics and politics, or the politics of form, is to understand the historical moment in which narratives are written. Similar to the ways in which "the sixties" has come to define both a historic decade and a radical ethic, the period after the twentieth-century civil rights and Black Power movements has come to be associated with certain defining sensibilities. The most familiar term designating the period, "post–civil rights," has come to be associated with a celebratory story culminating in the 1964 Civil Rights Act of 1964 and the Voting Rights Act of 1965. However, recent laws and challenges that unravel these same civil rights gains—from voter suppression and mass incarceration, to the war on drugs and the war on education, to name a few— have made that triumphant narrative now seem premature, if not pyrrhic.

Political retrenchment characterizes the current historic moment, alternately dubbed a Second Reconstruction and the New Nadir.[12] The social movements emerging out of Ferguson, Missouri, in the summer of 2014 challenge what some have called the "post-modern malaise" or the "rupture with politics" supposedly characteristic of this era, as a new generation continues civil rights struggles that many thought were already won.[13] In this study, I therefore avoid the triumphalist term *post–civil rights* in favor of *post-"Brown"* for several reasons. First of all, the latter better historically locates the period, specifying that the project focuses on black life and culture after the passage of *Brown*. In addition, using *post–civil rights* reinforces the already contested heroic narrative of the civil rights movement (1954–1968) and encourages the erroneous idea that the fight for civil rights is a single era or a particularly modern phenomenon, rather than a reaction to conditions. The abolitionist movement during the late eighteenth to mid-nineteenth century, for instance, was a civil rights struggle. And despite the proclamations of a postracial America following the historic election of the nation's first black president, the fight for civil rights is ongoing, as the post-Ferguson movements show. The term *post-"Brown"* also serves to clarify the confusion the prefix often engenders. For some, *post* suggests the idea of *after*, as if the era is over and past. For others, *post* signifies *beyond*, registering as a repudiation of prior values and strategies. While *Words of Witness* examines these autobiographies with an eye for the creation of a progressive politic, the study acknowledges that any future black politic must recognize the past. In using the term *post-"Brown,"* the intent is not to discredit the movement's aims and accomplishments but to address the inadequacy of the traditional political discourse that *Brown* now represents.

The select autobiographies included here are not meant to be representative of a post-*Brown* black women's autobiographical canon, for autobiographies and eras do not necessarily correlate. Cultural context certainly shapes personal circumstance and experience, but individual responses are unique and thus generate a variety of life narratives. Some writings reflect a dominant discourse; others, an alternate one; and still others are emergent narratives. Life histories, rather, map the broad contours of an era—its continuum of cultural shifts, social discourses, and political thought.[14] Johnnie Stover's scholarship on select nineteenth-century African American women's autobiography as social discourse influences the way I conceptualize *Words of Witness*. Stover writes, "The creative aspects of autobiography suggest the importance that place and time have on the development of the author and on the way in which that author then reinterprets the self for the reading of others. The self of the author is very much a part of the autobiography, so we as readers need to know out of what

social, spatial, and temporary locations that self emerged."[15] Because cultural
assumptions and preoccupations determine the idioms that writers use, *Words
of Witness* examines these autobiographies as contemporary case studies that
demonstrate how critically reading authors' self-fashioning strategies—the
narrative personas created and scenes constructed—can illuminate an era's
emergent ethics.

The project of examining how black women writers craft their lived experience to shape contemporary political discourse echoes the first book-length
study of black autobiography, Rebecca Chalmers Barton's *Witnesses for Freedom:
Negro Americans in Autobiography* (1946). Barton used her analysis of twenty-three
authors to interpret the significance of Gunnar Myrdal's *An American Dilemma:
The Negro Problem and Modern Democracy* (1944), extrapolating from these intellectual texts various ethical standards that might help improve race relations.[16]
Similarly, *Words of Witness* shows black feminist intellectuals theorizing about
traditional political subjects, such as the meaning of political formation and
action. The study also explores how these texts engage more contemporary
preoccupations around the place of affect, such as love, mourning, and joy in
the public sphere, reflecting an "affective turn" in black-feminist thought. Traditionally, political theory has opposed bringing emotion into the public sphere
for fear it might destabilize the rationality upon which liberal societies supposedly
operate, ultimately undermining freedom. In *Political Emotions: Why Love Matters
for Justice*, however, Martha Nussbaum argues that justice-loving societies, and
movements, for that matter, must cultivate emotional support of their political
culture and discourse if they are to be sustained.[17] The political implications for
doing this emotional work have been explored powerfully in *Sister Citizen*, as
Harris-Perry assesses how encountering, and deflecting, stereotypes engenders
both shame and stress, curtailing black women's full participation in the public
sphere. Scholars Darlene Clark Hine and Evelyn Higginbotham have noted
how black women have assumed a "culture of dissemblance" and the "politics of
respectability," respectively, protective strategies of emotional self-concealment
to fight against racism and sexism. In some instances, the unintended consequence has been a body of black feminist thought and praxis estranged from
affect and desire. Part of the project of articulating a black women's intellectual
tradition, then, is "to recover wholeness and sentience" and "to reclaim the
tender side" of black women's intellect[18] in service of a progressive future politic.

Many scholars argue that the breadth of such a future politic is hampered
because the dominant narrative of the civil rights movement (1954–1968),
whose protests and freedom songs still provide the template for contemporary
black political engagement, has been divorced from the progressivism of the

preceding New Deal era and the subsequent radicalism of the Black Power movement.[19] To recover these hidden politics, policies, and institutions of the "long civil rights movement," Jacqueline Dowd Hall has called on writers and scholars to produce personal narratives that supplement and challenge received movement history. In recent years, scholars have taken up this charge through biographies of famous activists, such as Chana Kai Lee on Fannie Lou Hamer, Barbara Ransby on Ella Baker and Eslanda Robeson, Gerald Horne on Shirley Graham Du Bois, Carol Boyce Davies on Claudia Jones, and Sherie Randolph on Florynce Kennedy. The edited essay collection *Want to Start a Revolution?* profiles unsung activists such as Esther Cooper Jackson, Victoria Garvin, and Johnnie Tillmon, shattering the "leading man" narrative of the black freedom movement and expanding notions of radicalism beyond self-defense and separatism. *Words of Witness* joins this critical conversation by examining the way autobiographies and memoirs of contemporary literary figures, both well and lesser known, contribute to this effort to broaden the understanding of black identity and politics.

In terms of form and narrative pattern, autobiographies are as varied as their authors. To provide a point of reference for interpreting the diverse personas and politics articulated in these texts, the study relies on cultural memory: the ways societies reconstitute themselves by recalling a shared past. A guiding assumption here is that the modern civil rights movement is such a master narrative:

> It usually begins with *Brown v. Board of Education*, quickly followed by the murder of Emmett Till in 1955—both events spurring an already hopeful, if not angry, black community into action. Black anger and hopefulness are traced to black support for the Good War against fascism abroad a decade earlier; they were, after all, loyal to America, and now it was time for the state to grant black folk democracy and citizenship. Then Montgomery showed the world what black protest could accomplish, thus giving birth to the modern civil rights movement. Local and national campaigns waged by the Southern Christian Leadership Council (SCLC), the Congress on Racial Equality (CORE), and the Student Nonviolent Coordinating Committee (SNCC), to name only the big three, fought for citizenship, the right to vote, and desegregation and succeeded in getting the federal government to pass the Civil Rights Act (1964) and the Voting Rights Act (1965).[20]

Of course this consensus memory is a historical construction increasingly critiqued for perpetuating fixed, dated notions of black subjectivity and struggle.[21] Scholars rightly warn that uncritical reference to this heroic narrative to frame and understand current affairs and politics precludes developing a viable black politic. The tropes of sacrifice, suffering, and radical action embedded within the archetypal narrative are so familiar that "they, in effect, do our thinking for us," with outdated ideas about black identity and politics obscuring the complexities of today's political dilemmas and moral choices.[22] In engaging this familiar and contested narrative, *Words of Witness* draws on Houston Baker's formulation of critical memory, which avoids nostalgia ("a purposive construction of the past filled with golden virtues, golden men, and sterling events") in favor of a more probing perspective that "renders hard ethical evaluations of the past that it never defines as well-passed."[23] In this study, the narrative of the civil rights movement thus serves to assess the ways these autobiographies *retool* its parameters and assumptions, pushing against received representations of the past to reveal exigencies of the present.

Recalibrating the Political Lexicon

Modern black political thought differs from other major schools (for instance, the social contract theory of Hobbes, Locke, Rousseau, Kant, and later Rawls; ancient Jewish political thought; nineteenth-century French liberal thought) in that it is less interested in the nation-state than with regimes of white supremacy within the nation-state, such as plantation politics, colonialism, apartheid, Jim Crow. In the United States, black political thought has been concerned first with slavery, then segregation, and now this post-*Brown* moment of political retrenchment. Twentieth-century black politics has been defined by a charismatic, elite leadership model bequeathed from W. E. B. Du Bois's "talented tenth," as well as the idea of black politics emanating from a shared cultural ethos, "the souls of black folk." The integration/assimilation versus nationalism/separatism debate has been a defining theme, with respectability politics and mass mobilization the most central strategies.[24] *Words of Witness* joins a growing consensus among scholars that traditional political discourse and strategy have proven inadequate to address the realities and dilemmas of the post-*Brown* era. The plethora of terms coined in the recent years to define contemporary black identity and politics—*post–civil rights, post-segregation, post-soul*—reflects a more populist need to craft new discourses that account for the structural changes and cultural shifts following the passage of civil rights legislation in the mid-1960s.[25] Since then, black communities have begun to reflect an even greater multiplicity of identities, with "cross-cutting" issues such as gender and class, sexuality and ethnicity, complicating old agendas and allegiances based solely on race.[26] The increasing variation in black life demands a shift in the political lexicon: new vocabularies for conceptualizing black identity, new strategies for constructing progressive black politics. In the last generation, three political crises in particular have revealed the need for fresh mobilizing trope and tactics: the Clarence Thomas–Anita Hill hearings, Hurricane Katrina, and Obama's historic presidency.

For many, perhaps no crisis was as startling as Thomas's nomination and confirmation to the Supreme Court, and the subsequent sexual harassment hearings. His now-infamous imputation of the televised proceedings as a "high-tech lynching" tapped into a longstanding political discourse that viewed the lynched black-male body as the most charged symbol of racism and the reassertion of black male authority as the most strategic response.[27] Consequently, a majority of blacks nationwide rallied behind Thomas's beleaguered nomination. No matter that his charge was a cynical manipulation that cast a man who had fled associations with black America as a victim of racial violence. No matter that he stood poised, with mediocre legal record and neoconservative politics in hand, to preside over a generation of civil rights retrenchment. No matter that Anita Hill's claims of sexual harassment were indeed credible. The nationalist and sexist ideologies embedded within the lynching narrative masked competing concerns about gender, subsequently fueling a patriarchal and parochial politic of preserving the "black [male] seat" on the court.[28] Thomas's subsequent tenure on the bench, in which he has ruled against policies and legislation that would have continued to redress racial discrimination, has exposed the outdated integrationist logic of "symbolic representation, that is, the belief that if an African American receives a prominent appointment in the government, the private sector, or the media, that Black people as a group are symbolically empowered."[29] In the post-*Brown* era, with racial allegiances no longer trumping gender, class, or political differences, black Americans could no longer trust in a trickle-down blackness, in which having individuals in high public offices somehow translates into advancement for the group.

A decade later, Hurricane Katrina exposed stark class issues still lingering long after the abandonment of the Poor People's Campaign in the wake of Martin Luther King Jr.'s assassination. The horrific images of black Americans wading through the murky waters and waving U.S. flags from rooftops, awaiting government aid that came too late or not all, raised questions about the federal commitment to black citizens and what the 1960s black freedom struggle had actually accomplished.[30] Hip-hop artist Kanye West's infamous accusation that "George W. Bush doesn't care about black people" reflected, for many,

"what the federal response in all its absences and shortcomings seemed to suggest."[31] West's statement revealed the inadequacy of contemporary black political thought on at least two levels. On the one hand, it confirmed the absence of spaces for frank deliberation and the articulation of differing viewpoints outside those permitted and encouraged by mainstream arbiters.[32] On the other, its singular race narrative failed to describe the complex causes and impact of the devastation, to discuss the structural realities and the malign neglect that ensured those who lived in the poorest areas and were the most vulnerable to natural disaster were primarily black. As Eddie Glaude writes in *In a Shade of Blue*, "What was striking about this moment involved, among other things, the fact that many groped for language to describe the horrible images they saw. And as they searched, what was revealed with remarkable clarity was a startling inability on the part of many people, including black leaders, to avoid the easy trap of thinking about racism solely in terms of institutional prejudice. The structural dimensions of racism that revealed themselves in the very material conditions of poor black New Orleaneans could not be captured in a sound bite or in the traditional language of the civil rights establishment."[33] But perhaps what was even more unsettling was that there was no language outside of American citizenship to challenge the exclusion.[34] Many have discussed the marginalizing impact of calling those fleeing the storm "refugees," as if they were foreigners without claim to citizenship, people for whom the government might bestow humanitarian aid, if so inclined. Katrina victims consequently staked claims as law-abiding, tax-paying American citizens to protest the erasure. Staking claim to American citizenship through protest, what Glaude has called "soul-craft politics," has been a common political strategy since the nineteenth century.[35] However, Richard Iton suggests, at the dawn of the twenty-first century, this "compulsion to establish national borders" and evoke citizenship not only emanates from an exhausted politics of respectability but also a diminished political imagination. Creating a sense of black identity beyond the national, to something more cosmopolitan and diasporic, is needed, he argues, to reinvigorate a robust politics that might address the issues of this moment, given the realities of globalization and immigration.

Certainly the increasingly diasporic dimensions of black identity came to the fore with the candidacy and presidency of Barack Obama. As a first-generation African American, with a father from Kenya and a mother from Kansas, Obama pushed people to think beyond slave ancestry and national borders as definers of black identity. He has also made people reconsider blackness and its evolving relation to power. As United States president and "leader of the free world," Obama's visage has become the face of American imperialism. While the visuals prompted the declaration of a postracial era, the subsequent racial backlash throughout the country belied that wishful thinking. But as with Thomas's ascendancy to the Supreme Court, Obama's rise to high office, the highest in the country—some might argue the world—challenges the logic of integration and its attendant philosophy of symbolic representation, as his political success has not translated into group advancement. Obama's election and tenure have exposed, once again, the limits of a charismatic, elite leadership model of black politics bequeathed from Du Bois's talented tenth, as well as the biblical Exodus narrative that has framed the black freedom struggle since the nineteenth century.

With the 2008 election coming forty years after Martin Luther King Jr.'s assassination, that prophetic Exodus narrative has acquired even more resonance. As one political commentator wrote at the time, "Apart from our flirtations with Rev. Jesse Jackson and Minister Louis Farrakhan in the 1980s and 90s, we've been stuck in the wilderness without any sort of national Black leadership model for forty long and difficult years. . . . We've been stuck in this vacuum for so long that we expect Mr. Obama to fill it up for us."[36] Cultural and political scripts have fueled the hope that Obama would be "the One" to emerge from this vacuum of black leadership and absent mobilization. The Hollywood fascination with the "magical Negro," for instance, is one factor. David Remnick's *The Bridge: The Life and Rise of Barack Obama* talks about supporters who hoped Obama would be "the bridge" within an increasingly divided America.[37] However, Obama himself has encouraged the association of his political success with black struggle in that he, like King before him, has been very adept at evoking and playing up the Exodus narrative. King's final speech before his assassination famously, and eerily, evoked Moses on the mountaintop: "I may not get there with you but one day we will get to the Promised Land."[38] During Obama's first presidential campaign, on a return to the Edmund Pettus Bridge in Selma, he positioned himself as a modern-day Joshua to King's Moses: "As great as Moses was, despite all that he did, leading a people out of bondage, he didn't cross over the river to see the Promised Land. God told him your job is done . . . We're going to leave it to the Joshua Generation to make sure it happens. There are still battles that need to be fought; some rivers that need to be crossed . . . The previous generation, the Moses generation, pointed the way. They took us 90 percent of the way there. We still got that 10 percent in order to cross over to the other side."[39] John Lewis then reinforced the idea on the eve of Obama's first inauguration when he said, "Barack Obama is what comes at the end of that bridge in Selma," referring to the march that led to the passage of the Voting Rights Act. In essence, Obama's historic presidency has too often been mistaken for the Promised Land itself. And yet, with the nation's first black president in the White House, social realities mock the civil rights movement's most celebrated milestones: schools are more segregated today than they were at the time of *Brown*. "Jail, no bail," the civil disobedience tactic used to dismantle Jim Crow, could just as easily refer to the contemporary incarceration epidemic.[40] The largest black middle class in history is dwarfed fourfold by its underclass. Sixty years after passage of the Voting Rights Act, arguably the movement's zenith, it is both the best and worst of times for black America.

Calls for the creation of progressive politics and movement have come from all quarters, with a focus on rebuilding a black public sphere, or a black counterpublic, as the way to facilitate progressive politic to confront today's realities and conditions.[41] Some question invoking public-sphere theory to reinvigorate black politics, given the exclusionary terms under which the theory was first conceived.[42] Others debate whether a contemporary black counterpublic, or a black politic for that matter, even exists now, given the lack of a visible social movement before the Black Lives Matter campaign since Ferguson; the structural changes in the political economy that have redefined black communities; and the seeming impossibility of a unifying political interest, as Jim Crow was for an earlier generation.[43] But I suggest that these concerns emerge from an outdated philosophy of black politics as necessarily rooted within notions of a priori black unity. Undoubtedly there has been a decline in all public spheres since the nineteenth century. Arguments about the "declining significance of race," however, have been premature. From the incarceration epidemic that legal scholar Michelle Alexander calls the New Jim Crow to the racial backlash in the wake of the election of the nation's first black president, race still matters and is still the major galvanizing force within black America.[44] What is more, multiplicity of experience and worldview has never negated the reality of shared black interests, in the United States or throughout the diaspora. People of African descent have always been defined by multiple identifications and varied affinities.[45] There does not need to be a unified, collective black identity or experience before there is action or a policy. Rather, politics can be the vehicle through which solidarities, racial or otherwise, are forged, the spaces of deliberation and debate that inspire like-minded people to take a collective stand.

Thinking of politics as occurring within counterpublics, within institutions and cultural spaces, rather than emanating from a charismatic individual, shifts the idea of black politics and leadership from the "One" to a sense of collectivity. Traditionally, black counterpublics have been found in the church and the press, and increasingly in social media, such as Twitter.[46] But culture and its institutions also constitute public spheres, what Iton prefers to call "locations":

virtual public squares and plazas, theaters of debates where voices come together and politics are incubated and generated. Contrary to the common scholarly practice of locating social movements within the visible emergence of a political contest, resistance struggles have cultural dimensions. Before any push for political rights, "freedom dreams" must be envisioned. Emergent political discourse begins beyond the state, within the registers of culture, for "if the nation is an imagined community"—as observed by Benedict Anderson—"then this is where it is brought into being."[47] Black counterpublics have long chronicled the history of black people bonded together against or—in the case of hip-hop—despite state power to make change in their communities, from Reconstruction and the nineteenth-century club women's movement, to Du Bois's Talented Tenthers and the hip-hop heads who emerged in the dying embers of the Black Power movement. In the absence of social movements, one can still find the deliberation and debate integral to democracy within cultural institutions, including literature.

Reading Culture as Politics

In *In Search of the Black Fantastic*, Richard Iton argues that because black Americans have been historically disenfranchised from formal politics but overrepresented within the cultural realm, they have had to use culture to achieve political aims and to theorize the relationship between culture and politics, both formal and informal.[48] Nowhere is this more evident than in the black autobiographical tradition. Besides its special place within black letters and political thought, autobiography as a genre lends itself to political theorizing in general and is, therefore, particularly useful for crafting a progressive black politics. Traditional political discourse tends toward the quantifiable and known, the ordered and disciplined.[49] In a search for "seamless coherency," it therefore often succumbs to extremes, such as dogmatism and cynicism, or rigid binaries that fail to account for the actual messiness of political action.[50] For instance, through the integration-separatism binary, the history of black political thought has been represented as an ongoing conversation between the two camps. But black politics, as all politics, is too nuanced for such rigid frameworks, with contemporary political theorists proposing other schema and calling for more flexible approaches.[51] Iton argues that the imaginative registers that fuel revolutionary ideals and break free from the paralyzing dead ends of traditional political discourse can be found in the "nuance, dadaesque ambiguity, and contrapuntality" of popular culture.

As a form of storytelling, autobiography rejects notions of universal and absolute truth in favor of an approach that replicates human experience in all its inconvenient complexity. A storytelling methodology avoids the pitfalls of rigid schematics and ideology as it keeps narratives free from explanation and dogma. But it perhaps also offers the most radical insights for addressing political dilemmas in that it demands critical engagement from readers, an ethical witnessing of what is said and unsaid, as the story facilitates the deliberative space necessary for creating politics, both theory and practice.[52] It is within this space of dialogue and debate that the "black fantastic"—what Iton calls those "agonistic, postracial, and post-colonial visions" generated from the most marginalized—arises. One of culture's most important functions, according to Iton, is "to establish and maintain space for substantive, open-ended deliberative activity and the related commitment to *the nurturing of potentially subversive forms of interiority through and by which private geographies are made available to the public.*"[53] This book's rationale rests on this very premise. In putting these five, select autobiographies in conversation with one another, *Words of Witness* simulates another deliberative space where readers weigh and witness a plurality of perspectives simultaneously and, drawing from each, imagine the new vocabularies and strategies that the moment demands.

In the early twentieth century, mainstream literary study disparaged autobiography as an inferior literary form without generic coherence. As its Greek etymology suggests ("self," "life," "writing"), the genre is a pastiche of personal narrative, history, and fiction whose hybrid nature encourages attention to form. And form attunes us not only to aesthetics but also to politics. In his study of political thought of W. E. B. Du Bois in *The Souls of Black Folk*, Gooding-Williams argues that literary criticism has provided closer attention to the political implications of aesthetics than political theorists.[54] Interestingly, the shift in black feminist thought's preoccupation with gender and other identity politics to a more engaged conversation with power relations and political thought more generally arguably began with scholarship on black feminism as a mode of critical reading. In *Not Just Race, Not Just Gender: Black Feminist Readings*, Valerie Smith builds on legal scholar Kimberlé Crenshaw's work around intersectionality. Smith argues that black feminist criticism was a mode of reading "simultaneity," the overlapping subjectivities within and among people, and the resulting and varying power dynamics. This reading strategy in turn has informed newer fields of literary criticism, as well as analyses of film, theater, music, media, and politics. For instance, in *Activist Sentiments*, P. Gabrielle Foreman explores the layered reading practices in black women's nineteenth-century writings, in which "reading" refers not only to literary production, reception, and consumption but also to how authors "read," or "signify" on, their audiences and their times. Scholars have since extended Smith's "simultaneity" argument from reading practices to cultural production, showing that, in creating works that are conscious of the overlapping, multiple, and socially constructed nature of identity, these creative texts in fact construct theory, their own "guiding principles of the subject's becoming and undoing."[55] The black feminist mode of reading power relations provides a theoretical basis for understanding contemporary autobiography as political thought.

The irony of looking for a progressive politic within works that are themselves products of neoliberal forces, as talk shows, reality TV, and scandals about literary "hoaxes" stoke public desire for "authentic" life stories, does not escape notice here. While situated within a longstanding literary and political history, *Words of Witness* arrives during a contemporary cultural fascination with autobiography. Since the late twentieth century, a "memoir boom" has monopolized the publishing industry, with scholars, media commentators, and cultural critics all noting a proliferation of first-personal narratives of new voices challenging established histories. These demographic changes have sparked both popular and academic demand for "true life stories" that explain America's changing face and political reality. In academia, the field of autobiography studies has consequently become one of the fastest growing. Disciplines across the humanities are seeking personal narratives as globalization increases cultural encounters and reader appetite for information about other ways of life. Consequently, the genre is rapidly becoming a place of curricular convergence as disciplinary boundaries merge and overlap. The elastic, hybrid nature of the autobiographical project itself only amplifies this rising critical and cultural currency. Life writing is about crafting a persona, selecting and shaping incidents of one's life to articulate an ethic about how to move in the world, and then finding narrative strategies to represent that worldview on the page. Autobiography has thus become a favored theoretical space to think through issues of self-disclosure, memory, and performance, as well as the relationship between autobiography and its audience and how it intersects with questions of identity and agency in a world in which people feel increasingly powerless.[56] In popular culture, celebrity memoirs by public figures, from politicians and entertainers to journalists and academics, constitute a large percentage of publishing's current memoir boom, with autobiography appearing in spaces other than books: museum exhibits, films, videos, and other media. Certainly the current contemporary technological milieu, "all those informational micro-memoirs tweaked for Facebook, YouTube, cell phones, blogs, and Webisodes . . . in 140 characters or less,"[57] stokes the circulation of, and desire for, stories about the self.

Increasingly, there are critics who decry what they see as the politically de-
mobilizing effects of these autobiographical intimacies in the public sphere.
Leigh Gilmore well argues that, in addition to coarsening our communities and
cultures, the proliferation of these self-disclosures stoke market forces that
compel certain subjectivities, narratives, and politics—a formula that she labels
the "neoconfessional," a style in which once-private issues (child abuse, depression, addiction, domestic violence) are made public.[58] Certainly contemporary
black autobiographies mirror this market trend, from celebrity memoirs to
tell-alls. Whereas canonical texts once maintained strategic silences—whether
Frederick Douglass and Assata Shakur refusing to disclose how they made their
escapes from slavery and prison, respectively, or Harriet Jacobs underreport-
ing the sexual abuse she endured for fear of alienating her northern female
audience—there has been a contemporary shift to disclosure, with Maya Angelou's then-stunning revelations of sexual abuse in *I Know Why the Caged Bird Sings*
perhaps leading the way. However, fears that the neoconfessional has monopolized the market, stoking proliferation of solipsistic stories that prevent the
publication of more political narratives, are premature, given the spate of post–
Vietnam War captivity narratives, prison memoirs, and political manifestoes
published in the last generation.[59] Representing the self as connected to material
conditions and to communal, even global, histories continues to be a significant
element in contemporary black life writing.

Among these contemporary political narratives are those that employ civil-
rights cultural memory such as the ones explored here.[60] The use of such a
familiar narrative assumes an implicit audience who has "come to expect certain
discourses of identity and history that conform to certain criteria. . . . The inclusion of certain identity contents and the exclusion of others; the incorporations
of certain narrative itineraries and intentionalities, the silencing of others, the
adoption of certain autobiographical voices, the muting of others."[61] By invoking
the classic narrative, then using lived experience to invert the received meaning
of its scope and significance, the autobiographies under study cultivate a reading
audience, presumably constituents of an emergent black public, to prompt new
ways of thinking about black politics and identity. Critical attention to the "use
of aesthetics for ethical purposes can become, in itself, a theory of reading ethically. It is the power of the audiences' response—how we read and shape a
community of readers—that finally enables a redefinition of community itself."[62]
Words of Witness thus asserts that, through engaging civil-rights cultural memory,
these memoirs create a collective intimacy with readers, beyond solipsistic disclosure and market exchange, where mediated shared experience can forge
new political discourses and allegiances.[63]

The Chapters

The book's chapters chart an arc of contemporary black cultural formation. The first two chapters focus on "movement narratives," autobiographies of those who came of age during the civil rights movement but whose lived experiences revise the received understanding about its scope and significance. The next two chapters broaden the purview to immigrant narratives, given that one of the movement's major legislative victories, the Immigration and Nationality Act of 1965, and its implications for black identity and citizenship, is often omitted from the classic civil-rights movement story. The final chapter explores hip-hop memoirs, for perhaps no narrative has so inverted the politics and poetics of the civil rights movement than this Bronx-born youth culture gone global.

The project embraces the idea that, as the etymology shows, autobiographies are constructions, a pastiche of literary forms, cultural idioms, and rhetorical acts. Consequently, each chapter maps the relationship between narrative pattern (childhood memoir, bildungsroman, immigrant narrative, *testimonio*, auto/biography) and identity construction (martyr, "the least of these," poet, mother, hip-hop head). My close readings of narrative personas and patterns show how these writers recalibrate the conventional political lexicon and, thereby, make an array of contributions to modern political thought, from challenging traditional civil rights discourse and rethinking the meaning of political action to theorizing the place of affect, such as love and mourning, alienation and joy, in the public sphere.

To interrogate the movement narrative is to grapple with the religious idioms embedded within it. The book thus opens with a discussion of Melba Beals's *Warriors Don't Cry: A Searing Memoir of the Battle to Integrate Little Rock's Central High*. Of all the texts featured, it is the one that most invokes the pieties of sacrifice and suffering, as well as the biblical images of Exodus and Ethiopia, that have animated black freedom struggles since the nineteenth century. Structured by canonical scripture, particularly Psalms 68:31, and by the African American spiritual "On the Battlefield for My Lord," *Warriors* depicts the movement as a religious revival animated by a liberationist theology. The classic civil rights narrative usually casts the martyred King as the messianic Moses. In Beals's retelling, however, the martyrs are the nine teenagers on the frontlines of this desegregation campaign. The sacrificial imagery used to effect this narrative inversion prompts a reconsideration of traditional civil rights discourse as it engages long-standing debates about rights and citizenship and the meaning of political action—from the Hannah Arendt–Ralph Ellison post–Little Rock exchange about "citizenship as sacrifice" to critical race theorists who decry the "unshared sacrifice" that traditional civil rights discourse demands. Millennial childhood memoirs often traffic in tropes of violated children to explore cultural anxieties. In *Warriors*, Beals's martyred persona serves to weigh the cost of integration against *Brown*'s lost promise.

Like many 1990s memoirs that incorporate the movement's cultural memory, Beals's text emerges out of a "racial divide discourse" that circulated as the O. J. Simpson trial and the Los Angeles uprising/riots polarized the nation.[64] Often highly gendered melodramas, these texts incorporated a feminine aesthetic associated with healing and social harmony to promote racial reconciliation and/or protest politics.[65] It also responds to another cultural flashpoint: Clarence Thomas's Supreme Court nomination and the subsequent sexual harassment hearings with Anita Hill. At the time of the first publication of *Warriors*, in 1994, black feminists were organizing against rape and sexual violence to create a political narrative that might counter the outdated lynching narrative Thomas deployed during the hearings. Black feminists nationwide sought to make rape the corollary to lynching in the black political imagination, so that women's concerns might have as much resonance and support within black politics.[66] I argue in this chapter that Beals's memoir reflects this social discourse of a renewed black feminist public that sought to place women's issues at the forefront of any future black politics. The day of the *Brown* ruling, a teenaged Beals suffers an attempted rape, which the narrative represents as retaliation for the landmark ruling, much like the lynching of Emmett Till.[67] The mythic narrative of the civil rights movement is that Till's death lit the fire that sparked the movement, rendering Till a political martyr. Through the portrait of the adolescent Beals, who was about the same age as Till when he was murdered, the textual figure of the "rehistoricized, politicized female child"[68] asks readers to rethink black politics in light of her trauma and sacrifice. The trope of sacrifice at the heart of social contract theory draws on the Old Testament story of a soldier, Jepthah, who acquires citizenship, inclusion into a national polity, through his unnamed daughter's sacrifice (see Judges 11).[69] Chapter 1, "Moving beyond the Strong Black Woman: Melba Beals's *Warriors Don't Cry*," argues that gendering debates about citizenship and political heroism serves to recognize anonymous sacrifices and losses in black politics. Critics charge Beals's memoir with reckless use of literary license as she crafts a countercultural memory of the Little Rock desegregation campaign. Some see an attempt to recoup a personal legacy that had been lost in official histories. But I suggest here that the memoir's political value and work lie in the ways it centers black women in the discussion of how to create a future black politics in the wake of an exhausted civil rights discourse.

Chapter 2, "Reclaiming Radical Interdependence: Rosemary Bray's *Unafraid of the Dark*," demonstrates how Bray's memoir genders the CRM narrative not only to make black women's lives a factor in defining black politics but also to promote social responsibility for "the least of these." *Unafraid of the Dark* also emerges out of the resurgence of black feminist organizing in response to the Clarence Thomas–Anita Hill hearings. But whereas these activists were addressing what Paula Giddings has called "the last taboo," bringing questions of gender and sexuality into black political discourse,[70] Bray's chronicle of her journey from the welfare roll to the *New York Times Magazine* masthead tackles the gendered violence of poverty and economic inequality, a central theme of contemporary black political thought.[71] Published in the wake of welfare reform, the memoir equates the saving grace of federal public assistance in the 1960s with the era's other iconographic victories, invoking the influential but little studied welfare-rights movement. Many have argued that class is the unfinished business of the civil rights movement, with the abandonment of the Poor People's Campaign in the wake of King's assassination. In detailing her experiences as a black girl growing up amid the trauma of poverty, Bray casts her life as representative of "the least of these," in solidarity with poor women pilloried in the public sphere. As she maps her memoir onto well-known representations of the modern civil rights movement—the heroic political narrative of 1954–1965, as well as its quintessential literary representation, Lorraine Hansberry's *A Raisin in the Sun*—Bray takes a narrative associated with black political advancement and infuses it with concerns often coded as feminine. This narrative strategy reflects the black feminist project of putting women's concerns at the heart of a black politic, but it also engages contemporary social ethics and political theory regarding the place of affect—such as love, care, and interdependence—in the public sphere.[72] In privileging women's experiences and values, Bray promotes a social ethic of interdependence based in "feminine" sensibilities of love and care, reclaiming "the tender side" of black women's intellect in service of a post-*Brown* politic and delineating modes of political radicalism beyond traditional activism.

Like many contemporary autobiographies by women and people of color, Rosemary Bray's *Unafraid of the Dark* appropriates the bildungsroman to create a place in public life and discourse for women's concerns. But the text is also a conversion narrative, like Augustine's foundational *Confessions*, as well as Malcolm X's and Angela Davis's Black Power–era autobiographies, as it charts the process by which Bray becomes radicalized: from "poor, afraid" to "unafraid of the dark" (even as the radical subjectivity that she outlines in *Unafraid* is contrasted quite consciously with that of the Black Power era). Those earlier memoirs give readers little detail about the interior, psychic dimensions involved in political struggle. Bray's text seeks to illuminate the spiritual dimensions of radical black subjectivity and politics, converting the bildungsroman of the self-made man to a theological meditation on social responsibility for the poor, a message as relevant in the Occupy era as it was during welfare reform.

In chapter 3, June Jordan's memoir, *Soldier: A Poet's Childhood*, serves as a bridge between the book's discussion of "movement memoirs" and "immigrant narratives." Most known as a writer and activist within the civil rights movement, Jordan is of Jamaican descent and among a second-generation immigrant cohort who "played an integral role in the evolution of African American politics and culture, largely as 'African Americans,'" along with figures such as Shirley Chisholm and Stokely Carmichael, Malcolm X and Audre Lorde.[73] *Soldier*, a self-conscious meditation on identity formation, chronicles how growing up the only daughter of West Indian immigrants shaped her into what she often called a "dissident American poet" in the vein of Walt Whitman and Phillis Wheatley.

As a millennial childhood memoir like *Warriors Don't Cry*, *Soldier* also mines traumatic history as Jordan recounts becoming a poet in the home of a violent father and a mother whose abject meekness was as devastating as any outright malice. However, rather than inverting iconographic civil rights history to craft an alternate, progressive politics, as Beals and Bray do in their memoirs, *Soldier* challenges the movement's animating pieties of sacrifice and redemptive suffering through her parents' story of thwarted immigrant striving. By displacing the movement's conventional pieties onto an earlier decade and within a discourse of war and immigration, Jordan links the black American freedom movement with global struggles as the narrative persona of the child-poet "June" becomes a figure for the world's dispossessed. In describing the young poet as finding personal power through the acquisition of her poetic voice, this ostensible *Künstlerroman* theorizes the possibility of agency within seemingly overwhelming matrices of power. Through the portrait of the child-poet as agent, rather than victim, Jordan recalibrates the much-invoked "struggle," known more for moral and pyrrhic victories than actual ones, in favor of what she calls "the good fight" and "working to win." *Soldier* seemingly focuses on Jordan's father as the influence behind this politic: the nickname he gave her christens the book; the narrative itself is dedicated to his memory. However, in chapter 3, "Honoring the Past to Move Forward: June Jordan's *Soldier*," I contend that the portrayal of Jordan's mother, figured in imagery of absence and abjection, is central to the humanist ethic the memoir promotes. In her study of Black Power memoirs, Margo Perkins notes that, "given the extent to which movement activists suffered massive repression at the hands of the state, it is curious that the reality of death and loss is not explored more extensively in their texts."[74] Indeed, Angela Davis recalls "one of the things that we [activists] didn't do is mourn. Our strength was often defined by our ability not to allow the death of someone we loved to set us back."[75] I argue that *Soldier* demonstrates the importance of mourning to renew one's commitment to revolutionary struggle. Jordan is among a contemporary generation of philosophers who argue that developing viable progressive politics requires first confronting past trauma, whether the Holocaust, apartheid, or slavery.[76] *Soldier*'s representation of the mother's death-in-life as an "inconsolable, irreplaceable loss," which Jordan's child-poet must face before boarding a train to her future of becoming a dissident American poet, is such an act of political mourning. One of the generic conventions of autobiography is that the writer knows the end of the story because the narrative has been written at the end of a life. Jordan, who completed *Soldier* in the face of her own imminent death, presupposes that "the story" does not end with her. When read as a companion text to her posthumously published collection of essays, *Some of Us Did Not Die, Soldier* models an act of cultural mourning to reinvigorate progressive politics in the post-*Brown* era.

Chapter 4 demonstrates that as much as Edwidge Danticat's *Brother, I'm Dying* is about mourning her father's and uncle's deaths, and Haiti's travails since independence, it also revisits Danticat's own immigrant odyssey and the very personal consequence of diaspora. The memoir chronicles a triad of events: the author's unexpected pregnancy, her father's terminal diagnosis, and her uncle's tragic death while in custody of U.S. Customs. The dying "I" of the title is thus a collective one, as this *testimonio* continues work done in Danticat's earlier novels to inscribe Haiti's national history onto familial and personal ones. In this chapter, "Storytelling as Diasporic Consciousness: Edwidge Danticat's *Brother, I'm Dying*," I draw on Danticat's essay collection *Create Dangerously: The Immigrant Artist at Work* to show how her memoir performs the cultural and political work of storytelling in service of social justice as it explores the diasporic dimensions of contemporary black cultural formation.

The influx of immigrants from the African diaspora since passage of the Immigration and Nationality Act of 1965—one of the bookends of the civil rights movement, along with the Voting Rights Act—has had a transformative impact on contemporary black cultural formation. One significant paradigm shift has been the creation of "a broader space" for works that are "not directly connected to the concerns of the 'movement'" as it has been represented in the historical record and popular imagination.[77] As discussed above, shared cultural tropes, particularly the civil rights movement, have defined black identity and politics. However, given the range of histories and geographies experienced by people of African descent throughout the world, there is no commonly shared history that can link everyone. In this chapter, I draw on the work of Michelle Wright in *Becoming Black: Creating Identity in the African Diaspora* to show the way Danticat develops a model of African diasporic identity and politics based in a shared intellectual tradition. According to Wright, the story of the black nation and subjectivity has traditionally been the story of men, with women serving only as mothers and mates who created male heirs. By excluding the role of the mother, this nationalist discourse creates a notion of identity and citizenship that is in the realm of metaphor rather than material reality. In creating subjectivity through nonlinear, dialogic structures in the vein of black feminist writers such as Mae G. Henderson and Audre Lorde, *Brother, I'm Dying* joins an intellectual tradition of black feminist writing on diaspora. Chronicling her subject formation at the hands of her father and uncle, all the while positioning herself as a mother-to-be, Danticat creates a black diasporic subjectivity beyond gender and nation.

Much has been written about hip-hop culture as an extension of the black musical tradition, but it is an extension of the black autobiographical tradition as well, serving as a forum for both self-assertion and social commentary. The culture has a primarily masculine aesthetic, with many of its coming-of-age tales echoing the life trajectory presented in *The Autobiography of Malcolm X*.[78] Hip-hop autobiographies by women, like Harriet Jacobs's *Incidents in the Life of a Slave Girl*, the first slave narrative by a black woman, often introduce a counternarrative through an examination of the unique perspective of women within the culture. Eisa Davis figures herself as such a "hip-hop head" in her play *Angela's Mixtape*, a coming-of-age tale that is as much about growing up the niece of radical icon Angela Davis as it is about the political awakening of the hip-hop generation.

The play stages an intergenerational dialogue with her famous aunt about how to materialize Black Power movement ideals of love and revolution in the post-*Brown* era. According to Kevin Powell in *Step into a World: A Global Anthology of the New Black Literature*, the intergenerational dialogue is an emergent genre.[79] Written by "children of the dream" who are both beneficiaries of the movement's gains and now custodians of all its losses, these dialogues reflect a "postsoul" aesthetic, a postmodern self-consciousness about historical tensions and distance as their contemporary works repurpose civil rights/Black Power iconography and styles.[80] Davis facilitates this dialogue through the play's episodic, "mixtape" form—with short scenes sliding into new ones, themes and motifs recurring like sampled tracks on a rap record—as well as a conceit of time travel borrowed from the film *Back to the Future*. In the final chapter, "Cultivating Liberatory Joy: Eisa Davis's *Angela's Mixtape*," I argue that the play dramatizes

Iton's idea of the "black fantastic": popular culture's "willingness to engage time, space, and other modalities outside of the given parameters" of traditional politics and identity to imagine new possibilities.[81] One of the founders of the hip-hop theater movement, Davis argues that hip-hop theater attempts to transcend the death that has gripped the commodification of popular culture and to bring a sense of joy back to revolutionary politics.[82] I argue here that, in restaging the Black Power era alongside the present moment, the play indeed tries to "Free Angela" from the prison of nostalgic movement iconography and, in turn, free her namesake, as well as the hip-hop generation Eisa Davis represents, from narrow notions of politics. Angela Davis has recalled that the civil rights generation never mourned its losses. Her namesake reimagines that past to create a future politic animated by joy and a renewed sense of solidarity.

Since the 1970s, the contemporary field of black women's writing has developed as a cultural space to create alternative worldviews. The writers examined here are an extension of this black-feminist public sphere, or counterpublic, contemplating the relationship between black women's cultural productions and their material lives. The ways black women writers craft autobiographical identities to engage contemporary political discourse has significance for evolving debates in autobiography studies about the nature of the self. Early critics of autobiography, often historians, were concerned with *bios*, the "truth" of a life. A second critical wave argued that writing could recover *autos*, an authentic self "truer" than any factual one. Finally, the critic-as-philosopher deemed the self a discursive fiction with no reality outside of language.[83] This strand of autobiography criticism suggests that narrative identities and politics, as mere discursive constructions, can be no more subversive than the social discourses out of which they emerge—in essence, that there is no way to write a radical self or politic outside of language, which can only reflect that status quo.[84] Today, however, a growing concern with agency—how can one act if one does not exist?—has scholars grappling with ways to articulate a concept of self that avoids narrow essentialism while acknowledging that identity matters, that lived experience does shape one's self-concept without determining it. The autobiographers featured in *Words of Witness* are part of a black feminist tradition that recognizes that selves, even narrative ones, are conditioned and created by particular forms of embodiment, which extends itself into the world around it. The signature mode of reading and interpretation in black feminist thought— its interrogations of the intersections of race, gender, and class that never lose focus on experience and condition; its understanding that identity is fluid and varied, creating the unruly spaces from which agency arises—provides an intellectual foundation necessary to ground political thought and action, to use story in service of social justice.

1

Moving beyond the Strong Black Woman
Melba Beals's *Warriors Don't Cry*

> Although there was always generosity in the Negro neighborhood, it was indulged on pain of sacrifice. Whatever was given by Black people to other Blacks was most probably needed as desperately by the donor as by the receiver. A fact which made the giving or receiving a rich exchange.
>
> Maya Angelou,
> *I Know Why the Caged Bird Sings*

Once celebrated as a watershed moment in American legal history, *Brown v. Board of Education*, the landmark ruling that deemed segregation in public schools unconstitutional and laid the foundation for Jim Crow's collapse, is now regarded as more symbol than substance. Commentators across the political spectrum agree that the liberal legal ideology that culminated in *Brown* has little traction today. Like the catchphrases that express the nation's ideals—all men are created equal, liberty and justice for all, out of one many—the legislation has become part of "America's rhetorical legacy," shorthand for its egalitarian, if elusive, principles.[1] In the sixty years since its passage, there has been a flurry of political commentary on how to achieve the racial equality that *Brown* promised.[2] For instance, Danielle Allen's *Talking to Strangers* revisits the 1954 decision to argue that it might have been successful had the nation as a whole embraced the ethos of "citizenship as sacrifice" that the civil rights movement modeled. The reasoned dialogue and deliberation that sustain democracy, says Allen, can flourish only in "a context of civic trust," within the "politics of friendship" nurtured through reciprocal sacrifice.[3] Whereas Allen views *Brown* as a missed opportunity to reinvent the republic into indeed "a more perfect union," critical race theorists such as Derrick Bell and Charles Ogletree decry it as yet another example of the "unshared sacrifice" that civil rights laws demand blacks shoulder to tether America's fragile democratic project.[4] The relationship between sacrifice and citizenship is understandably at the heart of this commentary on forging a progressive post-*Brown* politic, given its centrality to various schools of political theory, from early modern social contract theory to black political thought enacted by the civil rights movement. This chapter reads Melba Beals's *Warriors Don't Cry: A Searing Memoir of the Battle to Integrate Little Rock's Central High* as an interlocutor in these ongoing debates about the limits of traditional civil rights discourse and strategy, as she centers black women's lived experience within conversations about the meaning of political action and citizenship.

Warriors remembers one of the most celebrated milestones of the modern civil rights movement: the 1957 campaign to integrate Central High School in Little Rock, Arkansas. It was one of many school desegregation battles that the NAACP Legal Defense Fund, under the leadership of Thurgood Marshall, waged to implement *Brown*. When the Supreme Court struck down the half-century-old doctrine of "separate but equal," establishing equality under law, the ruling was thought to signal the end of Jim Crow. A year later, however, the Warren court essentially reneged on its unequivocal endorsement of racial equality with *Brown II*'s infamous "all deliberate speed" injunction, allowing southern states to comply on their own terms, or not. Little Rock was emblematic of the subsequent "massive resistance." Flouting the court order, Arkansas governor Orval Faubus summoned the state's National Guard to block students' entry into Central, rather than to protect their passage. In turn, President Eisenhower sent troops to enforce federal law and, incidentally, demand equal protection for African Americans for the first time since Reconstruction.[5] As one of the famed Little Rock Nine, Beals tells of being caught in the middle of this volatile face-off as state and federal interests played out on a world stage. Her behind-the-scene reportage recalls Anne Moody's classic movement memoir, *Coming of Age in Mississippi,* for its intimate, quotidian details: the august Thurgood Marshall dining with the teenagers in a neighborhood diner after a day in court; Daisy Bates, president of the NAACP's Arkansas branch, conducting news conferences at her rambling ranch-style home. *Warriors* takes readers past the tanks and soldiers stationed outside the schoolhouse door to provide a rare glimpse into the lives of the children placed on the front lines of the battle to integrate Central High School.

Beals's representation of this historic desegregation campaign mines the religious tropes of sacrifice and suffering, as well as a prophetic tradition that understands God as working on behalf of a chosen people, which have framed black political agendas since the nineteenth century. During the civil rights movement, twentieth-century reverberations of this black prophetic tradition

could be seen as churches hosted strategy meetings, with the discursive traditions of prayer, songs, and sermons structuring the organizing sessions.[6] The
contemporary narrative most often figures the Reverend Martin Luther King Jr.
as a Moses leading his people to the Promised Land. However, in Beals's retelling
of Little Rock, the nine teenagers conscripted for the campaign symbolize the
messianic martyrs who sacrificed their innocence to achieve a racial equality
that has yet to be secured. Through these tropes of sacrifice, Beals creates a
narrative inversion of the civil rights movement, a countercultural memory,
which revives a longstanding debate about the role of "political children" in
social movements.

Perhaps the most famous schoolchildren associated with the desegregation
efforts of the civil rights era are those who were a part of the 1963 Birmingham
campaign. Almost one thousand black children marched in the face of Bull
Connor's fire hoses and canines, singing freedom songs such as "Ain't Gonna
Let Nobody Turn Me Around" as they knowingly and willingly rode off to jail.
King and his Southern Christian Leadership Conference (SCLC) came under
harsh criticism for drafting youth for the cause, but the photographs and footage
of children attacked with fire hoses and by police dogs galvanized the American
conscience. The archetypal narrative suggests that it was because of their actions
that the civil rights movement succeeded in Birmingham. The "children's
miracle" is thought to have ushered in two of the movement's culminating
moments, the 1963 March on Washington and the 1964 Civil Rights Act, as
well as one of its most tragic, the bombing of the Sixteenth Street Baptist
Church.[7] Today, the Birmingham student protesters and the "four little girls"
are the best-known martyred youth in civil-rights cultural memory. But it was
the experience of the Little Rock Nine that first ignited the political children
debate in a very public exchange between the political theorist Hannah Arendt
and the novelist Ralph Ellison.

Arendt opposed putting children on the front line of a political campaign
for fear that federal intervention in the "social" realm of education might re-
create the totalitarian regime she experienced in Hitler's Germany. Ellison
countered that Arendt, as a European intellectual, misunderstood the ethic of
Christian sacrifice framing traditional black American political thought and
practice. Beals's portrait of the civil rights movement within the black prophetic
tradition, as an extension of Christian commitments, embraces Ellison's arguments, even as underlying textual tensions seemingly endorse Arendt's objections
to political children and forced integration. These tensions complicate discerning
the memoir's operative ethics. For instance, the colliding arguments arguably
reflect the anxieties about agency and the political paralysis that have come to

define the post-*Brown* period, and the narrative inconsistencies have elicited strong challenges to the memoir's authenticity.

Through strategies of indirection and displacement, however, the textual tensions serve to trouble traditional civil rights discourse as Beals weighs the cost of integration against *Brown*'s failed promise. The memoir is more than a modern-day take on the perennial integration versus separatism debate that has been a defining characteristic of traditional black political thought. Rather, close reading of the sacrificial imagery Beals uses to convey the desegregation campaign's traumatizing impact on the Little Rock Nine reveals that she genders the political children debate. In concert with a burgeoning black-feminist social discourse around rape as a corollary to the lynching narrative invoked during Clarence Thomas–Anita Hill hearings, *Warriors* engages the rape trope to center black-female lived experience within debates about creating a future politic in the wake of an exhausted civil-rights discourse. The autobiography charts Beals's political formation into a "warrior who does not cry"—the proverbial "strong black woman," what political scientist Melissa Harris-Perry defines as "the most pervasive and widely accepted" mode of contemporary black-female agency.[8] However, its textual tensions reveal that Beals in fact challenges this self-sacrificing mode of citizenship, offering instead a model of political action that reclaims vulnerability yet eschews victimization, reflecting the "affective turn" in contemporary black feminist thought.

Before exploring the political uses to which Beals puts her memoir, I first discuss how she capitalizes on two 1990s publishing trends, movement and childhood memoirs, to craft her countercultural memory of the Little Rock campaign.

Creating a Countercultural Memory

The era following the wave of reforms launched by *Brown* has come to be known as the Second Reconstruction, a historical parallel to the period of black political gains following the Emancipation Proclamation. The Reagan presidency of 1980–1988 orchestrated this conservative shift by co-opting the egalitarian language of traditional civil rights discourse to defeat *Brown*'s race-conscious remedies to discrimination.[9] As Alan Freeman has written, "It took thirty-three years to go from the promise of the Emancipation Proclamation in 1863 to the bleak reality of 'separate but equal' endorsed by *Plessy v. Ferguson* in 1896" and "thirty-five years to go from the glowing promise of *Brown v. Board of Education* in 1954 to the [conservative counterrevolution] that enshrined the principle of 'unequal but irrelevant.'"[10] *Warriors Don't Cry* is among a spate of 1990s civil rights narratives that sought to inspire oppositional discourse in this era of political retrenchment and increasing social discord.[11]

In "Debating the Present through the Past," Jennifer Fuller argues that many 1990s memoirs that incorporate civil-rights cultural memory emerged in response to a "racial divide discourse," as the O. J. Simpson trial and the Los Angeles riots polarized the nation.[12] Often highly gendered melodramas, these texts incorporated a traditionally feminine aesthetic associated with healing and social harmony to promote racial reconciliation or protest politics.[13] *Warriors*'s sentimental, melodramatic style reflects this literary moment. A popular text in elementary-and secondary-school curricula, the memoir reads like genre fiction, replete with car chases, action-packed getaways, and cliff-hanging chapters designed to captivate its young-adult target audience. Beals casts her narrative persona "Melba" as a fanciful teenager fond of "white lace pillows," "stuffed animals," and other sentimental trappings of a "normal girl."[14] This idealized portrait of childhood contrasts sharply with the depiction of childhood as traditionally represented in black autobiographies. Nellie McKay has written that black autobiographers present alternative representations to challenge notions of a universal, innocent child.[15] In a revision of that autobiographical tradition, Beals reifies the fiction of childhood innocence to better fashion her narrative persona of a martyr who paid the price integration exacted. A recurrent refrain in *Warriors* is "integration stole my," with myriad childhood joys filling in the blank: "my sixteenth birthday" (217), "my Christmas shopping fun" (227), "even my daydreams" (243). These sentimental themes of adolescent angst morph into markers of psychic trauma: "My eight friends and I paid for the integration of Central High with our innocence. During those years when we desperately needed approval from our peers, we were victims of the harshest rejection imaginable. The physical and psychological punishment we endured profoundly affected all of our lives. It transformed us into warriors who dared not cry even when we suffered intolerable pain" (2). Consistent with other 1990s movement memoirs, *Warriors* concludes with a call for racial harmony so the teens' suffering will not have been in vain. Fuller argues that these memoirs draw on the dominant civil-rights cultural memory to remind readers of the movement's successes, of the possibilities of progressive politics.[16] Beals, too, hopes to recover a sense of political immediacy and urgency with her text, by evoking not the era's successes but, rather, its unfinished business of racial equality.

To present the questions of citizenship and equality that *Brown* and Little Rock posed in the 1950s as "current affairs," Beals structures the narrative around newspaper clippings from the period. With *Arkansas Gazette* articles chronicling the unfolding firestorm—FAUBUS CALLS NATIONAL GUARD TO KEEP SCHOOL SEGREGATED (40); JUDGE ORDERS INTEGRATION (46); FAUBUS, U.S. GOVERNMENT HEAD INTO CRUCIAL COLLISION IN FEDERAL COURT TODAY (92)— reading *Warriors* is like scrolling through the morning headlines, as if the past were present and hugely pressing. And of course it is. That integrated public schools are "still not a reality" is a prime impetus for this memoir: "Why have we not devised a workable plan for solving a problem that has so long plagued this nation?" (310). Beals writes at autobiography's end, "We put a man on the moon because we committed the resources to do so" (310). The allusion to a lack of government will speaks to the conservative political moment of the memoir's publication but still has relevance a generation later. Sixty years since *Brown*, with schools more segregated than ever, achieving integration, by race or gender or disability, has ceased to be a priority in education reform, and *Brown*'s sense of collective purpose for schools—laying the "foundation of good citizenship" and teaching the habits of democracy," such as reason, deliberation, tolerance, fairness, and compromise—seems largely forgotten.[17] It is perhaps fitting and understandable that Beals exploits media tropes to inspire a renewed commitment to progressive politics. She is a former broadcast journalist whose career was inspired by reporters who covered the Little Rock desegregation campaign. The rhetorical strategy also recalls that unprecedented media coverage played an enormous role in launching the most successful social revolution of the twentieth century, rendering it a celebrated if fading part of the national consciousness. The photograph of Emmett Till's mutilated corpse, broadcast across the globe, is widely credited for igniting the outrage that sparked the movement's direct-action phase. Within a year, there were worldwide reports of Rosa Parks "sitting down" on a segregated bus in Montgomery, Alabama, to "stand up" for civil equality.

Just as the movement's narrative has its iconographic elements—*Brown*, the Montgomery bus boycott, Little Rock, the sit-ins—each of these historic moments has its own emblematic stories. For Little Rock, it is the famous photograph of Elizabeth Eckford, walking grim faced and terrified through a would-be lynch mob on the first day of the campaign. Eckford's harrowing encounter has been seared into the national memory because Will Counts, a sharecropper's son and a new hire at the *Arkansas Democrat*, captured the moment in a now iconographic shot. *Warriors* alludes to her walk, but then supplements the received story with the "searing memories" of the memoir's title. For instance, Beals shares that, as Eckford ran that gauntlet of bigots hurling epithets, off camera she and her mother were barely escaping equally murderous vigilantes set on lynching them. Her version in *Warriors* of that fateful day differs markedly from the dominant Little Rock narrative in established historical sources, such as the *Eyes on the Prize* (1987) documentary series; in fact, there is some doubt whether Beals actually was present at all that day.[18] But for audiences familiar with Little Rock's broad strokes, Beals's narrative revision unsettles official history and intimates to readers that that half of civil rights history may well not yet have been told. The narrative strategy enlivens "the narrative behind the still photos of historic moments,"[19] reviving the immediacy of the era as the past reverberates in the present through provocative new images.

The revised Eckford scenario is just one of many stories that Beals shares in *Warriors* that expand the dominant narrative associated with the Little Rock campaign: a KKK attack on her family's home; an unlikely friendship with a white classmate, Link, who is the liberal son of a White Citizens Council member; and an attempted rape (discussed below). Throughout the narrative, Beals repeatedly asserts that these stories are coming to light only now because her family demanded silence at the time for fear of retaliation. Fellow Little Rock Nine members reportedly have since deemed the text "untrustworthy," with critics branding its account as revisionist, or worse. For instance, according to David Margolick in *Elizabeth and Hazel*, a study of the campaign and the history since, Eckford herself has complained that the made-for-TV memoir of Ernest Green, another member of the Little Rock Nine, downplays the students' difficulties, while Beals's narrative goes to the other extreme. Eckford appreciates that each version of events does some personal or cultural work. In Green's case, she suggests that "he wasn't exactly fibbing; it was just that, in the process of becoming . . . an 'acceptable Negro,' he'd blocked out anything unpleasant." As for *Warriors*, Eckford recognizes that the text "filled an important hole in the literature" by focusing on the difficulties the Nine faced, but she objects to the way Beals "seemed to claim for herself the experiences and traumas of them all."[20]

Narrating traumatic history is always an act of reinterpretation, because trauma is in fact a repeated narrative, a recurring enactment. The "searing memoir" phrase of the subtitle conveys trauma's indelible imprint as the amalgamated, and oft-told, stories that we have come to associate with Little Rock become shared metanarrative. Of the nine students, the best known are Eckford, for that harrowing walk; Green, the senior who would be the first black American to graduate from Central High; and Minnijean Brown, who was expelled for retaliating against her teenaged tormentors and was the only student who did not complete the year.[21] As discussed above regarding Eckford, and as will be shown regarding Brown, Beals consistently places herself at the center of these iconographic events, "claim[ing] for herself," as Eckford charges, "the experiences and traumas of them all." Skeptical readers speculate that this is to recoup a personal legacy reminiscent of Elaine Brown's *A Taste of Power*. Before this memoir, Elaine Brown had less visibility than other Black Power era activists such as Angela Davis, Ericka Huggins, Assata Shakur, and Kathleen Cleaver. And the contemporary autobiography of another Black Panther leader, David Hilliard's *This Side of Glory* (2001), barely mentions her.[22] When first published, *A Taste of Power* was criticized as heavily revisionist. However, as Farah Griffin has argued, Brown's ultimate assertion of power may be the writing of a text in which she inserts herself into the history in a way that popular recognition of her actions has not. Ironically, the most riveting autobiography of the Black Power era, which has been dominated in popular memory by militant black men such as Stokely Carmichael, H. Rap Brown, Eldridge Cleaver, Bobby Seale, and Huey Newton, may in fact now be that of a woman whom many have never identified with this period.[23] Critics have suggested similar arguments about the representation of civil-rights cultural memory in *Warriors*. Perhaps the speculation derives from a reputation for self-aggrandizement that apparently followed Beals even as a teenager. Midway through the year, Dr. Kenneth Clark, the psychologist whose findings on the harmfulness of segregated education had buttressed the NAACP's case in *Brown*, interviewed the Nine to see how they were faring in Central. His appraisals of each student were omitted from his final report, but records indicate that he assessed Melba and her mother as "unduly conscious of their celebrity role in this situation."[24]

In seeming anticipation of the critics, *Warriors* gamely alludes to Beals's celebrity-hound reputation, recalling a press conference where Daisy Bates chastises the teenaged Melba for wearing sunglasses inside; one of the Nine then quips, "Some of you'all think we're stars" (95). The rather belabored author's note prefacing the memoir also takes great pains to assert the truth of her narrative and the purity of her motives: "all the incidents recounted here are based on the diary I kept, on news clippings, and on the recollection of my family and myself" (xviii). The assertion establishes equality among source materials so that her personal diary and thirty-year-old recollections are deemed as credible and verifiable as the newspapers collected by her mother, "Dr. Lois Pattillo, a high school English teacher." One understands efforts to validate sources, given that autobiography is an indeterminate genre whose literary value lies in its claims to truth. Memoirs work only through "common cultural consent," what theorist Philippe Lejeune calls "the autobiographical pact": a tacit contract between reader and author affirming the truth of a narrative.[25] However, the peculiar emphasis placed on her mother's elite credentials and professional training for the mundane task of clipping articles perhaps points to authorial anxieties regarding reconstructed, if not flatly fictive, elements within the text. For instance, Beals allows that "some of the conversations have been re-created." Sophisticated readers understand that, at thirty years' remove, it is probable that all conversations in *Warriors* are wholly reconstructed. This overly conscientious acknowledgment of having partially indulged in what is an assumed and expected practice in life writing begs the question of sincerity. Take the diary entries threaded throughout the narrative. They are purportedly as authentic as the headlines. At times, however, they sound like an adult approximating the voice of a child rather than a child's actual writing. One illuminating entry finds an eight-year-old Beals meditating on theodicy after her attempt "to go 'potty'" in a segregated bathroom results in a brush with local police: "What if God can't fix things. What if white people are always gonna be in charge. God, now, please give me some sign that you are there and you are gonna do something to change my life. Please hurry!—Melba Beals— age eight—a Sunday school student" (18). The closing tagline might indeed be the gesture of a child who imagines God needs help keeping straight supplicants' prayers. In terms of a writer-reader dynamic, however, the salutation more likely serves to cultivate the impression of childhood innocence, which is presumably the purpose behind the colloquial "gonna." The irony, of course, is that translating spoken vernacular into written form is as sophisticated a literary skill for a third grader as the "potty" baby talk is developmentally delayed.

These inconsistencies of voice, along with the surprising narrative turns that the memoir takes, have fueled concerns about the memoir's factual reliability, especially considering *Warriors*'s ubiquitous presence in secondary and college curricula as an authoritative text on civil rights history. Some objections to the liberal poetic license Beals takes with her memoir stem from our present "memoir boom." The current "neoconfessional" publishing market, competing with talk-show culture and reality TV, has become ever wary of the literary "hoax," from James Frey's *A Million Little Pieces* and Margaret B. Jones's *Love and Consequence* to even Elie Wiesel's critically acclaimed *Night*, as "bad readers and rude journalists" demand "true" stories, having much less tolerance for the self-mythmaking that has always been central to autobiography.[26] And one cannot ignore the degree to which the burden of authenticity under which black authors have labored since the slave narratives shapes readers' and critics' expectations.[27] Indeed, many autobiographies that are known to contain fictive elements, such as Augustine's *Confessions* and *The Autobiography of Benjamin Franklin*, are now considered "canonical" and "classics."

Scholars of the genre have long argued that, for the autobiographer, there is a difference between meaning and fact. Focusing solely on fact misses the motivations behind, and meanings within, a text. Arguments that Beals is seeking a personal legacy, for instance, overlook the actuality that her legacy was arguably assured long ago. She is prominently featured in the Little Rock segment of the *Eyes on the Prize* documentary, as a talking head in interviews completed for the segment, as well as in footage from an even earlier documentary that filmed a teenaged Beals preparing for school. In essence, long before *Warriors*'s publication, Beals's personal story framed the Little Rock narrative, during the actual campaign and then afterward in its historical reconstruction. Achieving some personal legacy, then, seems the least of her concerns in *Warriors*. More interesting and productive than fact-finding is examining how, and why, Beals uses her memoir to construct a counter civil-rights cultural memory.

In some ways, *Warriors* functions like its slave narrative predecessors in its use of a personal story for a communal aim. The stories that some have called "revisionist" and "unreliable" could in fact be an amalgam of narratives, just as slave narrators created composite stories and characters to convey slavery's scope and terror. The way Beals amasses newspaper clippings, diary entries, and composite stories to evoke the civil rights era is in fact reminiscent of how slave narrators "very deliberately accumulated diverse materials—anecdotes, newspaper clippings, work descriptions, character sketches, sections of slave codes—to illuminate vividly all aspects of the socio-political-economic-psychological environment."[28] The cover art for *Warriors*'s first edition suggests this communal aim: a print of a famous Norman Rockwell painting of soldiers flanking Ruby Bridges, the first black child to attend an all-white elementary public school in the South. Using an illustration of a 1960 desegregation campaign that followed Little Rock seemingly signals that Beals intended *Warriors* to have significance beyond her personal story, and even beyond the 1957 campaign. And the print's title, *The Problem We All Live With*, fittingly conveys the breadth of her message and audience.

In the wake of the criticism, however, Beals, or her publishers, seemingly bows to genre rules, emphasizing the "truth" of her story in subsequent abridged editions. In "The Entangled Self: Genre Bondage in the Age of Memoir," Nancy Miller notes the role photography plays in validating the truth claims that the tacit autobiographical pact promises.[29] The cover art of subsequent *Warrior* editions works to appease contemporary readers' desire for "truth" as it replaces the Norman Rockwell print with photographs that were part of the original edition's seven-page photo spread. One cover has a drawing of a photograph of the teenaged Melba, designed to look like a formal, painted portrait. Another has an actual photograph of her leaving Central High, surrounded by soldiers, books held close to her chest, in a posture very much like the iconographic Eckford photo. The covers' increasing verisimilitude serves to bolster the memoir's claims. Even the subtitle in subsequent editions has been changed from "*a* searing memoir" to "*the* searing memoir," emphasizing the tale's personal singularity. While these changes perhaps serve as authenticating devices in a skeptical age, Beals has not let criticism of her text as factually "unreliable" undermine her personal truth. The abridged edition still contains the singular, some say "suspect," stories that alter Little Rock's dominant narrative. Indeed, it is as if in repackaging her countercultural memory within the conventional trappings of truth, Beals doubles-down on her assertion in the original author's note that if autobiography is understood as a performance designed to articulate a message, then all that matters is that *Warriors* "conveys [her] truth of what it was like to live in the midst of a civil rights firestorm" (xviii).

Scholars have written of the ways writing autobiography creates both personal autonomy and useful political interventions.[30] With *Warriors*, Beals's self-fashioning arguably makes the self-conscious point that civil-rights cultural memory is already a mythic narrative that has been put to varying personal, cultural, and political uses. As mentioned above, Eckford reads Ernest Green's sunny portrait of the Little Rock campaign as performing respectability politics: "becoming . . . an 'acceptable Negro.'" Margolick notes that Daisy Bates's biographer, Grif Stockley, considered numerous passages in her memoir, *The Long Shadow of Little Rock* (1962), to be "either incomplete, unverifiable, misleading, or incorrect," inconsistencies that he attributed to her publisher wanting "a heroic self-portrait."[31] And Charles Guggenheim's 1964 film, *Nine from Little Rock*, commissioned by the United States Information Agency to counteract images of church bombings and fire hoses, is sheer Cold War propaganda that also somehow managed to avoid faulting Faubus for fear of alienating the segregationist congressmen funding the project.[32] With *Warriors*, Beals introduces her own countercultural memory, a narrative whose tropes of sacrifice, I argue, serve to critique the traditional civil rights discourse and strategies that *Brown* launched.

Troubling Traditional Civil Rights Discourse

Millennial childhood memoirs often traffic in tropes of violated children to explore cultural anxieties.[33] In *Warriors*, Beals's martyred persona serves to weigh the cost of integration against *Brown*'s lost promise. That *Warriors* intends to trouble sacred cows about traditional civil rights discourse and strategy is clear from the way Beals depicts the day of the *Brown* ruling, customarily celebrated as one of the finest hours in American jurisprudence. Thurgood Marshall's legal team invoked the incantations of prevailing legal opinion to harness state power and dismantle more than a half century of American apartheid, prompting a widespread sense of triumph. Those in the legal community were, of course, jubilant. In her memoir, Legal Defense Fund lawyer Constance Baker Motley recalls an impromptu victory party the night of the ruling: "No one associated with us in preparing the briefs or oral arguments called to see if there was going to be a victory party. Those who knew Thurgood knew that 'party' was his middle name. Everyone converged on LDF's offices. . . . It was bedlam; the party went on most of the night." Motley, known for her "New England cool" and reserved demeanor, "remember[s] being there when the clock struck 3:30 a.m."[34] Derrick Bell, who was not yet the critical race theorist skeptical of the liberal legal ideology *Brown* represents, also recalls the widespread sense of triumph: "For black Americans long burdened by our subordinate status, there was, to paraphrase the spiritual, the sense of 'a great day a-coming.' Among black people, at every level, that was the majority view."[35] A famous photograph of a mother, Nettie Hunt, and her daughter Nicki sitting on the Supreme Court steps the day after the historic ruling captures that hopefulness. Hugging her child with one hand, the mother holds in the other a newspaper trumpeting the headline HIGH COURT BANS SEGREGATION IN PUBLIC SCHOOLS. The gaze the two hold—the mother peering down; the daughter, expectant, smiling up—speaks of the deferred dreams that the civil rights generation fought to pass on and realize in their children.

Warriors's representation of the ruling and its aftermath pointedly contrasts with this popular perception. Published on *Brown*'s fortieth anniversary, but amid the virtual defeat of its reforms, the memoir characterizes May 17, 1954, as a day of apprehension and trauma. Once news of the Supreme Court decision hits the wires, Beals's seventh-grade teacher professes pride in the historic decision, but "her face didn't look at all happy" (22). The middle school issues an early dismissal, presumably to protect students from any retaliatory violence: "Pay attention to where you're walking," the teacher instructs. "Walk in groups, don't walk alone" (23). Beals fashions her narrative persona as an innocent who fails to register the full import of her teacher's warning. Walking home alone through an isolated field, while daydreaming "about being a movie star or moving North to New York or out West to California," Melba is attacked by a would-be rapist angered by the *Brown* ruling. Mercifully, the neighborhood bully, Marissa, also lurks in the shadows, arriving not a moment too soon to rescue Melba from harm's way (24, 25–28). In this scene, Beals consciously develops her theme of childhood innocence shattered ("I had figured out [that the near-rape] was something awful and dirty"), and introduces themes of trauma in relation to *Brown* and the ensuing desegregation battle. As the narrative progresses, to show integration's traumatizing impact on the tender sensibilities of children, childhood daydreaming morphs into dissociative states, as in a courtroom proceeding to decide the fate of the Little Rock campaign: "The attorneys for the United States made repeated references to the May 1954 decision. I had to stop listening. The very mention of that decision always made me sad. It brought back the face of the angry white man who had chased me down that day. Panic-filled recollections flooded my mind, blotting out the courtroom proceedings" (100). From this point in the narrative, Beals figures herself and her cohorts as martyrs in the black freedom struggle.

As discussed above, in the normative movement narrative, Martin Luther King Jr. is usually portrayed as the messianic figure. Biographer Lerone Bennett has noted that this is due partly to the biblical tropes that have long defined black freedom struggles, and partly to King's own deft depiction of himself as a Mosaic figure.[36] Perhaps there is no better example than his eerily prophetic final sermon: "I just want to do God's will. And He's allowed me to go up to the mountain. And I've looked over. And I've seen the Promised Land. I may not get there with you. But I want you to know tonight, that we, as a people, will get to the Promised Land."[37] The historian Taylor Branch argues that this "King-centric" representation of the civil rights movement perpetuates a myth of racial progress, with America's nationalist rhetoric "claim[ing] King's antiracism as its own," even as inequality and imperialism continue unabated.[38] In *Warriors*, however, Beals assumes the messianic role: "Okay, God, so Grandma is right. It's my turn to carry the banner," reads a diary entry after the judge orders Arkansas public schools and Governor Faubus to comply with *Brown*. And, then, in an echo of King's "mountain-top" sermon, she writes: "Please help me to do thy will" (102). As the narrative progresses, the efforts of all the Little Rock Nine to integrate Central are linked with sacrificial images of hanging (107, 116, 144), "victims" (235, 241, 243, 274), and even a reference to Christ: "Not everyone approved of what Jesus did," her mother reminds her in the face of segregationist violence (85).

The sacrificial imagery not only displaces King, challenging contemporary myths of racial progress. It also alludes to the political children debate Hannah Arendt and Ralph Ellison waged during and after the campaign. Beals's restaging of this exchange occurs during renewed interest among political theorists in Arendt's work, whose peculiar blend of "obtuseness and insight" renders her perennially provocative opinions uncannily prescient.[39] For instance, our increasingly technological and globalized world, characterized by cyberspace surveillance and "the genomization of the human condition," has revived interest in her analyses of totalitarianism.[40] Contemporary political theorists increasingly put civil-rights movement history in conversation with her scholarship to reassess her objections to *Brown* in light of the law's unintended consequences and failures.[41] At the height of the Little Rock campaign, Arendt penned a controversial essay, "Reflections on Little Rock," that took the NAACP to task for putting schoolchildren on the front line of a political campaign. Children prematurely politicized, Arendt argued, become indoctrinated zealots rather than the freethinking, rational agents democracy requires.[42] Her opposition to *Brown*, especially as executed in Little Rock, derived from earlier writings in which she outlined her political theory about the distinct categories—the private, social, and political—that define "the human condition."[43] In this schematic, intimacies such as marriage, love, and parenting constitute the private sphere; places of employment, education, and free association, where we choose friends for ourselves and for our children, constitute the social; public spaces to exercise civic rights such as voting, organizing, and marrying whom we please constitute the political.[44] Failure to distinguish the three realms, Arendt believed, threatened political freedom, as she witnessed living in Hitler's Germany, where Nazis drafted young people into that totalitarian cause against their parents' wishes. While education does serve a political function as it prepares children for civic participation, according to Arendt this government interest should not trump parents' "private right over their children and the social right to free association."[45] "Reflections on Little Rock" challenged the liberal consensus that had emerged around *Brown* and desegregation, as the prospect of a Jew who decried anti-Semitism seemingly endorsed racist policies, provoking a firestorm of controversy.

One of her major critics was the novelist Ralph Ellison, who charged that Arendt's projection of her European experience onto U.S. racial dynamics led her to misunderstand the longstanding ethic of Christian sacrifice that underwrote political action within traditional black political thought. Subsequent scholarship has since delineated the ways religious narratives have often framed political struggles in the United States. The Puritans used biblical language of "God's new Israel," "Canaan," and the "Promised Land" to create their group identity as a New World "chosen people."[46] In different ways and to different ends, subsequent generations of Americans of all ethnic backgrounds have adopted and adapted this convention.[47] In the African American tradition, the historic black church provided the stage for these Christian discursive traditions to be used for political ends, with the biblical images of Exodus, Egypt, and Ethiopia characterizing the burgeoning language of nationhood.[48] This spiritual vocabulary served to reimagine black history and struggle in terms of a prophetic tradition in which God played an active role in history on the side of the oppressed. For instance, as Eddie Glaude notes, David Walker's 1829 jeremiad believed black civic inclusion would come through providential intervention: "But has not the Lord an oppressed and suffering people among them? Does the Lord condescend to hear their cries and see their tears in consequence of oppression? Will he let the oppressors rest comfortably and happy always? Will he not cause the very children of the oppressors to rise up against them, and oftimes to put them to death? God works in many ways his wonders to perform."[49] This interplay of piety and politics soon evolved into a liberationist theology that saw "the mission of the darker peoples of the world" as ushering in a better America, with Psalms 68:31, "Princes shall come out of Egypt, and Ethiopia shall soon stretch forth her hands unto God," serving as the scriptural basis.[50] By the nineteenth century, black Christians, who comprised the majority of African Americans, "believed that the present and the future were shaped by God's providence, in which they were assigned a particular role . . . and destiny [in which their suffering] had meaning."[51]

Warriors's depiction of this interplay between piety and politics within the civil rights movement embraces Ellison's model of democratic citizenship. For instance, the figure of Beals's pious grandmother India most embodies this prophetic tradition that has long animated the black freedom struggle. When church members and neighbors object to Little Rock's school desegregation campaign for fear white backlash would jeopardize jobs and lives, she stokes Beals's faith: "God's voting on your side—so march forward, girl, and don't look back" (41). And when neighbors refuse to join a boycott of a white grocer who overcharges black patrons, she tempers her disappointment by invoking Psalms 68:31: "Then she picked up her Bible and read aloud the verse that cleared away the tears in her eyes: 'And Ethiopia shall stretch forth her wings'" (17). Some of the memoir's more lighthearted scenes involve Grandmother India training Melba and her brother, Conrad, in everyday sacrifices, what Danielle Allen calls the "habits of citizenship": "She always said God had pointed a finger at our family, asking for just a bit more discipline, more praying, more hard work, because He had blessed us with such good health and good brains" (4). Consequently, at Thanksgiving and Christmas, she insists the children "donate" beloved belongings to needy families during the Easter season and supervises their commitments during Lent. Unlike the social gospel of liberalism, an ethics that asserts society progresses as people improve in decency and acquire more knowledge,[52] the black prophetic tradition taught one must work, or sacrifice, for change: "Even when the battle is long and the path is steep, a true warrior does not give up. If each one of us does not step forward to claim our rights, we are doomed to an eternal wait in hopes those who would usurp them will become benevolent. The Bible says, 'WATCH, FIGHT, and PRAY'" (3). The representation of Grandmother India training Melba and her brother in the ways of sacrifice represents Ellison's rejoinder to Arendt that, in black politics, young people are apprentice citizens who are inculcated into a shared civic culture of Christian sacrifice.

Readers' first introduction to Beals's portrait of her narrative persona, Melba, epitomizes Ellison's democracy-as-sacrifice model of citizenship. For instance, the idea of a providential purpose, a destiny for the "darker peoples of the earth" as the foundation of black political action, is explicitly evoked in the messianic representation of Melba's birth. Born on the momentous day of Pearl Harbor, she fell ill with a forceps-induced infection that bigoted nurses refused to treat. Ministers and church ladies stood vigil while her grandmother hummed "On the Battlefield for My Lord," the African American spiritual whose pieties of providential guidance and redemptive suffering animate the black prophetic tradition. The intervention of a janitor who overhears the doctor's prescribed treatment of Epsom salts facilitates Melba's subsequent and, indeed, miraculous recovery. For Grandmother India, the Little Rock desegregation campaign fourteen years later is "proof positive that destiny had assigned [a] special task" (4), that there was indeed a redemptive purpose for the suffering surrounding the birth: "Now you see, that's the reason God spared your life. You're supposed to carry this banner for our people" (5). It is at this point in the memoir that Beals highlights the overlap between traditional political theory and black political thought. As the 101st Airborne soldiers escort the Little Rock Nine into Central High, their "forward march" command echoes her grandmother's mantra of providential black progress: "Forward is the only way our people can march" (12): "We began moving forward. . . . We approached the stairs, our feet moving in unison to the rhythm of the marching click-clack sound of Screaming Eagles. Step by step we climbed upward—where none of my people had ever before walked as a student. We stepped up to the front door of Central High School and crossed the threshold into that place where angry segregationist mobs had forbidden us to go" (132–133).

In an interview with Robert Penn Warren, Ellison described desegregation campaigns like Little Rock as "a rite of initiation" that black parents train their children to endure so that they will know how to confront and master the racial tensions and terrors of Jim Crow.[53] Crossing the color line of segregation, thus, epitomizes the ethic of democratic citizenship as sacrifice. In *Luminous Darkness*, a meditation on the moral evil of segregation, Howard Thurman defines the "redemptive work of nonviolent direct action": "The segregated persons, in this instance the Negroes, who are aware of the fear, may put forth genuine effort to help white persons to see their behavior for what it is and what it is doing to them, their children, and the total world of their values. All available resources must be brought to bear to release them from their enforced bondage."[54] In the face of massive resistance to the integration campaign within and without the walls of Central, Melba strives to become the warrior of the memoir's title. To the reporters of the Associated Press, she remembers her first, hellish day in Central High School as a turn-the-other-cheek parable of radical love: "I was slapped by one girl. I turned and said, 'Thank you' and continued on my journey to class" (123). When dodging ink darts, acid bombs, and live firecrackers as she navigates the treacherous halls, she hears her grandmother's voice, urging her to recite Psalm 23 (20, 57, 153, 208), scriptural reassurance of a God active in history and on the side of the oppressed. As Danielle Allen writes in *Talking to Strangers*, "Whereas Arendt developed a political theory that might protect children from politics," Ellison's account of democratic citizenship argued that children are never spared.[55]

Beals's portrayal of her inculcation into Jim Crow ethics not only embraces Ellison's argument that children are never spared politics but also roundly counters Arendt's dismissal of Little Rock as apolitical. Will Counts's photo of Eckford, unaccompanied and menaced by the mob, prompted Arendt's charge in "Reflections on Little Rock" that the parents and NAACP had abdicated their adult authority: "The girl obviously was asked to be a hero—that is, something neither her absent father nor the equally absent representatives of the NAACP felt called upon to be."[56] As Allen writes, in accusing the students and their parents "of a lack of heroism, she also more specifically charged the desegregation movement with a failure to rise to the level of political action. Her position depends heavily on the argument . . . that politics, properly understood, is a heroic activity; Achilles, the Greek hero of the Trojan War, is her paradigmatic political actor."[57] Beals's repeated assertions that she and her peers were "heroes" and "heroines"—"warriors," in fact—names their actions as political, in Arendt's own terms, and insists upon recognition of their sacrifice in a political battle. In drawing on martial metaphors, *Warriors* evokes the soldier of classic republican political theory, who is considered the consummate political actor, the ultimate citizen.

Beneath this model of citizenship as sacrifice, however, are insistent if latent critiques of integration that recall the critical race theorist Derrick Bell, one of the most vocal critics of traditional civil rights discourse. One of Bell's most basic assertions on race and rights is that, in the resolution of racial issues in America, black interests are sacrificed or upheld so that whites may settle a dispute and establish their relationship. These pernicious social physics have been operative within American legal history from the ratification of the United States Constitution, as the founding fathers institutionalized slavery alongside democratic rhetoric of "liberty and justice for all," to virtually every piece of civil rights legislation since the Emancipation Proclamation. *Brown*'s two-part ruling illustrates this "racial fortuity principle." Many have argued that the 1954 *Brown I* decision was a preemptive salvo in the Cold War to protect America's democratic image, and imperialist interests, abroad. This foreign policy interest was in fact cited in the original brief, and one cannot forget then President Eisenhower's almost utter silence after the ruling, which in effect encouraged the massive resistance that followed. This reality makes the political, rather than principled, calculation of his unprecedented deployment of federal troops to Little Rock all the more obvious. Whereas the 1954 decision reflected the "white self-interest" rule of this two-sided principle, *Brown II* is an example of its corollary, "involuntary sacrifice": the erasure of black rights when the remedial impact of antidiscrimination law becomes burdensome to dominant interests. Bell's structural theory accounts for the "ebb and flow" of antidiscrimination law and the post-*Brown* era's mirroring of the nineteenth century's Reconstruction/Nadir pattern. Given that civil rights doctrine is easily manipulated to accommodate any interpretation on race and equality, as the Reagan counterrevolution made clear, Bell argues that blind adherence to integrationist ideals is, at best, naive, if not nihilistic. He couches his unorthodox views and searing critiques of liberal legal ideology within allegories, fables, and Socratic dialogues to challenge these political pieties "in terms that are less threatening and confrontational" for audiences.[58] In *Warriors*, Beals's countercultural memory employs similar indirection as she calls the political project of integration into question.

In the dominant Little Rock narrative, Eckford's walk is regarded as the first event of that campaign. Beals's revision of that fateful day draws on themes of protection that seemingly endorse Arendt's objections to political children. The first day of school occurs just before her sixteenth birthday, so Melba is not yet legal to drive. In this scene, the need to escape the lynch mob forces her to learn before she is even capable. Literally, as Hannah Arendt would say, Melba has been put prematurely into the public realm. In this moment, her mother relinquishes parental authority, telling Melba to escape alone if she must (50). Perhaps one could consider this an example of parental authority in that the mother instructs her child how to survive. But the mother nonetheless does relinquish all responsibility for physical protection of her child from the mob, and in fact it is the child who saves the parent. In these moments, the memoir seemingly supports Arendt's assertion that the campaign reflects an abdication of adult authority, a failure of the parents and the NAACP black leadership to protect children. However, I argue that Beals draws on discourses of protection to elicit concern for the Nine's political sacrifice and decry the unshared sacrifice that traditional civil right discourse demands. One of the first things that readers learn about Beals's mother is that her husband cannot protect her from white men's sexual advances (14–15). This portrayal recalls Abbey Lincoln's classic essay "Who Will Revere the Black Woman?": "Who will keep our neighborhoods safe for innocent Black womanhood? Black womanhood is outraged and humiliated. Black womanhood cries for dignity and salvation. Black womanhood wants and needs protection and keeping and holding."[59] The yearning for patriarchal protection, while not feminist, exemplifies a traditional element of black thought that implies a social contract in which black women accept patriarchal norms in exchange for security.[60] Despite the respectability politics some critics see operating in the memoir, I argue that Beals does not invoke this discourse of protection in the traditional way. Rather, in the context of debates about the meaning of political action and citizenship, the call for black-female protection speaks to the violence inherent in liberal legal ideology. Arendt faults these parents for supposedly abdicating adult authority, but Beals takes great pains to show that her participation in the desegregation campaign was not forced: She signed up willingly. Her mother and grandmother gave her the opportunity to withdraw. Her father, in fact, sought to intervene. But just as Jim Crow ethics prevent him from protecting his wife from white men's constant sexual overtures, the structure of the campaign itself prevents parents from protecting their children. *Warriors* recounts a well-documented meeting between Central High's superintendent and a group of parents angry about the unchecked violence directed toward their children: "'These folks had best do something really big to show me they wanna make this integration work.'" Another replies: "'I'm tired of them counting on us to make all the sacrifices. . . . We need to know what they're willing to sacrifice'" (188).

Besides echoing Bell's arguments about the unshared sacrifice inherent in civil rights law, the memoir suggests that Melba's naïveté about integration is a reflection of the strategy itself. While the choice is hers, it is portrayed as emanating less from political conviction than from a longing rooted in girlish fantasy. On Sunday afternoon drives, the family would pass the high school, and its formidable façade—"so tall, so majestic, like a European castle"— would stoke Beals's "wish to see what's inside" (21). Her grandmother's response, "Don't you ever dare say that, girl; curiosity gets a body in a whole lot of trouble," recalls all the "curiosity killed the cat" warnings Melba receives for other forays across the color line (21, 20). The autobiography's introductory chapters recount Melba's numerous attempts to experience social equality as a child: trying to be seated on the merry-go-round at the Fair Park on the Fourth of July, sneaking a sip from the WHITES ONLY water fountain, ducking into a segregated bathroom to see if "it was just as bright and pretty as I imagined it to be" (18). Beals suggests that a similar naïveté inspires her decision to join the Little Rock campaign: "As I signed my name on the paper they passed around, I thought about all those times I'd gone past Central High wanting to see inside. I was certain it would take a miracle to integrate Little Rock's schools. But I reasoned that if schools were open to my people, I would also get access to other opportunities I had been denied, like going to the shows at Robinson Auditorium, or sitting on the first floor of the movie theater" (28). Here, Beals emphasizes her minimal understanding as a young girl of the political stakes or personal dangers involved. The naïveté of her decision reveals the naïveté behind the political project of integration. When Beals enters Central High, she discovers the "castle" to be in fact a "hellish torture chamber" (xx). As she awakens from these fairy-tale delusions, she realizes that "integration is a much bigger word than I thought" (154). Traditional civil rights discourse, invested in liberal legal ideology, views integration as an end of struggle. However, as segregationists' violence keeps her housebound on the weekends, Melba reconsiders that notion, writing in her journal, "Freedom is not integration."

Beals's engagement of the political children debate critiques not only the project of integration and its liberal legal ideology but also traditional, top-down black politics as represented by the NAACP. As Charles Ogletree writes in *All Deliberate Speed,*

> For many in the African-American community, however, integration was viewed with suspicion or something worse. Many communities at the center of the battle for integration, represented by the crusading lawyers of the NAACP, would have welcomed something less than the full integration demanded by the civil rights lawyers. Instead, these teachers, school principals, and janitors

would rather have kept their schools, their jobs, and their positions of power and influence than see their charges bused to white schools run by white principals where white educators often made the children all too grimly aware of their distaste for the new state of affairs.[61]

Beals's critique begins by framing the tactic of legal redress as a reflection of the ideals of "elite public interest lawyers rather than the actual interests of black communities and children."[62] *Brown* was the culmination of a twenty-year NAACP campaign. After winning a series of Supreme Court cases related to segregation in higher education, Thurgood Marshall's legal team decided to make public schools the next stage of the campaign, despite substantial disagreement in black communities. As Constance Baker Motley concedes in her autobiography, *Equal Justice under Law*, "The NAACP's national-office files document the long-running controversy between the NAACP and many black communities, even in the North. However, the NAACP and LDF were sufficiently buoyed by the Supreme Court's decisions [leading up to *Brown*] that there could be no turning back."[63] Many communities at the center of the desegregation battles, however, would have rather kept their jobs, schools, and prestige. According to Motley, there were various camps of detractors. There were those familiar with the civil rights legislation of the late nineteenth century and aware of the setbacks that followed, and some who thus feared the Supreme Court would *extend* the *Plessy* standard beyond public schools. Others simply preferred a policy of gradualism. And then there were those who actually opposed integration, either for fear of the harm that would be done to their children or for black-separatist politics. A church scene in *Warriors* powerfully portrays the dissension. When the minister declares from the pulpit that "the judge's positive decision for integration was God's will," invoking traditional liberationist theology, there are mumbled affirmations in an amen corner (103). Most congregants, however, have yet to be converted, having lost jobs as Faubus's segregationist forces squeeze livelihoods to quell the campaign. One recently fired woman, a domestic, corners Melba in a bathroom to vent her fury. Her mother intercedes, preaching the ways of sacrifice: "Look . . . there's a price to be paid for freedom; we pay it now or we're in 'ball and chain' forever." The fellow parishioner sees this noble rhetoric as mere privilege talking: "Easy for you to talk. . . . You're an educated woman. I ain't got no sheepskin on my wall" (104). Although Beals's parents live paycheck to paycheck like their neighbors, surviving on store credit for groceries and a yearly bank loan during the summer to make ends meet, her mother's graduate degree and status as a teacher confer middle-class status. Beals's emphasis on these trenchant class tensions is one of the autobiography's most significant interventions: challenging myths of a unified black community in the days of segregation.

It has been said of sixties' desegregation battles that black communities "got what we fought for but lost what we had."[64] However, the themes of death and loss that accompany the portrayal of the campaign in *Warriors* intimate that perhaps even the fight was futile. Ironically, rather than ushering in the "beloved community," the integration campaign is portrayed as resulting in a social death greater than any suffered under Jim Crow. Old friends no longer invite the Little Rock Nine to parties or outings: "Some of them feared for their safety when we were around—others didn't agree with what we were doing and refused to have anything to do with us. Still others didn't mean us any harm; it was a case of 'out of sight, out of mind'" (205). But the sense of exclusion they felt inside Central created a far worse spiritual death: "Nothing in my life was the same anymore. I felt so empty inside, like somebody had scooped out the warm sweet part of my spirit that made me smile and feel grateful to be alive. Integration hadn't at all worked out the way I'd planned. I didn't know it would eat up so much of my time—and so much of my life" (155). Scenes portraying life before and after *Brown* convey the false promise of integrationist ideals and liberal rights discourse. In the early chapters, there is an allusion to the lone black man who integrated the University of Arkansas's law school: "In the classroom, he was forced to sit confined by a white picket fence erected around his desk and chair. When he needed to come or go, he sometimes stumbled over that fence. White people around him sometimes stumbled over that fence, too. And still each day when he arrived, there it was, encircling him, keeping him separate but equal" (12). The image of the "white picket fence," evocative of the American Dream, alludes to another American institution in the pre-*Brown* era: legal apartheid. In relating the mutually corrosive effects of segregation, with "white people . . . stumbl[ing] over that fence, too," Beals captures what Howard Thurman calls segregation's "zones of agreement," the putative fellowship that allows for interaction but no genuine human exchange.[65] It is significant that, after the *Brown* ruling, Beals describes her sense of isolation within Central in remarkably similar terms: "I was treated as though I were an outside observer, sitting and looking into a glass room that held all the white students, separate and apart from me" (160). This portrayal articulates a common critique of antidiscrimination law's indeterminacy: "while abstract principles of formal equality removed the symbolic manifestations of racial oppression, the material subordination of blacks persisted under the illusion of equal opportunity."[66] The "glass room" separating Beals symbolizes the structures of racial inequality that were erected once the formal "fences" were dismantled, insidious barriers rooted in class and geography, making discrimination harder to identify and therefore less easily remedied. The latent critiques of liberal civil rights discourse and strategy align with critical race theorists who urge racial justice advocates to "rely less on judicial decisions and more on tactics, actions, and even attitudes that challenge the continuing assumptions of white dominance."[67]

"Sister Citizen"

Beals's countercultural memory of the Little Rock campaign perhaps is most significant for the way she centers black women in the discussion of how to create a future black politics in the wake of an exhausted civil rights discourse. In *Sister Citizen: Shame, Stereotypes, and Black Women in America*, Melissa Harris-Perry writes that "black women are rarely recognized as archetypal citizens,"[68] even though centering their lives in politics improves the lives of many since black women experience multiple, interlocking oppressions that others may face as well, if only in part. In *Warriors*, the relationship between the black female body and political discourse is made most explicit in the attempted-rape scene that occurred on the day of the *Brown* ruling. As Allison Berg writes in "Trauma and Testimony in Black Women's Civil Rights Memoirs," "Beals' decision to recount this traumatic episode in print . . . marks the private experience of a pre-adolescent black girl as pertinent to the public record of *Brown*'s legacy."[69]

Beals's revelation recalls disclosures of sexual violation in two well-known black women's autobiographies, Harriet Jacobs's *Incidents in the Life of the Slave Girl* (1861) and Maya Angelou's *I Know Why the Caged Bird Sings* (1969). Jacobs's narrative is known for the way she understates her experience of sexual abuse as an enslaved girl from her master, Dr. Flint. Writing within the parameters of nineteenth-century "true womanhood," Jacobs sought support for abolition among her northern white female readers without offending their Victorian sensibilities and reinforcing stereotypes about black women's promiscuity.[70] Darlene Clark Hine has argued that this studied reticence, what she calls the "culture of dissemblance," has been a hallmark of black women's narratives as they strive "to protect the sanctity of the inner aspects of their lives."[71] A century after Jacobs's narrative, Angelou's *I Know Why the Caged Bird Sings* revolutionized black autobiography when she challenged the prevailing culture of dissemblance and its respectability politics by disclosing that she had been raped at age eight. Angelou's text ushered in an era of black women writers' daring to break silences and address their inner lives, and Elaine Brown's *A Taste of Power* went even further, exploring issues of mental illness, drug addiction, and sexuality. As Berg contends, Beals's revelation of sexual assault the day of the *Brown* ruling is a part of the larger trend of challenging the politics of respectability that often structured black women's memoirs in which they hide or minimize sexual and gendered violence.

I would also argue that the scene reflects the social discourse of a renewed black feminist public around the place of gender within any future post-*Brown* black politics. In addition to the "racial divide discourse" that Jennifer Fuller names as a catalyst for 1990s movement memoirs, another cultural flashpoint is Clarence Thomas's Supreme Court nomination and the subsequent sexual harassment hearings with Anita Hill. At the time of *Warriors*'s first publication in 1994, black feminists were seeking to create a political narrative around rape to counter the outdated lynching narrative Thomas deployed during his confirmation hearings. Just as Thomas evoked the spectacle of lynching to garner widespread black support, feminists sought to make its corresponding narrative, the trope of rape, as galvanizing a force in the black political imagination. They hoped to create a metaphor about black women's lived experience that would resonate as powerfully as lynching so that women's concerns would factor into public debates about black politics and social action. In a similar vein, *Warriors*'s near-rape scene asks readers to rethink the state of contemporary black politics in light of Beals's trauma and sacrifice. Political theorist Danielle Allen argues that sacrifice must be shared and recognized for the democratic social contract to work.[72] Allen explains that decisions for "the common good" always have those who benefit less or who are actually harmed. In democracies, the practices and habits by which citizens accept communal decisions with which they disagree, or that disadvantage them, must rest on a highly developed notion of reciprocity, of mutual sacrifice. The passage from Angelou's *Caged Bird* that serves as the epigraph for this chapter illuminates that ideal of mutual sacrifice for communal progress, "a fact which made the giving or receiving a rich exchange." Too often, however, the reality is more like the Old Testament story of the soldier Jepthah who secures citizenship through his unnamed daughter's sacrifice (see Judges 11).[73] The martyred persona Beals cultivates in this attempted-rape scene, in displacing King in the dominant movement narrative, emphasizes the anonymous sacrifices of ordinary others, especially black women.

In *Contesting Childhood*, Kate Douglass maintains that childhood memoirs provide a way "to write back to paradigmatic historical representations of childhood."[74] In the heroic civil-rights movement narrative, Emmett Till's lynching is said to have lit the fire that sparked the movement, rendering him a political martyr. *Warriors* represents this near-rape as retaliation for the landmark ruling, much like the story surrounding the animus behind Till's murder. At the time, Beals was about the same age as Till was when he was murdered. The martyred persona she creates in *Warriors*—a "rehistoricized, politicized *female* child," as Douglass writes[75]—recovers a black feminist knowledge that campaigns against sexual violence have been central to the freedom struggle. McGuire's *At the Dark End of the Street*, for example, details how the women behind the Montgomery Improvement Association, including Rosa Parks, first organized as antirape activists in the 1930s and '40s. Therefore, "what is mythically regarded as the start of the civil rights movement," McGuire writes, "is actually part of a decades-long struggle to protect black women from sexualized violence and rape."[76] *Warriors* itself is part of a growing tradition of black women's narratives charting the movement's gendered dynamics, alongside Daisy Bates's *Long Shadow of Little Rock* (1962), Septima Clark's *Echo in My Soul* (1962), Anne Moody's *Coming of Age in Mississippi* (1968), Jo Ann Gibson Robinson's *The Montgomery Bus Boycott and the Women Who Started It* (1987), and Endesha Ida Mae Holland's *From the Mississippi Delta* (1997), among others.[77]

The near-rape scene and its aftermath also speak to the political formation of the traditional black female subject, showing "how black women's internal worlds are constituted by the political and cultural realities in which they live."[78] From this moment in the text, readers witness Beals morph from an "innocent" child into a "warrior who does not cry," otherwise known as "the strong black woman." Harris-Perry argues that histories of slavery, Jim Crow, urban segregation, racism, and patriarchy have constructed black women's citizenship and identity around the theme of "self-sacrificial strength" that is characteristic of the strong black woman.[79] In the national and black political imagination she is the hypervisible social scapegoat (think "welfare queen") whose citizenship remains unrecognized, like Ralph Ellison's invisible man. Beals's narrative portrayal of "the growing warrior within"—the social and cultural dynamics that make this stance a political imperative—correlates with the trajectory of political formation that Harris-Perry outlines. First, Harris-Perry writes that the strong black woman role serves to shield black women from the shame of daily assaults—some physical, many psychic—and the attempted rape clearly symbolizes those daily assaults and their emotional impact. The teenaged Melba first experiences utter powerlessness: "A voice inside my head told me I was going to die, that there was nothing I could do about it. White men were in charge." She summons the strength to fight back by hearing her grandmother's prophetic voice: "God is on your side." Religion dictates this position, which is later bolstered by social and legal imperatives. For instance, once her father learns of the attack, he sheds rare tears but refuses to "call the law" for fear "those white police [might] do something worse." Ironically, traditional civil rights law such as *Brown* stems from equal-protection clauses, but it is the law that actually incites sexual violence against her. Lack of social or legal protection for black women's lives is a theme throughout the narrative. To Harris-Perry, this reality often engenders a subsequent sense of shame for black women, with the mantle of impervious strength a "shame management strategy."[80] Throughout *Warriors*, Beals enumerates the "many times when I felt shame, and all the hope drained from my soul as I watched the adults in my family kowtow to white people. . . . It frightened me and made me think a lot about how, if I got into trouble with white people, the folks I counted on most in my life for protection couldn't help me at all" (15, 17). This sense of helplessness and shame culminates in the near-rape scene, with Melba resorting to the impervious self-reliance that is the hallmark of the strong black woman to deflect it, as she vows "to keep up with what the men on the Supreme Court are doing. That way I can stay home on the day the justices vote decisions that make white men want to rape me" (28).

In her reading of the self-representation of rape in Jacobs's and Angelou's narratives, Mary Vermillion asserts that both writers "reclaim their bodies" in the wake of sexual assault.[81] Jacobs asserts her agency over her own body by choosing to have an affair: "It seems less degrading to give one's self, than to submit in compulsion. There is something akin to freedom in having a lover who has no control over you except that which he gains by kindness and attachment."[82] Angelou does the same; although the experience leaves her pregnant at sixteen, she emerges in full control of her body and its powers: "I had a baby. . . . I had help in the child's conception, but no one could deny that I had had an immaculate pregnancy."[83] As Vermillion notes, Angelou's use of the word "immaculate" not only challenges racist stereotypes that associate black women with illicit sexuality but also indicates that she sees in herself the beauty and power that she sees in her mother, whom she perceives as looking like the Virgin Mary.[84] A central difference between *Warriors Don't Cry* and these two earlier works is that Beals never recovers from her trauma. This split consciousness emerges in the restaging of the Arendt–Ellison debate through a double-voiced narrative that never directly resolves its textual tensions, a schizophrenic impulse that perhaps reflects the author's anxieties about her own critique. However, I argue that the dissociation becomes embodied in Beals's portrayal of her relationship with Minnijean Brown, a literary foil who represents a model of political action beyond the strong black woman.

Early on in the memoir, when Beals describes the other students integrating Central High, she represents Minnijean as an alter ego: "Best of all, my special friend Minnijean Brown was going. She lived only a block away from me; we saw each other almost every day. We had much in common; both of us were tall for our age, and we shared daydreams—our worship of Johnny Mathis and Nat Cole, and our desire to sing" (35). A later reference to a full-page photograph in *Life* magazine ("It wasn't the first time we'd seen ourselves in print or on television, but we giggled at the wonder of it all—Miss Minnijean and Miss Melba could be seen on the pages of *Life, Look*, or *The New York Times*") intimates that the two are doppelgängers who become literary foils, given the very different tactics they take to survive that year, and the opposing models for crafting a contemporary politic that they embody. As with other narrative particulars in *Warriors Don't Cry*, it is uncertain how close the two girls actually were. In *Elizabeth and Hazel*, David Margolick's interviews with the Nine (except for Beals, who refused) reveal that they "were not particularly close, either at Central or for decades afterward." According to Eckford, however, if Minnijean Brown was anyone's "special friend" throughout the campaign, she was hers, suggesting that Beals, as with the iconographic walk, has once again appropriated another's experience as her own.[85] Some readers may discount the narrative outright if they conclude Beals alters facts for self-aggrandizement, to center herself within the narrative, which is always a possibility in this age of celebrity. But the memoir's value may in fact lie in the very ways that the narrative privileges black female experience in political discourse. In both Arendt's and Ellison's models of citizenship, the students have little to no political agency. Rather, as Kenneth Warren notes, they are described respectively as "victims of misplaced adult activism or cultural apprentices being trained into the disciples of the Negro's life world." Beals, on the other hand, presents an account of citizenship that recognizes the students as full-fledged political actors whose challenges to their elders' authority and traditions offer a different model of citizenship and political action.[86] I argue that, in Beals's countercultural memory of the Little Rock campaign, the story of Minnijean Brown's campaign for full inclusion in student life at Central intimates an ethic of political agency beyond the strong black woman.

Of the Nine, Minnijean is adamant that she will participate in the school talent show and Christmas pageant. The Central High Mothers' League, presumably some of the same women seen hot on the heels of Elizabeth Eckford, is just as adamant that she will not (the Nine were unable to participate in extracurricular activities for fear of race-mixing). Segregationist students retaliate against Minnijean with renewed fervor, just as their parents do against Little Rock's black community at large: The *Arkansas State Press*, the weekly newspaper Daisy Bates and her husband, L.C., published, ultimately went bankrupt as a result of her role in the Little Rock campaign.[87] State officials pressured local NAACP chapters to disclose membership lists and threatened their tax-exempt status.[88] Black families continued to lose jobs. Given the echoes between Minnijean's personal campaign and the political one of the Little Rock Nine, Melba's critique of her alter ego registers as a repudiation of "forced integration": "It was as though these objections fueled her need to do what wasn't wanted" (193), an objection that echoes those Melba received from family and neighbors for her involvement in the desegregation campaign. When Minnijean is ultimately expelled, Melba presents her own less-solicitous social approach as being more effective: students who frequented morning chapel, apparently exercising their freedom of association, voluntarily invite her as a guest speaker: "I kept my invitation to myself. I didn't want to hurt Minnijean's feelings, giving the heroic effort she was making to convince school officials to allow her to sing onstage" (195). On its narrative surface, Beals's retelling of Minnijean's "19-day ordeal" seems to endorse Arendt's controversial views about the perils of "forced integration" and the benefits of "free association." But in naming Minnijean's actions "heroic," Beals evokes the archetypal soldier-citizen whose ultimate sacrifices make the republic possible.

In tracking the "growing warrior within" Melba (182, 184), alongside Minnijean's unorthodox campaign, Beals critiques the culture and traditions of sacrifice and redemptive suffering that have required the strong black woman mode of citizenship. Harris-Perry argues that the strong black woman posture handicaps black women's citizenship practice and possibility as much as it helps. The memoir in fact initially characterizes Melba's transformation from a fanciful teenager cradling stuffed animals to a "growing warrior" as strongly positive: "I tried to remember everything Danny had taught me. I discovered I wasn't frightened in the old way anymore. Instead, I felt my body muscles turn steely and my mind strain to focus. I had to take care of myself. I could really depend only on myself for protection. A new voice in my head spoke to me with military-like discipline" (182). And the chapter ends with her resorting to self-defense, celebrating her newfound self-reliance: "I suddenly felt surging inside of me a strength that matched my determination . . . I felt better because at least I wasn't a whining wimp anymore" (191). In an effort to get Minnijean to "stop pushing to participate," Melba encourages her to take on the same "warriors don't cry" stance: "I tried to impress upon her that our being able to make it through the year was the biggest talk-back and fight-back we could give them" (233). Of the two, however, it is in fact Minnijean who best thrives, contrary to Grandmother India's counsel that "if you fight, you have a battle, and you will be the loser." Though expelled from Central, she receives a scholarship to a northern prep school, where she completes the year living with the famed Kenneth Clark. Melba's fate, on the other hand, undercuts the political pieties that she has championed. As she strives to embody the dictates of the strong black woman/citizenship-as-sacrifice, a rhetoric of victimhood creeps into the narrative, with the remaining Little Rock Nine alternately described as "victims" of "ridicule" (235), of "a dousing with raw eggs" (241), of "another devilish deed" (234), of "ostracism" (274). Absorbing white fear and hatred to transform it, as Thurman defined the role of redemptive suffering, actually takes a devastating toll. Time and again, her teenaged daydreams became dissociative states, leaving her vulnerable to attack and, metaphorically, exposing the violence undergirding traditional civil rights discourse. By narrative's end, Melba has been consumed, body and soul: "I think only the warrior exists in me now. Melba went away to hide. She was too frightened to stay here" (246). The dissociation that began on the day of the *Brown* ruling is now complete.

All the suffering seems to have been in vain. Melba must spend her senior year attending school in California because Faubus closes all Arkansas schools for a year to prevent integration. Even as she expresses gratitude and love for her white host family for having taught her "the true meaning of equality" (308), she reveals a profound alienation from black communities and the religious ethos that inspired the movement. After leaving Little Rock, she has returned only "five times in thirty years," even though her birth family still lives there (xxi). And the autobiography closes not with the voice of her grandmother as the standard bearer of the black prophetic tradition but with "Namaste," a greeting from Eastern religious traditions. If asked whether she would join the integration campaign again, knowing the political stakes and its physical dangers, Beals insists that her reply would be "Yes, unequivocally, yes. I take pride in the fact that, although the fight for equality must continue, our 1957 effort catapulted the civil rights movement forward a giant step" (3). Beals strikes a transcendent mood as she recounts a return to Little Rock for an NAACP convention held on the thirtieth anniversary of the 1957 campaign. Bill Clinton, not Faubus, is in the governor's mansion. Little Rock has its first black woman mayor. Beals's brother is the first black captain of the state troopers. And Central High has a black student-body president, who welcomes the Little Rock Nine through doors segregationists once blocked. That these examples of individual success have not translated into national black progress, a reality the autobiography acknowledges, belies the tables-turned narrative. This textual tension, alongside Beals's troubling of "warriors don't cry" / "strong black woman" politics, latently argues against notions of self-sacrifice and reveals a critique of the citizenship-as-sacrifice ethic the memoir purportedly champions. The portrayal of Melba's alter ego Minnijean Brown suggests that relinquishing notions of unparalleled strength provides a first step in crafting an alternate model of political agency. In the chapters that follow, I examine texts that explore a range of affect—love and care, mourning and joy—that autobiographers embrace in service of developing post-*Brown* politics.

2

Reclaiming Radical Interdependence
Rosemary Bray's *Unafraid of the Dark*

Hope is a word in a tuneless ditty—
A word whispered with the wind,
A dream of forty acres and a mule,
A cabin of one's own and a moment to rest,
A name and place for one's children
And children's children at last . . .
Hope is a song in a weary throat.

Pauli Murray,

excerpt from "Dark Testament"

The 1990s witnessed a resurgence of black feminist organizing in the wake of the Clarence Thomas–Anita Hill hearings. A decade earlier, the creative explosion of black women's writing that emerged out of the civil rights and women's movements gravitated to academia with the formal study of black women's literature and history.[1] While debates over canon formation certainly constituted new sites of struggle, the new focus marked a shift from life on the barricades to life of the mind as the country moved rightward under the Reagan revolution. The hearings were a collective call to action. In succeeding Thurgood Marshall, a prime architect of the major civil rights legislation of the second half of the twentieth century, Thomas was poised to preside over an era of retrenchment to rival the collapse of Reconstruction. The irony, of course, is that his now-infamous manipulation of the lynching trope exposed the inadequacy of the traditional political lexicon: a man who had fled associations with black Americans was now claiming to be a victim of racial violence. Black feminists saw a "teachable moment" in this historical juncture in which traditional black political discourse proved yet again inadequate to address post-*Brown* realities. From a national network of academics that organized in the wake of hearings to ad hoc grassroots coalitions, black feminists mobilized conferences, media campaigns, and mass demonstrations. To center black women's lives into public debates about black politics and social action, they deployed the rape trope to serve as a corollary to lynching and an extended metaphor for violence against black women and girls—from physical rape and domestic violence to sexual harassment and character-defaming cultural stereotypes.[2] A call for papers issued for a conference at MIT, "Black Women in the Academy: Defending Our Name, 1894–1994," described the impetus for this collective outrage: "Black women have come in for a large share of negative criticism in the form of both open and coded discourse generated by the Anita Hill/Clarence Thomas hearings last year, and political discourse generated by electoral campaigns over the course of the last year largely centered on the issue of welfare reform and 'family values.' These events have generated the most intense public consideration of the character and morality of Black women that this country has witnessed since the 1890s."[3] The 1990s resurgence of black feminist organizing recalled earlier waves: nineteenth-century clubwomen who mobilized against stereotypes about black female promiscuity and immorality; 1940s organizing against rape and sexual assault;[4] and the 1970s publication of many of the foundational texts of black feminist thought, when dialogue in the academy paralleled conversations at the grassroots as black women across the political spectrum discussed the relationship between black feminist thought, politics, and the material conditions of black women's lives.[5]

Rosemary Bray's *Unafraid of the Dark: A Memoir* emerged out of this renewed black feminist public sphere. But whereas these activists were addressing what Paula Giddings has called "the last taboo," bringing questions of gender and sexuality into national black political discourse, Bray tackles the gendered violence of poverty.[6] The memoir was published in the wake of the 1996 Personal Responsibility Act, otherwise known as "welfare reform." The legislation, which dismantled the social safety net for all by scapegoating poor women of color, represented thirty years of antiwelfare rhetoric: from Daniel Moynihan's attack on the "matriarchal black family" as a "tangle of pathology" to Reagan's "welfare queen" slander during his 1976 presidential campaign and Bill Clinton's subsequent sloganeering "to end welfare as we know it."[7] Bray uses her life story of growing up on welfare to create an ethic of social interdependence that challenges the ideologies behind the discourse of "personal responsibility." *Unafraid* builds upon the 1990s black feminist project of centering women's concerns in the social construction of black political reality by theorizing the impact of bringing sensibilities traditionally associated with women, such as love and care, into public life. The social interdependence that the memoir promotes both reclaims "the tender side" of black women's intellect in service of a post-*Brown* politic, reflecting the contemporary "affective turn" in black feminist thought, and offers a vision of political radicalism beyond traditional notions of activism.

A central argument in the memoir is that, as black feminist intellectuals retreated into the academy during the 1980s, a group of neoconservatives stepped into the vacuum, with Thomas simply the most visible among a band of policy-makers, such as Thomas Sowell, Glenn Loury, and Shelby Steele, building public profiles by denouncing social insurance programs, such as welfare and affirmative action:[8] "Men like Thomas—and they were largely men—seemed determined to co-opt the traditional strengths of the black communities from which they came, to cast those strengths in a more individualistic and conserva- tive mode."[9] To counter this "'bootstrap' theory of personal responsibility" fueling the debate on welfare reform, the memoir employs a bit of rhetorical gamesmanship as its narrative arc compares Bray's formative years with Thomas's: both experienced childhood poverty, attended Catholic schools and the Ivy League, and attained a measure of public achievement. However, in his public narrative of ascent from sharecropper's grandson to Supreme Court nominee, Thomas donned the guise of the self-made man, as if "he had done it all himself; there was no one who helped, it was all his strength of will and his own faith in God" (263). Having been raised by a woman who once resorted to welfare to care for her family in the face of poverty and unreliable male support, Bray chafed at self-interested neoconservatives who sought to "make my life and the lives of others an unfortunate aberration, a misguided attempt at social engineering, a lie" (xvi). A self-described witness to the saving grace of public assistance, she writes that she felt a moral imperative to testify "about the good that could happen—and that did happen—under the welfare system of the 1960s" (xvi). Acts of ethical witnessing such as Bray's are often written after great trauma, such as Art Spiegelman's *Maus* (on the Holocaust), Antjie Krog's *Country of My Skull* (on the Truth and Reconciliation Commission in South Africa), Ishmael Beah's *A Long Way Gone* (on being a child soldier in Sierra Leone), Maria Rosa Henson's *Comfort Woman: A Filipina's Story of Prostitution and Slavery under the Japanese Military* (on World War II sex slavery), and Doris Pilkington's *Rabbit-Proof Fence* (on the forced separation of Aboriginal children from their families in Australia).[10] While the precipitating catalysts are past, the narratives themselves are written with hope for the future, utilizing a myriad of autobio- graphical modes to create what Lauren Berlant has called "intimate publics," a community of readers whose shared experience inspires social action.[11] Bray's memoir, a coming-of-age story that also tracks a radical transformation from "poor and afraid" to, as the title proclaims, "unafraid of the dark," draws primarily on the bildungsroman and the conversion narrative to cultivate a progressive post-*Brown* politic.

The terms *autobiography* and *memoir* are often used interchangeably, but there are formal differences. Whereas traditional autobiography chronicles the life arc of the self-interested individual, usually male, from sinner to saint, rags to riches, memoir is a collective story, with the narrator situated within a particular historical moment, among a community of people, using the self simply as a lens through which to view broader histories and concerns.[12] Bray's pointed subtitle, *A Memoir*, perhaps reflects a publisher's exploiting the contemporary "memoir boom," giving the text a popular tag to whet reader appetites for the "true." However, the subtitle perhaps also suggests that this former book review editor is attuned to generic conventions and how they help achieve her project of creating an ethic of social interdependence. True to form, *Unafraid* catalogues repeated incidents in which people and circumstance facilitate Bray's ascent from public assistance to public achievement: "I have been lifted up by hands both seen and unseen, both individual and governmental. People, institutions, governments—all of them have something to offer people, something particularly important to the least among us" (xvii). That final phrase echoes the biblical injunction in Matthew 25 to care "for the least of these," a phrase theologians interpret as figuratively designating society's most vulnerable.[13] In detailing her experiences as a black girl growing up amid the trauma of poverty, Bray casts her life story as representative of, and in solidarity with, poor women scapegoated during the welfare reform debates. Like many contemporary minority and women autobiographers seeking to create a place in public life and discourse for the marginalized,[14] Bray appropriates the bildungsroman to chronicle her journey from the welfare rolls to the masthead of the *New York Times Book Review*. Traditionally, the bildungsroman has been regarded as a novel of development of a young man. The plot involves an escape from some repressive, outsider status into a larger world where encounters with mentors and life lessons lead the protagonist to relinquish youthful idealism and embrace social norms. Bray's use of its upward trajectory to chronicle her up-from-welfare narrative serves not to assimilate into a status quo but to signify on the individualistic narrative arc that has been characteristic of American autobiography since Benjamin Franklin's foundational eighteenth-century text, to transform the narrative of the self-made man into a spiritual meditation on social responsibility for the poor.

To champion an ethic of social interdependence, Bray's revisionist civil rights history of a Chicago family on welfare first invokes the understudied but influential welfare rights movement of the 1960s, equating it with the era's other iconographic victories. As she maps her life story onto well-known representations of the civil rights movement, from the heroic political narrative of 1954–1965 to its quintessential literary representation, Lorraine Hansberry's *A Raisin in the Sun*, Bray infuses this narrative of black political advancement with ethics of love and care, concerns often coded as feminine. This strategy reflects the larger 1990s black feminist project of putting women's concerns at the heart of a black politic, but it also engages political theory regarding the place of affect in the public sphere.[15] The debate about the relationship between politics and affect dates back to Saint Augustine, whose writings are considered foundational in Western autobiography and political thought. For instance, *Unafraid* owes its conversion-narrative arc to Augustine's pioneering *Confessions*, as do many contemporary memoirs.[16] But unlike Augustinian notions of grace that have animated conservative, even hostile, stances toward the poor, Bray draws on love-centered theologies that promote an ethic of social interdependence and redefine notions of political radicalism.

The Civil Rights Movement: A Mise-en-Scène of Performativity

Autobiographies construct their narrative selves on multiple mise-en-scènes to capture "a location, a moment in history, a sociopolitical space in culture."[17] In the opening lines of the memoir's preface, Bray situates her narrative in the modern civil rights movement as she lays claim to the activist sensibility attributed to the period: "In the very best sense, I am a child of the 1960s—not a direct participant in the maelstrom of events, but a human being whose life and culture, politics and identity were formed in this crucible of American change" (viii). More than a historical period that encompasses a discrete decade, "the sixties" has become shorthand for activist politics. Just the mere mention, then, of the year 1960, invoked five times in Bray's preface alone, conjures images of sit-ins, voter registration campaigns, and Freedom Rides for those even faintly familiar with the metanarrative. In her representation of the civil rights movement in *Unafraid*, Bray takes pains to summon the conventional story only to frustrate readers' expectations with odd silences surrounding pivotal moments. For instance, there is not a single explicit mention of *Brown v. Board of Education*, the landmark civil rights legislation that paved the way for the end of legal segregation. References to the movement's other legislative victories are omitted as well, and the sole mention of the Montgomery bus boycott is in a black history book (62). Rather, in Bray's retelling, 1960 is noteworthy because that is the year her mother hauled her brood to the Cook County Department of Public

Aid in Chicago. At the height of the movement, with sit-ins across the South dramatizing the principles of nonviolence, and with African nations waging decolonization battles across the Atlantic, her mother's "concerns were more mundane: food and clothes and a place to sleep for herself and her family" (vii).

Throughout *Unafraid*, Bray invokes, and then inverts, the conventional history to revise received understanding about the movement's scope and significance. Use of such a metanarrative always assumes an implied audience who has "come to expect certain discourses of identity and history," so that when known parts of the story are excluded or revised, new histories are formed.[18] Conjuring the familiar narrative only to omit defining elements allows Bray, for instance, to disrupt the false North-South dichotomy that often frames conventional civil rights history as she inserts her northern, working-class experience into a social movement considered southern and middle class. With television cameras trained on Little Rock and Greensboro and Birmingham, the era's most lasting images have portrayed the civil rights movement as a southern struggle. However, when Bray recounts her family marching with Martin Luther King Jr. in his unsuccessful protest against still-segregated Chicago public schools, she suggests that northern racism rivaled, if not surpassed, that of the South: "Bull Connor was one thing. But this was *Chicago*, with Gage Park and Bridgeport and a dozen other neighborhoods that nobody black would walk through, even in daylight" (64). And when the memoir does finally invoke the watershed year of 1954, it is to note not *Brown* but the structural changes in the post–World War II industrial economy that left blacks trapped in vulnerable sectors of the economy (ix). In *There Is a River*, historian Vincent Harding outlines three stages of the twentieth-century black freedom struggle: survival, mass protests, and radical action.[19] The civil rights movement is most often remembered for the last two. In Bray's retelling, she depicts what the sixties struggle looked like for poor and working-class people for whom the domestic dramas of day-to-day survival took precedence over the momentous political change sweeping the nation. The narrative inversion serves to recover the significance of the welfare rights movement, one of the most important but understudied social movements of the postwar period. It gained national prominence in June 1966 when six thousand welfare recipients and their supporters marched on state capitols and welfare departments all over the country in a national day of solidarity.[20] At its peak, it had an estimated following of between thirty thousand and one hundred thousand, the same number of followers of the Students for a Democratic Society (SDS). But the movement began years earlier, in the late 1950s and early 1960s, as poor black women like Bray's mother confronted caseworkers in local welfare offices, "the first site of contestation."[21]

Bray's memoir is among a group of recent scholarly works repositioning the welfare rights movement in civil rights histories. Before *Unafraid* was published in 1997, the welfare rights movement had received little attention outside of Guida West's *The National Welfare Rights Organization* (1981) and a chapter in Frances Fox Piven and Richard Cloward's *Poor People's Movements* (1978). Since then, there have been Premilla Nadasens's *Welfare Warriors*, a study of the movement's origins, and Lisa Levenstein's *A Movement without Marches*, which chronicles local organizing in Philadelphia. Reclaiming survival as a form of freedom struggle addresses one of the civil rights movement's unfinished goals and a major theme of contemporary black political thought: economic justice.[22] But it also challenges conventional movement history in two significant ways. First, the expanded narrative shows that the concerns about class and economic justice predated the 1968 Poor People's Campaign (whose plan of camping out on the National Mall in a show of mass disobedience predated the Occupy movement almost a half century later). In fact, King sought the endorsement and participation of the National Welfare Rights Organization and its leaders, including Johnnie Tillmon, a mother of six who founded the Los Angeles–based Aid to Needy Children–Mothers Anonymous before becoming NWRO's executive director, and deferred to these antipoverty advocates on welfare policy.[23] Second, recontextualizing the civil rights movement in relation to the welfare rights movement provides an opportunity to rethink the emergence of radicalism in the 1960s. Conventional histories cite the summer of 1964 as a time of polarization, when militant activists began to abandon King's nonviolent vision, veering off into black nationalism (as well as the women's movement and the antiwar movement). However, the very month Stokely Carmichael unleashed the call for "black power," June 1966, welfare recipients marched in their national day of solidarity. Rather than armed self-defense, their version of radicalism was based on the idea that poor black women, who had never been respected or valued for their work as mothers, as nurturers and caretakers of their *own* children, were deserving of government assistance for this indispensable social role.[24]

In *Unafraid*, Bray seeks to recover this argument about the radical politics that emanate from love and care in the public sphere. Generally, in black feminist thought, radicalism, if discussed at all, has been confined to militancy, stoking stereotypes of black women's unparalleled strength, or made more palatable by subsuming it under notions of the maternal that conform to politics of respectability.[25] But, as Vivian May reminds in her reevaluation of radical icon Harriet Tubman, references to the maternal can also reflect a "black feminist countermemory at work," one that recalls the radical legacies of black women during slavery who led what Angela Davis has termed "household[s] of resistance."[26] The ethic of social interdependence that Bray promotes in *Unafraid* is such a countermemory. Throughout the memoir, she frequently resorts to "strategic essentialisms," essentialist notions in service of a "visible political interest,"[27] which privilege values traditionally associated with the maternal and feminine, not to maintain a chauvinist belief in women's superiority but to reclaim social interdependence as a radical politic.

Toward this aim, the memoir engages debates within mainstream feminist social ethics of the 1980s and 1990s regarding purported gender differences in moral reasoning. Like its black feminist counterpart, the larger feminist movement sought to make women's experiences a necessary component in devising any model of political action. Carol Gilligan's seminal work, *In a Different Voice*, launched the notion of a gendered moral dualism, known as a feminine ethics of care and a masculine ethics of justice, to legitimize women's "ways of knowing." Influenced by Gilligan, feminist social ethicists in the 1980s and 1990s often privileged attributes associated with an ethic of care, disparaged and discredited as they are within society at large, to imagine "alternative form[s] of genuine moral reflection such that care for children or the infirm, customary occupations of women in our society, become matters for ethical reflection as important as issues of war and peace."[28] In recent years, scholars have distanced themselves from this essentialist model, for, as Katherine Tanner notes in "The Care That Does Justice," when examined in isolation, each ethic can be problematic: care can become paternalistic; justice, authoritarian and inhumane.[29] Privileging an ethics of care reproduces sexist images of men that disregard social structures and the gendered racism of black men's lives. Although *Unafraid* arguably works to integrate these constructs toward memoir's end, essentialist gendered spheres indeed structure the narrative as the actions and values of men are depicted as hurting black families and, by extension, black communities. For instance, the precinct captain who threatens her mother's welfare benefits unless she votes for Mayor Daley recalls the contemporary context in which the memoir arrives, with black male politicos exploiting gender politics to consolidate their personal power at the expense of broader black communities: "Mayor Daley's machine hacks did a great many things akin to threatening women and children. . . . Precinct captains like the one who threatened my mother were commonplace: this was one of the few positions of relative power reserved for blacks in the Daley organization. Of course there were a few other black people who had been rewarded for their faithful service to Daley, my father said, frequently referring to them as 'those handkerchief-head Negroes' and 'Uncle Tom sumbitches'" (59–60). On the one hand, the scene dispels any nostalgic visions of a mythic, unified black community under segregation, a common theme in post-*Brown* movement narratives, as we saw with Melba Beals's *Warriors Don't Cry*. But the scene also provides a larger political context in which to understand how "the public spheres of work and government" are intimately connected to "the interpersonal relations of family life."[30]

Bray's strategic use of essentialist gendered spheres to advocate a political ethic that honors female experience and values is most evident in her parents' portrayal. From the memoir's earliest pages, her mother is celebrated for her "genius at making do" (10), whether improvising a grill out of a bucket and oven rack to cook dinner and warm the house when the gas is cut off (14–15) or making the proverbial dollar out of fifteen cents. In *Black Womanist Ethics*, Katie G. Cannon has argued that black women regard "survival against tyrannical systems of oppression [as] the true sphere of moral life,"[31] and Bray indeed portrays her mother's resourcefulness in the face of dire poverty as a reflection of moral strength. In response to welfare-reform advocates convinced that the benefits to the poor and, therefore, "the unworthy," must be policed, she writes, "Not one of them could survive for a week on what my mother raised four children on every month for more than twenty years" (13). A Pentecostal who hums spirituals throughout the day, Bray's mother could in fact be one of the activists profiled in Rosetta Ross's *Witnessing and Testifying: Black Women, Religion, and Civil Rights*. For Ross, civil rights movement organizers like Fannie Lou Hamer and Diane Nash, steeped in the traditions of the black church, embraced a spirituality that linked survival and well-being with racial uplift and social responsibility.[32] Bray inserts her mother into this tradition as she links her familial caretaking to racial uplift. A case in point is another mise-en-scène that inverts the civil rights movement narrative of the Freedom Summer of 1964. Known for the voting-registration drives that launched Fannie Lou Hamer to prominence, the Freedom Summer narrative is employed here to suggest the intensity with which her mother worked, through a rigorous regimen of black respectability, to achieve some upward mobility for her family. Bray writes, "In the summer of 1964, and for many summers after that, there were precious moments of freedom amid the work of the household" (43). Saturday chores were rewarded with trips to the library, a ritual so valued that her mother keeps her children's library cards filed with birth certificates, vaccination records, food stamps, and medical cards. At day's end, there would be methodical preparations—hair styled, clothes laid out—for church on Sunday: "Nobody looking like a bum was going to church with Mama" (50). Critics have argued that respectability politics has a conservative cast,[33] but in a world where black mothering is disparaged and criminalized, the portrait is a radical one.

Bray's father is rhetorically positioned throughout the narrative to occupy the dialectically opposed authoritarian ethic of justice. A news junkie whose favorite program is *Meet the Press*, he "believed in America—at least on paper. He talked about the Declaration of Independence and the Constitution at every opportunity, if only to point out the error of white folks' ways" (38). But whereas her mother is portrayed in terms of uplift, her father is described as "Walter Lee's evil twin" (16), in dubious homage to the character of Walter Lee Younger from Lorraine Hansberry's *Raisin in the Sun*. Like Walter Lee, Bray's father exemplifies "shadow men" (46): would-be patriarchs turned abusive in the failed attempt to attain white male privilege. Other men in their Chicago neighborhood "saved their outbursts for weekends, or a night of heavy drinking," but her father, a gambler with a hustler's entrepreneurial instincts, exploded in random rounds of domestic violence rooted in an authoritarian "need to control" (15).

Bray, who describes her childhood as "like being on the set of *A Raisin in the Sun*" (16), meticulously maps these family dynamics onto Hansberry's play, one of the most famous movement narratives in American literature. Bray's appropriation of it in *Unafraid* is yet another example of the way the memoir invokes and then inverts classic movement stories to theorize an ethics of interdependence. As Walter Lee's maturation symbolized a nation coming of age in the 1960s, Bray's development and transformation serve as a discursive model for a post-*Brown* politic, though reconfigured through a feminist perspective. There are indeed several pointed parallels between the play and this memoir about poor, black families living on Chicago's South Side at the dawn of the civil rights movement. Thwarted dreams torment her father, as they do Walter Lee. Bray's feminist politics mirror those of Beneatha, Walter Lee's spirited sister. Even the Sisyphean striving of the Younger household, captured in Hansberry's opening stage directions, is mirrored in Bray's description of her family's cramped kitchenette: "Our front door opened from the hallway into the living room. The room was furnished with a couch covered in a green-blue faintly iridescent fabric, where Mama slept each night, and a stuffed chair, a bookcase I pretended was mahogany, and a gigantic console radio. To the left, through a set of curtains, was the children's bedroom. To the right was an enormous room with built-in cabinets. This clearly used to be the dining room; for us, it was both dining room and kitchen" (6–7). Most significantly, both play and memoir open with mothers waking the household in preparation for a new day.

In *Raisin*, at the sound of an alarm clock that echoes the reported bombs exploding like "dreams deferred" throughout the play, Ruth wakes Walter Lee along with their son, as if both are children. The image links black progress to the maturation of black manhood, with the nation metaphorically coming of age as Walter Lee assumes his father's mantle as patriarch. In the memoir, however, Bray presents an image of social interdependence animated by a feminine, spiritual aesthetic. In the memoir, Bray's mother also wakes her children, although it is the middle of the night. The broiler is out again, and she wants them to stand in the warmth of the stove, its door open and burners on, as she sets pots of water to boil for their morning routine. Long after the children return to bed, however, Bray's mother stands vigil over the lit stove until morning. "As long as the stove was on, someone had to stay awake. That someone was always Mama" (4). The image of a woman standing vigil through the night to keep a fire burning serves as a metaphor for the ethics of interdependence that is at the heart of *Unafraid*. It recalls the African American spiritual "Keep Your Lamps Trimmed and Burning," which is based on the New Testament parable of the wise and foolish bridesmaids,[34] a narrative prelude to the injunction to serve "the least of these" in Matthew 25. After that night, at daybreak, Bray recalls, "I stumbled through the dark into the dim kitchen lit only by the burners on the gas stove and the faint flicker from the broiler" (3–4). In the scenes that follow, Bray chronicles her maturation from being a "poor, afraid" little girl on welfare to a "writer, wife, mother" who is now "unafraid of the dark."

The autobiography's seemingly bourgeois trajectory—with Bray transformed from the outsider status of welfare recipient to "writer, wife, mother" by narrative's end—is more subversive than the traditional bildungsroman narrative arc suggests. Given the ways black mothers are vilified in the welfare reform debate, to position herself as a mother in a memoir meant to solicit reader support of public assistance is to walk as fine a line as Harriet Jacobs did in *Incidents in the Life of a Slave Girl*. In addition, the unconventionality of her identity construction as a "writer" troubles traditionally gendered ideas about what it means to be a wife and mother. Historically, the autobiographical act has challenged the socially constructed category of "woman."[35] In this space of seeming conventionality, Bray charts a model of black female political formation that provides an alternative not only to the self-sacrificial strength that Beals critiques in *Warriors Don't Cry* but also to the "radical black female subjectivity" portrayed in the memoirs of Black Power activists such as Angela Davis, Assata Shakur, and Elaine Brown.[36] The Black Power memoirs, in chronicling the evolution of a radical political consciousness, hew to the era's militant ethos, the "gospel of blackness": a psychological and cultural transformation in the way black Americans radicalized in the sixties understood themselves as political actors and their relationship to the state.[37] Bray, who served as a Unitarian Universalism minister for thirteen years before becoming president of Starr King School for the Ministry, imagines political agency as emanating from the reorientation of self through "encounters with the divine," or what some theologians call grace. The narrative arc of *Unafraid* ends before Bray becomes a minister, and the memoir acknowledges her "affinity for feminist theology" (249) only in passing. However, the radical transformation from "poor, afraid" to "unafraid of the dark"—the classic conversion-narrative arc of a "faulty" to an "enlightened" self—provides a theological meditation on the relationship between affect and justice, what Martha Nussbaum calls "political emotions." Katie Cannon suggests that the love-centered writings of Howard Thurman and Martin Luther King Jr. may enrich the development of feminist social ethics.[38] I now examine the way Bray's memoir merges the bildungsroman trope of coming-of-age through serial lessons with the conversion narrative's arc of radical transformation to take up Cannon's charge.

"A Radical Reorientation of Personality"

Suspicions regarding the relationship of love to politics in modern political theory date back to Saint Augustine. His concept of grace, a redemptive state granted by divine mercy rather than good works, has been said to contribute to the political apathy that de Tocqueville predicted would be the fate of all liberal democracies, "a growing sense of impotence about the possibilities of collective action."[39] Recent scholarship suggests that the more antiliberal strains of Augustinian thought animate the social conservative stances of late twentieth-century American evangelicals. Bray alludes to these debates about religious social ethics when she describes "Christians whose faith had led them, not to a larger embrace of the world, but to a profound sense of hopelessness. . . . What was it about the mercy of God as they had experienced it that made them so merciless toward their fellow human beings?" (262). To combat this cynicism, progressive political theorists increasingly consider the place of affective sensibilities in the public sphere to revive the creative imagination that inspires engaged citizenship and political action, what Robin D. G. Kelley has called "freedom dreams."[40] *Unafraid* has a similar agenda and, consequently, implications for these new directions in modern political theory. Like Augustine's spiritual autobiography, *Confessions*, *Unafraid* recounts repeated instances when, by strokes of great providence, people and circumstance facilitate Bray's journey from "poor, afraid" (4) to, as the title testifies, "unafraid of the dark." *Unafraid* works within the confessional conventions that are the genre's foundation and the contemporary memoir's template. In sync with "neoconfessional" market trends, Bray divulges various childhood "sins": stealing at school, lying to social workers to protect her family's welfare benefits, indulging in spending sprees as "profligate" as her father's gambling.[41] But as Rita Felski argues in *Beyond Feminist Aesthetics*, confessions such as Bray's often serve to "constitute feminist community and provide alternative knowledge based in the authority of personal experience."[42] For instance, the Augustinian notions of grace that once cautioned against misplaced virtue and "utopianism" in the public sphere have devolved to political apathy and even hostility toward the poor.[43] The social ethics that underwrite *Unafraid* understand that a providential encounter, or grace, should inspire, if not require, service to others.

In the seminal essay "Love," which influenced Martin Luther King Jr.'s formulation of the "beloved community," Howard Thurman argues that cultivating "an attitude of respect for personality" is the key to nurturing a social ethics of interdependence. According to Thurman, one is awakened to a sense of personal power and collective purpose through spiritual experience, or encounters with the divine, which he thought occurred through everyday interaction with others.[44] In chronicling her life story, Bray dramatizes Thurman's belief that a "radical reorientation of personality" through everyday encounters with the divine engenders moral agency with political consequence that is "constitutive of all forms of meaningful freedom."[45] While an earlier generation equated freedom with the abolition of slavery, for her parents, strivers of the Great Migration generation, "a little more freedom" meant greater opportunity for their "children, many of them still unborn, who might know a world of more possibility than theirs" (ix). In the memoir's opening scenes, Bray associates her mother in particular with this child-centered ethos to model an ethic of social interdependence seemingly lost in the contemporary political moment. The linkage rhetorically and strategically draws on gendered ethics, although Bray regards "the qualities of common struggle, of collective action and mutual dependence [as] legacies of African American life" (263). A scene where a three-year-old Bray learns to read reflects this past value of self-sacrifice and collective struggle on behalf of future generations: "Mama printed the letters of the alphabet on notebook paper, then tacked the sheet to the wall near the pantry door with a tiny nail. She would go over and over it with me. Then she would choose words that she liked, and ask Miss Holmes what they meant, and how to spell them. She would write everything down, then teach me what Miss Holmes taught her. This way, Mama and I learned together. The first word we learned was *opportunity*; I spelled it out loud in a singsong voice as often as anyone would allow me. . . . In a few months, I could spell words out when I saw them on signs, or labels, or posters. Mama and I were on a bus one afternoon, and I began to point out letters and words that I knew" (24). Such scenes of instruction, in which narrators detail the pains endured to come to literacy, have been a slave-narrative convention since the eighteenth-century text of John Stuart or Quobna Ottobah Cugoano. The setting of an integrated bus in the early 1960s, as well as the word learned, *opportunity*, arguably evokes the civil rights era. In the nexus of these tropes of "literacy as freedom" and "freedom as opportunity," Bray creates a space to craft her counterculture memory, to re-imagine the meaning of freedom in the post-*Brown* era. From this moment of literacy, as she depicts her eclectic education in Catholic schools, prep school, and the Ivy League, Bray suggests that, in the contemporary moment, freedom requires an expansive identity beyond singular or nationalist notions of "black-ness." In the sixties, "blackness became a determining category in how African Americans understood themselves as agents," as political actors in relation to the state.[46] In *Unafraid*, Bray imagines political agency emanating from the reorientation of self toward the divine.

Bray's journey from welfare to writer, from wounded to whole, begins in a childhood defined by poverty and domestic violence, invoking the "dark night of the soul" that often begins the conversion narrative.[47] On yet another wintry Chicago night, she lies awake, chilled to the bone by the cold and the "slapping sounds of flesh on flesh" (8) as her father fought her mother. In its evocation of the lingering effects of racial trauma on the black modern subject, the scene once again echoes Frederick Douglass's 1845 *Narrative*, as he describes the horror of hearing his aunt Hester whipped by a slave master jealous of her suitors, and the misery of feet "so cracked with frost that the pen with which I am writing might be laid in the gashes."[48] The emergence of the writing black subject as constitutive of freedom defines the African American autobiographical tradition, and Bray couples the literacy-as-freedom trope with the conventions of the bildungsroman as she stages her conversion.

In 1961, when Bray starts first grade, Chicago schools are still segregated, despite the passage of *Brown*. Chronicling her elementary and secondary education does more than dramatize *Brown*'s conclusions that segregation had a "deleterious and warping effect upon the minds of children."[49] It also illustrates what Thurman called the "zones of agreement," the patterns of fear and hate that keep segregation in tact.[50] For instance, at Saint Ambrose, a black parochial school, the bookish Bray faces daily harassment from peers threatened by her smarts. When she transfers to Parker, a white prep school on Chicago's North Side, she anticipates starring in her own Little Rock Nine episode, with racists hurling epithets while blocking passage to the schoolhouse door: "I literally backed away from the door. 'Mama, those people are white!' I couldn't believe she looked so unexcited. 'They'll kill me!' She watched the same news I watched; she knew white people had thrown bricks at us in demonstrations in Chicago years earlier. She knew as well as I did that white people sicced dogs on little boys in Selma and blew up churches in Birmingham while little girls were in Sunday school" (72–73). Once again Bray conjures iconographic images— attack dogs in Selma, the bombing of the Sixteenth Street Baptist, and implicitly Little Rock—only to frustrate readers' expectations: "Girl, these kids ain't going to bother you" (73), her mother says, dismissing the protest. To be sure, Bray encounters racism at Parker, where students who feared her singular black body in their midst hatefully dubbed her the Black Plague (94). But it is her own sense of shame, the self-rejection that Thurman called segregation's "real evil,"[51] that Bray emphasizes here. As Hortense Spillers writes, the fear of blackness "identifies the terrain of racism and the racist. . . . [But] inasmuch as the white problem redounds on black personality, the burden is generously shared."[52]

A pivotal confession of kleptomania while a student at Parker—"I didn't plan to become a thief, but I became one nonetheless" (78)—best illustrates the influence of Thurman's theology on this memoir (despite its echoes of theological antithesis in Augustine's pear stealing in *Confessions*). The one poor student amid privilege, Bray begins to steal money from her peers to pass as middle class. The ethics of this revelation are intriguing, for, when finally caught, she felt, "The theorists were right about me, and it hurt to find myself living out the stereotype. I was doing just what white people always said black people do whenever we got the chance—steal, cheat, lie" (79). A cursory reading suggests a troubling embrace of the pernicious culture-of-poverty stereotypes that the memoir seeks to displace. However, an earlier admission of lying to the welfare authorities to protect her family has established a dramatic irony in which readers understand this childhood confession to be an indictment of racist theories, not so-called black pathology. The hassles and hurdles of welfare required families to run outside hustles and calculated games lest benefits be cut and families fractured: "To keep ourselves together, we needed a common story, a common set of lies, to be told at appropriate times, a common under-standing of what was at risk" (57). Thurman calls this "age-old technique by which the weak have survived in the midst of the strong" the "sinless sin."[53] Within this ironic framework, readers realize that Bray's spate of kleptomania reflects the psychic effects of structural inequality rather than her character.

A further suggestion that Bray's confession serves to theorize Thurman is that it echoes a story he recounts in *Luminous Darkness*, his meditation on the evil of racial segregation. Another six-year-old, Ruby Bridges, integrates a New

Orleans school. As the only black child, she is segregated "as though she were the carrier of a disease"—as if she too were, like Bray, a Black Plague—in a class of her own, "insulated from the other children, with her own special teacher." Over the holidays, when school staff finds the child's locker stuffed with months' worth of uneaten lunches, they realize the "terrible burden" placed on her and incorporate her into the regular life of the school. At year's end, "the children presented a program, and she was naturally and unself-consciously a part of the program, and nobody thought twice about it."[54] Similarly, a school production follows Bray's confession of her own psychic, "terrible burden," with both revelations serving to dramatize the transformative encounters of everyday grace that Thurman defines as "religious experience." Through the intervention of a theater teacher who "saw me, knew me for who I was and who I might be" (88), Bray is cast as the lead in *Alice in Wonderland*, another coming-of-age narrative of chrysalis and change. The rationale was that, if she were allowed to show her peers "what kind of person" (96) she was, they'd be able to transcend the barriers of race, culture, and class that kept them enemies: "[The experience] did a lot more than show them what kind of person I was. [It] showed *me* what kind of person I was. Until then, I had remained ashamed of who I was. I knew I shouldn't be. I knew I didn't want to be. But I was ashamed, and all I could do was turn that shame into anger and silence, except in the classroom. Mr. Griffith helped me find my voice, glimpse my real self without shame" (96). The star turn evolved into Bray's directing a schoolwide Christmas tableau, a metaphorical vision of the "beloved community": "There were Glass Wax murals everywhere: a black Jesus, a glowing menorah, a multiracial heavenly host. It was different and real and very beautiful. This is the world I want, I thought. This is what life should be like all the time" (109). From this point on in the narrative, Bray registers "something in me growing broader and deeper" (102). This expanded consciousness continues at Yale after an encounter with a compassionate dean who refuses to attribute her flunking grades to racist notions of black inferiority. Instead, he intuits "what kind of person [she is, one] of those students with strict parents who spends her whole life studying, then comes to college and spends the whole time partying" (134). Rather than presumptuous or paternalistic, the dean's response is depicted as providential: he extends the grace that allows Bray not only to recover a squandered semester but also to reject the careerist trajectory expected of black Ivy Leaguers and follow her heart's desire: to be a writer.

Through these serial scenes of instruction, Bray recasts the literacy-as-freedom trope as the freedom to embrace an identity that is "inclusive of all the meaning of his life," as Thurman puts it:[55] "Sixteen years of school were over and my real life could begin: I was free, black, and twenty one" (170). In equating blackness with an expanded consciousness, Bray directly challenges the Du Boisian "double consciousness" (251), whose gendered formulations of identity and nation fail to account for a personality shaped by disparate impulses and loyalties beyond race and gender, what Mae Gwendolyn Henderson has called "multiple consciousness."[56] Arguably, then, Bray imbues this rearticulation of freedom with a black feminist perspective.

If education presents the vehicle for Bray to chart her "radical reorientation of personality," then her journalism career chronicles the political import of this consciousness. Fittingly, writing brings all aspects of her being into wholeness: "Of all the work I'd ever done, it was this job that came closest to my ideal life—a place in which all my interests and identities and passions came together" (250). Given the importance of religious experience in Thurman's thought, it is significant that Bray deems working at *Essence*, the nation's premiere magazine targeting a black female audience, as a "*spiritual experience*" (206). The convergence of personality and purpose was most evident during her tenure at the *New York Times Book Review*. As she shepherds into print a review of Darlene Clark Hine's historic collection of such nineteenth-century black women writers as Maria Stewart, Frances E. W. Harper, Anna Julia Cooper—outspoken women who used their voices and pens to proclaim a black feminist perspective on the issues of the day—Bray has an epiphany about her own calling: "There has always been, in much of the African-American community, a sense that God calls people to do certain work, certain things that are their tasks and no one else's. Some of those tasks are large, so large that they seem unachievable. Some of them are small things, links in a larger chain. This was my moment to be the link in a chain" (266). Through the meticulous ordering of her calling, Bray has argued that "nurturing a respect for personality," which she casts as a spiritual conversion, is a prerequisite for making political change. As Bray writes in her preface, "I know who I am. More important, I know who I was and I know who I became; I understand the journey from there to here. I am the great great granddaughter of slaves and the granddaughter of sharecroppers and the daughter of poor, proud, angry people determined to make more of me than they could of themselves. I have been given priceless gifts I have no right to squander. . . . I understand that these things were mine for a reason: to secure for others what was once secured for me" (xvi–xviii). Thurman argues that true personality only emerges within the context of interdependence, the context of shared community and fellowship. In charting the "journey from there to here," Bray articulates a theological vision that is also one of political justice.

Radicalism Redefined: Love in Action

In religious thought, the translation of God's grace, "vertical love," into social action, "horizontal love," is often mediated through an encounter with a neighbor.[57] The gospels, of course, extend the definition of "neighbor" to include the poor and marginalized, those "on the highways and byways, in the factories and slums, on the farms and in the mines," as Gustavo Gutierrez writes in *The Power of the Poor in History*. Transformative change begins with this broadened perspective, Gutierrez argues, for it demands not charity or relief but a call to "build a different social order."[58] In a chapter that narrates a budding friendship with Royce, a homeless man in her Harlem neighborhood, Bray models the radical impact of social interdependence, of love in action. Framed by two chapters that relate Bray's discovery and then her embrace of her literary calling, the Royce chapter develops a parallel story of Bray's brief foray into traditional political activism. Through these intersecting chapters that juxtapose "the life of the mind" and "life on the barricades," Bray expands the registers in which we understand radical politics.

In depicting Harlem, Bray draws a portrait of a fractured community torn by class warfare and returns once again to her theme of gendered moral dualism. An associate of the local drug dealers, Royce is branded the "enemy" (230), and even his homeless status indicates that he stands outside the community of homeowners in the block association of which Bray has become president. Like her earlier confession of stealing, Bray's portrayal works rhetorically to show a transformation; over the course of their encounters, the relationship moves from paternalism to equality, with the two sharing daily conversation on her brownstone steps. Their reconciliation reflects the recent direction of feminist social ethics, which seeks to replace "these ineffective or inappropriate strategies [of unreconstructed ethics of care and justice] with an open dialogue in which all bring their own highly situated particularities of perspective and concern into a public forum for mutual critique."[59]

Whereas the encounter with Royce serves to model social interdependence, the intertwined story line of Bray's foray into activism speaks to the alternatives to traditional notions of radicalism. Throughout *Unafraid*, Bray characterizes her engagement in traditional activism as "an adolescent search for identity" (61, 101), or the juvenile folly characteristic of the bildungsroman. This theme has its most prominent expression at a civic meeting in which Bray, as president of the block's tenant association, challenges city planners who are determined to make their Harlem community a dumping ground for yet another social service institution. She makes a telling distinction between "the heated remarks made by a group of Harlem residents who'd won their activist stripes on the battlegrounds of the late 1960s" and the "written speech" she delivered (240). City officials dismissed the militant rhetoric of these erstwhile activists, full of empty threats to demolish the building brick-by-brick. In contrast to the rhetoric of late-1960s militancy, Bray's prepared statement brought "listeners to their feet" and "total shock [to] the faces" of the city representatives (241). Admittedly, Bray traffics here in the caricature of the Black Power movement as the crazy uncle of the black freedom struggle that recent scholars challenge.[60] It is another strategic essentialism in service of an important point. In making this contrast, *Unafraid* seeks to delineate alternate registers—spiritual, affective, feminine—of political action. The scene in fact recalls "Where Do We Go from Here?," King's last presidential address to the Southern Christian Leadership Conference, in which he took militants to task for their failure to formulate pragmatic approaches to transforming society: "One of the great problems of history is that the concepts of love and power have usually been contrasted as opposites . . . so that love is identified with a resignation of power, and power with a denial of love. . . . What is needed is a realization that power without love is reckless and abusive, and love without power is sentimental and anemic. Power at its best is love implementing the demands of justice, and justice at its best is power correcting everything that stands against love."[61] King's message of how love accomplishes justice speaks to the memoir's exploration of political emotion. After this foray into life on the barricades, Bray realizes that she has been ordained "as a writer, not a politician" and that this calling has collective political implications. She concludes, "While activism was the heart of black political and social progress, writing and thinking was its backbone" (266). Or, what civil rights activist, poet, and priest Pauli Murray was fond of calling socially conscious intellectual thought: "confrontation by typewriter."[62]

To understand the alternate notions of radicalism that Bray recovers through theorizing the place of love and care in the public sphere, it is perhaps useful to consider *Unafraid* in relation to Murray's posthumously published autobiography, *Pauli Murray: The Autobiography of a Black Activist, Feminist, Lawyer, Priest, and Poet* (1989), originally titled *Song in a Weary Throat: An American Pilgrimage* (1987). Both are "movement memoirs" that detail how the twentieth-century black freedom struggle indelibly defined each writer's life. Murray's is the more traditional autobiography, covering the course of her life from birth to death, and its careful historical documentation and prosaic style less lend themselves to the rich close-readings than Bray's more belletristic narrative affords.[63] However, there is a literary unity to *Pauli Murray*. An excerpt from her epic poem "Dark Testament" (1943) serves as the autobiography's epigraph (as it also does for this chapter). The whole of "Dark Testament" tells of a history that has been silenced, suggesting that *Pauli Murray* represents such a history, a countercultural memory to the received civil rights story.[64] Readers learn, for instance, that one of Murray's seminar papers, written at Howard Law School, introduced the novel notion of challenging "separate but equal" as a civil rights strategy, which of course would later shape the foundational argument of *Brown v. Board of Education*. Her legal thinking was so essential that Thurgood Marshall is said to have nicknamed her reference book, *States' Law on Race and Color* (1951), "the bible" in the three years leading up to the *Brown* decision.[65] And after being denied entry into a graduate program at the University of North Carolina at Chapel Hill for her race, and then into Harvard Law School for her gender, Murray coined the term "Jane Crow" to describe what black feminists would later call "double jeopardy."[66]

Despite these bona fides, Murray, who was jailed in Virginia for refusal to move to the back of a segregated bus fifteen years before Rosa Parks, was dismissed during the Black Power era as a reactionary. Brandeis students newly converted to the era's "gospel of blackness" faulted Murray for failure to adhere to the tenets of its ideology.[67] Recently, Murray has enjoyed redemption, as scholars recognize the rigor of her intellect and writing, attributing to her a brand of radicalism beyond rhetoric and posture.[68] Murray's life thus epitomizes those personal narratives that historian Jacquelyn Dowd Hall has asked scholars to recover to broaden our understanding of the civil rights movement's breadth, scope, and radicalism. I argue that the uncanny echoes between Bray's and Murray's texts take up that charge. For instance, Bray's confrontation with ersatz radical activists at the neighborhood civil meeting recalls Murray's showdown at Brandeis, both moments challenging the traditional notion of militancy as the only form of political radicalism. Bray's oratory brought "listeners to their feet" and "total shock [to] the faces," much like a recitation of Murray's "Dark Testament" during a memorial for Martin Luther King Jr. reportedly brought a Seattle audience of more than ten thousand "to its feet in tribute to its eloquence."[69] These echoes work to recover and expand notions of radicalism during the civil rights movement, but they also serve to constitute activist community.

The memoir's sensitivity to reader-writer dynamics reveals Bray cultivating an audience for political ends. From her days as a writer at Scholastic Magazines crafting prose for "reluctant readers" (184) and at *Essence* influencing feminist politics, Bray understands how the rhetorical strategies of identification sway audiences. The scene of Bray reading Louisa May Alcott's *Little Women* might provide a model for the sense of identification she arguably would like to elicit from readers. On one of those radicalizing Freedom Summer library trips, she stumbles across this novel of four sisters anticipating a Christmas without presents. Also one of four siblings in a poor family, Bray is captivated from the first page: "It was about girls, for one thing, girls who could almost be like me, especially Jo. It seemed to me a shame that she wasn't black; then our similarity would be complete. She loved to read, she loved to make up plays, she hated acting ladylike, she had a dreadful temper. I had found a kindred spirit" (48). In *Unafraid*, Bray sets about forging a sense of identification with such "kindred spirits" and defining her community of readers, what Lauren Berlant calls an "intimate public," an audience she assumes has shared knowledge and experience.[70]

Presumably, *Unafraid* speaks to a black women's public sphere mobilized in the wake of the Thomas-Hill hearings (even as publishers may be courting a previously untapped black female readership "discovered" during the 1990s "black book boom," when Terri McMillan, Toni Morrison, and Alice Walker topped the *New York Times* bestsellers list). From her preface it is clear that she has a distinct audience in mind. As she laments the advent of welfare reform, Bray speaks to the complacency, and complicity, of her civil-rights movement generation: "My mistake, and the mistake many of us made, was in believing that we might best repay the system that saved our lives by just downplay[ing] the circumstances of our early lives. . . . We thought it would be enough to get an education and a job, to marry and start a family, to pay our taxes and vote, to be ordinary and unexceptional citizens. It now appears that we were wrong" (viii). The use of first-person plural pronouns *us* and *our* assumes shared experience: accomplished middle-class black women like herself who escaped poverty because of civil rights reforms. It is not simply the trauma of childhood poverty to which Bray alludes, however. In the memoir's opening chapter, she recounts how her husband's gestures of affection often trigger flashbacks of waking in the middle of the night to hear her father beating her mother. What is striking about the passage is that Bray frames this personal story in the second person: "Certain things shape you, change you forever. Years later, long after you think you've escaped, some ordinary experience flings you backward into memory, transports you to a frozen moment, and you freeze" (3). In Augustine's *Confessions*, *you* addresses God and the human reader who is edified through the narrative's witness. Bray's *you*, of course, is the reader. In this self-conscious act of ethical witnessing, the use of the second-person pronoun conflates the experiences of autobiographer and reader, eliciting identification around the issue of violence against women, the major issue of 1990s black feminist activism.

The narrative strategy demands that readers be ethical witnesses as well. In this first chapter, Bray seeks to create a sense of shared suffering and shared responsibility, for what follows is the scene of Bray's mother standing over the stove's lit burners, the memoir's central motif of interdependence. The juxtaposition suggests that this is the ethic that Bray hopes readers will glean from *Unafraid*, and it is to this ethic that she returns in the epilogue.

The epilogue opens in a day care center as Bray, pregnant with her second child, picks up her firstborn son. The focus on children evokes her mother's ethos of interdependence, as does the bedtime ritual of singing Jerome Kern's "Look for the Silver Lining," which she says distills the "ageless wisdom" of her mother's favorite spiritual, "Trouble Don't Last Always." In *Deep River: Reflections on the Religious Insight of Certain Negro Spirituals*, Howard Thurman notes that "Trouble Don't Last Always" and the series from which "Keep Your Lamps Trimmed and Burning" derives both reflect an ethos of "incurable optimism."[71] The hopeful sentiment evokes the excerpt from Pauli Murray's "Dark Testament" that introduces this chapter:

> Hope is a word in a tuneless ditty—
> A word whispered with the wind,
> A dream of forty acres and a mule,
> A cabin of one's own and a moment to rest,
> A name and place for one's children
> And children's children at last . . .
> Hope is a song in a weary throat.

Berlant argues that contemporary women's writing, steeped in sentimentality, often has an "optimistic ending pointing toward a better future waiting."[72] In that regard, *Unafraid* perhaps reflects its literary moment. But given the black autobiographical tradition of offering life story as a political intervention in which the memoir is also steeped, the "silver lining" attitude of its ending, its testament of hope for "one's children / And children's children at last," reflects the memoir's animating ethic of social interdependence.

The theological meditation on caring for "the least of these" embedded within *Unafraid* becomes explicit in a sermon Bray delivered about Occupy Wall Street, the radical movement against economic inequality for which she served as a chaplain. It was October 2011, a month after this reincarnation of Dr. King's Poor People's Campaign began in New York City's Zuccotti Park; debates about welfare reform had faded from public discourse, but concerns about rising poverty had only intensified in the fifteen intervening years. It was also the season of Divali, the Indian festival of lights. A contraction of the Sanskrit word *Deepavali*, which means "row of lamps," Divali involves all kinds of light—fireworks, bonfires, strings of electric lights, clay lamps filled with oil—to celebrate the triumph of light over darkness in the world. In her sermon, titled "Illumination," Bray notes that every culture has a tradition symbolizing that universal human struggle to, in essence, "keep your lamps trimmed and burning"—not in preparation for apocalypse, or some otherworldly encounter, but for the daily human interactions that inspire social responsibility on behalf of others.[73] As with *Unafraid*, she grounds the sermon's theological meditation in a personal narrative. Twenty years earlier, she was working the copy desk at the *Wall Street Journal*. At 7 p.m., editors turned on the network news to ensure that their top stories coincided with ones in the paper. Bray's top story that evening was about a crop of soybeans rotting on a ship anchored at sea, a cost-benefit analysis that found it more profitable to let the crop spoil than to unload and distribute it. The famine in Ethiopia led the network news. Of course the unconscionable reality of widespread starvation in a world of plenty emphasized the systemic nature of economic inequality. But as Gutierrez writes in *The Power of the Poor in History*, such a revelation is never "politically neutral" or "ethically innocent," for an ethic of social interdependence calls for not simply charitable relief, but radical action: it demands we imagine and create a better world.[74]

amazon.com

Your order of July 4, 2016 (Order ID 115-2890149-5286638)

Qty.	Item	Item Price	Total
1	Words of Witness: Black Women's Autobiography in the Post-Brown Era (Wisconsin Studies in Autobiography) Ards, Angela A. --- Paperback (°° 1-D-7 °°) 029930504X	$24.38	$24.38
1	Buttoned Up: Clothing, Conformity, and White-Collar Masculinity Casanova, Erynn Masi de --- Paperback (°° 1-D-7 °°) 1501700499	$19.95	$19.95

This shipment completes your order.

Have feedback on how we packaged your order? Tell us at www.amazon.com/packaging.

Subtotal	$44.33
Shipping & Handling	$4.98
Promotional Certificate	$-4.98
Tax Collected	$3.00
Order Total	$47.33
Paid via credit/debit	$47.33
Balance due	$0.00

Return or replace your item
Visit Amazon.com/returns

37/DXbFNHJOH/-4 of 4-//UPS-PHLPA-T/sss-us/7867627/0712-10:00/0707-10:06

A3

3

Honoring the Past to Move Forward
June Jordan's *Soldier*

> To whom do I owe the power behind my voice,
> what strength I have become, yeasting up like
> sudden blood from under the bruised skin's blister?
> Audre Lorde,
> *Zami: A New Spelling of My Name*

June Jordan is most often remembered as an international activist nurtured in the black American freedom struggle of the 1960s. She is among those activists of the civil rights and Black Power movements whose writings helped launch the field of contemporary black women's literature, such as Alice Walker, Sonia Sanchez, and Audre Lorde. Like her cohorts, Jordan gravitated to academia in the 1980s with the emergence of the formal study of black women's literature and history. But what distinguished her was her continued presence on the political front lines. When civil rights and Black Power collapsed, she found revolutions elsewhere: South Africa, Nicaragua, and Northern Ireland; El Salvador, Palestine, and Lebanon; LGBTQ issues, children's rights, and cancer awareness. Jordan writes that her experience in the black women's movement, as a black woman who "always had to invent the power my freedom requires," led her into solidarity with oppressed others around the globe.[1]

Less discussed, however, is the immigrant heritage and sensibility that infuse her writing.[2] Born in Harlem to West Indian parents, Jordan came of age when Cold War politics that encouraged insularity, alongside immigration policies that posed national quotas and restrictions on West Indians, created a hostile political climate that rendered immigrants "dangerous others," resulting in high-profile deportations and a diminished, if safer, domestic political discourse. As a result, second-generation immigrants—political figures Stokely Carmichael

and Shirley Chisholm; religious leaders Louis Farrakhan and Malcolm X; actors
Cicely Tyson and Harry Belafonte—engaged in U.S. black politics and culture
primarily as "African Americans."[3] Jordan's memoir—part immigrant narrative, part *Künstlerroman*, or portrait of artistic development—*Soldier: A Poet's
Childhood* (2000) chronicles how she, the only daughter of West Indian parents,
became what she often called "a dissident American poet."

    Soldier tracks the first twelve years of Jordan's life and reflects a contemporary
trend in childhood memoirs that mine trauma to explore larger cultural concerns.[4] Millennial works such as Frank McCourt's *Angela's Ashes* (1996), Mary
Karr's *The Liars' Club* (1995), Beals's *Warriors Don't Cry* (1994), and even Bray's
Unafraid of the Dark (1998) are steeped in confessions of childhood violation and
vulnerability. *Soldier*, however, refuses to indulge this commonplace trope.
Certainly, the narrative lays bare the devastation of a harrowing childhood.
Set in the 1940s, *Soldier* is permeated by images of war: World War II raging
abroad; Joe Louis fighting for black equality stateside; a young "June" battling
a father whose pursuit of "misbegotten American dreams" made him violent
and a mother whose abject meekness was more wounding than any outright
malice.[5] The memories and traumas narrated in *Soldier* are ones Jordan explored
time and again in various autobiographical poems and essays over her forty-
year career, revealing how indelibly seared into her consciousness they are. But
through the portrait of the child-poet "June" as agent, rather than victim, Jordan
recalibrates the much-invoked "struggle" that has long characterized black
political progress in favor of what she terms "the good fight" and "working to
win."[6] Whereas *Warriors* and *Unafraid* invert iconographic civil rights history,
reframing Little Rock and evoking the welfare rights movement, respectively,
to craft a post-*Brown* progressive politics, *Soldier* challenges the movement's
animating pieties of sacrifice and redemptive suffering through her parents'
story of thwarted immigrant striving. By displacing the movement's conventional pieties onto an earlier decade and within a discourse of immigration and
war, Jordan not only conveys the "long civil rights movement" but also links it
with broader struggles as the child-poet June becomes a figure for the world's
dispossessed. Jordan has acknowledged that she put this familial drama within
a global context to show the universally political nature of childhood: "These
are the years that determined my own ideas about power, about authority,
about children, about justice, about faith despite an insane environment, and
about the saving grace of my independent mind, my unruly stubborn spirit, as
well as the redemptive possibilities of language."[7]

    In this chapter, I demonstrate how Jordan's memoir pays tribute to the
immigrant heritage that made her into a "dissident American poet" while
crafting a progressive politic based on her philosophy about the relationship

between language and action. In the previous chapter, I discussed how Rose-mary Bray's depiction of her calling as writer utilizes theologies of love and grace to broaden notions of political radicalism. Jordan's "portrait of the artist as a little black girl," *Soldier*'s title when first announced for publication, promotes what she called a "secular version of the concept of grace": a humanist vision of how like-minded people find solidarity despite the totalitarian forces that threaten the autonomy of their lives. Jordan is among a contemporary genera-tion of intellectuals and philosophers who argue that attempting to create political alternatives divorced from the past is bound to fail, for such a project depletes any new ethics of the philosophical resources that might animate an emerging vision. For Jordan, the contemporary era is "an age of forgetfulness" that requires—"before going forward"—we "retrace our steps into an earlier attitude, an earlier certainty, about our American human rights. That grounding will make our love/our self-respect/our future days a likely, and a credible, ambition."[8] The portrait of her poet's becoming, a voice and sensibility forged in the crucible of her parents' immigrant striving, dramatizes what she calls "working to win": creating an ethic of honoring the past to move forward. *Soldier* seemingly focuses on the larger-than-life presence of Jordan's father as the animating influence behind this politic: The memoir's title comes from a child-hood nickname he gave her; the narrative itself is dedicated to his memory. However, it is actually Jordan's mother, a silent, fading presence throughout the memoir, who is central to the ethic of resistance and agency the memoir promotes. Jordan, who published *Soldier* two years before she herself died from breast cancer, negotiates her mother's memory, figured in imagery of absence and loss, in the shadow of her own death, modeling acts of cultural mourning that point to alternate politics in the post-*Brown* era.

"Of the Faith of the Fathers"

The immigrant narrative's traditional arc of "dream anticipation," in which a protagonist leaves the Old World and must confront the New World's utopia myths as he negotiates its realities, colors Jordan's portrayal of her parents' immigrant striving.[9] Granville Ivanhoe Jordan and his wife, Mildred, were among the many folks of color migrating to northern cities from the Caribbean and the American South during the interwar years. In the 1930s, they first settled in Harlem and then, after securing a job as an elevator operator, Jordan's father moved them to Brooklyn, to "raise him up a family" like men of "'The Frontier.'"[10] Immigrant narratives often use cultural myths, such as "rags to riches" and "the self-made man," to fashion American identities.[11] *Soldier* clearly favors frontier imagery, with the prologue's opening line invoking the Wild, Wild West: "I found the clothesline from the third-floor window of our brownstone more exciting than a rodeo" (xv). Interspersed with recollections of her favorite Zane Grey novels, where cowboys lived out on the range, "by their wits," the prologue describes the ingenuity and grit that her father brings to the annual ritual of erecting a clothesline, a clear metaphor for the immigrant striving to attain the American dream. A 1986 autobiographical essay originally published in *New York Newsday* to celebrate the Fourth of July, "For My American Family," pays tribute to her parents' "legacy of gifted intelligence and guts": "In general, the very word *immigrant* connotes somebody white, while *alien* denotes everybody else. But hundreds and hundreds of thousands of Americans are hardworking, naturalized Black citizens whose trust in the democratic promise of the mainland has never been reckoned with, fully, or truly recipro-cated. I know that my parents would have wanted to say, 'Thanks, America!' if only there had been some way, some public recognition and welcome of the presence here and then some really big shot to whom their gratitude might matter. . . . My parents lived in America, full of faith."[12] Here, Jordan not only challenges the exclusive American notion of *immigrant* but also expands tradi-tional concepts of black American identity to include "naturalized Black citi-zens." The faith the passage references becomes a major theme in *Soldier* as the memoir's early chapters show her parents cultivating faith in the American dream through their daughter.[13] For instance, the "ponderous pram" of her baby carriage sported one single decal of FDR, a symbol of American optimism and resilience. And as a girl, she fills her weekends with a relentless itinerary of museums, planetariums, and symphonies; her weekdays, with recitations of Paul Laurence Dunbar, Shakespeare, and Edgar Allan Poe, as well as the Old and New Testaments.

It is no coincidence then, for Jordan indeed knows her bible, that two scriptures preface this story of immigrant striving and identity formation:

Honor thy father and thy mother.
              (Exodus 20:12)

And straightway the damsel rose, and walked; for she was the age of twelve years.
                                  (Mark 5:42)

On a very basic, narrative level, the Old Testament injunction to "honor thy father and thy mother" and the New Testament parable of a daughter's resurrection and reincorporation into a new community frame the story of how this daughter of Jamaican immigrants became an American poet. The framing parable in the Gospel of Mark, the one that orients readers to the moral of all subsequent ones, is that of the sower who plants seeds, defined as "the Word," into different kinds of ground.[14] All the parables that then follow, including the one in *Soldier*'s second epigraph, describe people who did or did not respond to the "Word," who did or did not keep faith. In *Soldier*, this spiritual idiom of the Word comes to symbolize her parents' secular faith in America's civic religion of democracy. The portrayal of her parents' eclectic spiritual practices intimates that their religious affiliations met sociopolitical needs more than they expressed a convert's belief. For instance, just as her father "somehow got the mayor, Fiorello La Guardia, to hold [her] on his lap," Jordan was baptized in Harlem's Saint Philip's Episcopal Church so that its renowned bishop could be her godfather. After the ceremony, however, she was never again taken to that "august Anglican edifice" (11). The pomp and poetry of Anglican liturgies did not preclude her family enjoying the music and magic of the storefront churches favored by West Indians and black southerners migrating to Harlem in the interwar years. When not attending Father Divine's Peace Mission with her father, June and her mother frequented the Universal Truth Center ("I suppose it was a Christian congregation"), whose minister, Big Momma, preached a creed centered on the powers of the Word: "If you lost your wallet, you'd say, 'There is no loss in the Divine Mind,' and you'd believe that, and your wallet would turn up. If your neck was swollen with an elephantine thyroid disorder, you'd say, 'I am perfect in the Lord,' and you'd believe it and that disorder would shrink or disappear. At the Universal Truth Center, the Word was nothing to play with" (13).[15] This allusion to New Thought, a popular theology within twentieth-century millenarian movements that taught "to name a thing is to create it,"[16] conveys the discursive impact of these eclectic spiritual experiences on her identity as a poet. Through its tone of mischievous impudence, this passage, when read from the vantage point of the adult autobiographer recollecting the past, suggests amused skepticism toward New Thought theology. But when read in the voice of the credulous child, the budding poet, the passage captures the spiritual, faithful beginnings of her literary sensibilities. In such an environment, "the split between religious and regular words" dissolved, as she delighted equally in her mother's reading scripture ("Verily the Lord saith") or nursery rhymes ("Merrily we roll along, roll along, roll along"). Of the spiritual-secular sonic convergence she writes: "'Verily' and 'Merrily' sounded almost the same to me, and I was so excited about that! I marched around, shouting, 'Merrily and Verily!' 'Merrily and Verily!' for quite a while" (27).

   In *Blues, Ideology, and Afro-American Literature*, Houston Baker describes a vernacular tradition forged at this very nexus of faith, language, and political progress: "If faith is the substance of things hoped for, the evidence of things not seen, then *metaphor* is that which keeps 'the unseen' in the mind's eye of the believer."[17] Baker argues that for black America, and in African American literature more specifically, a prominent metaphor for faith in racial progress is the figure "at a railroad juncture . . . await[ing] the arrival of a much-delayed train."[18] Evidence of this blues vernacular reverberates in a scene in which Jordan invokes the train to symbolize the promise of her parents' faith being realized within her:

> We were waiting for the train. . . .
>
> Then we heard a moaning in the dark. And, as startling as a transitory signal from a hidden fire, the huge eye of a locomotive eased its promise into the night and, growing large, grew larger, and everything around me shook and shuddered as that engine pulled alongside the platform, lurching, awful, to a halt.
>
> I had never felt worshipful before that. But there was no arguing with the enormity of that black locomotive traveling, hell's bells, on two million steel wheels.
>
> I could scarcely believe the beauty of that solitary beam of light as it engorged itself inside my eyes.
>
> I completely forgot about Big Momma as my mother settled us on a fuzzy double seat of that long-awaited train. And presently she held me close. And I soon fell asleep, all the way home. (32–33)

According to Baker, in a blues text such as this, the "locomotive rhythms" of moans and groans, whistles and wheels reflect black America's striving. In this passage, Jordan frames this secular faith in terms both sacred and profane, "regular and religious," with "awful" and "hell's bells" describing "the enormity of that black locomotive." The train is figured here as an otherworldly presence that elicits a sense of fear and trembling "as everything . . . shook and shuddered" with its arrival at the platform. The phrase "transitory signal" can be read as punning on the verb "transit," which conjures the image of an electric current transmitted from the train to Jordan, a connection that is made all the more evident as the train's "eye" engorges her own, leaving her in a complete state of illumination: "I could scarcely believe the beauty of that solitary beam of light as it engorged itself inside my eyes." And finally, several shifts at the level of the sentence manifest this singular transformation. Consider, for instance, the line "the locomotive eased its promise into the night, and growing large, grew larger." The move from the past tense "eased," to the participle "growing," and back to the past tense "grew," suggests a process occurring within a discrete moment in time, as does the shift from the modifier "large" to its comparative, "larger." And while beginning in the first-person plural, after the encounter with the train, the passage concludes, emphatically, in the first-person singular, with the visual descent of the repeated "I" representing this secular faith being absorbed into her body, "all the way home."

This concluding phrase, "all the way home," echoes an earlier scene that also raises the question of embodiment, the way knowledge is acquired through bodily experience, a defining tenet of black feminist thought. As a baby, Jordan's mother sang Mother Goose nursery rhymes about piglets going to market, "connecting a particular part of my body to every noun": "It's fair to say that I could not help but fall in love with words. . . . My mother would wiggle [my toes] one at a time to identify each little pig, and, then, when she got to 'all the way home,' she'd bury her nose in my belly and giggle a soft sound that I liked to listen to. Pretty soon my body had absorbed the language of all of the Mother Goose nursery rhymes, and my mother's dramatization of the rhythms of these words filled me with regular feelings of agreeable intoxication" (8–9). In its most literal sense, *home* refers here to the physical spaces in which her family lived: first in the Harlem River Projects and later their Brooklyn brownstone. As Jordan writes in "For My American Family," in such a "house as that modest home created by my parents, I became an American poet."[19] Another sense of home, which thinks of "the human body as agent in all perception, so that movement or action is home," may also be operative here.[20] This concept of home is a significant metaphor throughout Jordan's oeuvre, in which the world becomes as intimate and sacred as our "living rooms," coincidentally the title of a poetry collection about revolutions in Nicaragua, El Salvador, and South Africa.[21] Expanding the meaning of home, from its nationalist notions to a concept of world citizen, is a central theme in Jordan's oeuvre that culminates in the memoir.

According to Carole Boyce Davies, "rewriting home" is characteristic of immigrant women's narratives,[22] with Audre Lorde's biomythography, *Zami: A New Spelling of My Name*, perhaps the most famous. Given the striking similarities between the two autobiographies, *Zami* seemingly serves as an intertext through which Jordan develops her humanist vision. Although *Soldier* ends at age twelve and *Zami* at age twenty-three, both are written by second-generation immigrants whose parents traveled to the United States from the Caribbean during the interwar years, the 1920s for Lorde's parents, the 1930s for Jordan's. Both texts are also *Künstlerromans*, meditations on "How I Became a Poet," as the childhood section of Lorde's memoir is subtitled.[23] Lorde's prologue acknowledges a desire "to be both man and woman" and echoes the theme of androgyny introduced in *Soldier*'s prologue, where her father treats his only daughter like "a sidekick, a son." The texts depart significantly, however, on the representation of home. While Lorde duly acknowledges her father's "psychic print," she focuses in *Zami* primarily on "the images of women, kind and cruel, that lead me home." For Lorde, *home* first refers to Carriacou, the small Caribbean island off the coast of Grenada whose legacy of women loving each other was legend. As the narrative progresses, *home* becomes relationships with other women—her mother, her grandmother, her childhood friends, her lovers—whose bonds were "like coming home to a joy I was meant for" (139). Finally *home* is her own body, a personal sense of self-discovery and acceptance, "an island that cannot be found on a map." Barbara Christian and Mae Gwendolyn Henderson have written that *Zami*'s mythic narrative creates a diasporic space and consciousness that stretches back to the women of West Africa, a mythic "matrilineal diaspora" (an idea explored further in the next chapter).[24] *Soldier* uses tropes of home to develop a humanist vision that is even more internationalist in scope. In Jordan's oeuvre, home is the place where voice and body, language and action merge for activism in the world, for "moving towards home," as she titled a collection of political essays. There are also deep resonances between Jordan's thoughts on the relationship between body and voice, language and action, and Lorde's writing, particularly the essays "The Uses of the Erotic" and "Poetry Is Not a Luxury."[25] However, in her foreword to Jordan's posthumously published poetry anthology *Directed by Desire*, Adrienne Rich describes Jordan as unusual among twentieth-century U.S. poets in that "she believed in and lived the urgency of the word—along with action—to resist abuses of power and violations of dignity in—and beyond—and her country."[26]

Soldier's two epigraphs telegraph this internationalist politic. The Exodus verse comes from the Ten Commandments, the covenant God established with the Israelites as they were transformed from an extended family, descendants of Abraham, into a nation. Numerous scholars have detailed how early African American communities adapted the Exodus trope to characterize their burgeoning language around nationhood and liberation.[27] With this first epigraph, Jordan gestures to these nationalist struggles and traditional notions of family and home in building a critique of contemporary political ethics. In *Autobiography and Black Identity Politics*, Kenneth Mostern argues that women writers countering nationalist narratives and the ideologies of masculinity inscribed within them is characteristic of the contemporary field of black autobiography.[28] Much as *Warriors Don't Cry* rehistoricizes civil rights narratives of political children from a female perspective and *Unafraid* challenges the gender politics behind the rhetoric of "personal responsibility," *Soldier* interrogates the historically gendered framework behind nationalist notions of black leadership and progress. For instance, the memoir's title refers to a childhood nickname bestowed by her father, who attended Marcus Garvey's "uplift the race" rallies in Harlem during the 1920s. Martial ritual and imagery that invoked black men as kings, emperors, and soldiers shaped the black-nationalist ideology of Garvey's Universal Negro Improvement Association. The race-man narrative of progress inspired the nickname and subsequent "military reconnaissance training" (20) that Granville Ivanhoe Jordan devised for his only child, a daughter:

> Regardless of any particulars about me, [my father] was convinced that a "Negro" parent had to produce a child who could become a virtual white man and therefore possess dignity and power.
>
> Probably it seemed easier to change me than to change the meaning and complexion of power.
>
> At any rate, he determined he'd transform me, his daughter, into something better, something more likely to succeed.
>
> . . . There was a war going on against colored people, against poor people. I had to become a soldier who would rise through the ranks and emerge a commander of men. (18)

Jordan's father means for his "military reconnaissance training" to foster a progressive politic, one that advocates for the marginalized and the poor, "the least of these," as Rosemary Bray would remind. The dissonance between his patriarchal projections against Jordan's reality as a girl calls the nationalist ideology into question and highlights the memoir's critique of outdated, ill-fitting political discourses. Jordan's concern with transforming nationalist notions of family and home first appeared in an essay, "Waking Up in the Middle of Some American Dreams": "Much of the American Dream . . . supposes that our children are, as we like to say, seeds. But, again, that is a peculiar metaphor for human beings must change and challenge the old order of things into which we are born."[29] While the memoir certainly critiques nationalist politics, the second epigraph, from the Gospel of Mark, develops the simultaneous message of honoring the past to move forward. Mark's most prominent theme is keeping faith in the Word even as traditions are broken to form new communities. Specifically, the second epigraph derives from a parable about a twelve-year-old girl who is raised from the dead because of her father's faith, which in turn envelops a companion parable about the woman whose faith cures her of a twelve-year hemorrhage. Ancient cultic laws would have considered both woman and child ritually unclean, their illnesses having resulted in a social death, on the one hand, and an actual death on the other. However, healed by faith, these formally outcast women are, against all law and tradition, addressed as daughters and restored to community. *Soldier* adopts this ethic of boundary-breaking and communal re-formation to articulate an ethic of honoring the past while charting new politics. In the twenty-first century, Jordan argues, racial progress is no longer animated by a liberationist theology of a God-chosen race redeeming the world through their suffering. Rather, allegiances are based on a "secular grace," a sense of moral and social justice: "This time we must name our own god. . . . There will be no skyborne imagery, no holy labels slapped around our wrists. Now we rise, alert, determining, and new among ourselves. We move into a community of moment. We will choose. But not as we were chosen, weighed and measured, pinched, bent backwards, and under heel. . . . Instead, we choose a real, living enlargement of our only life. . . . And it is here that we see fit to continue—as subjects of human community. We will bring back the person, alive and sacrosanct."[30] In Jordan's vision, a progressive, post-*Brown* politic moves from an outdated philosophy of black politics as necessarily rooted within notions of a priori black unity to humanist solidarity with like-minded others.

"A Child Shall Lead Them"

Although immigrant narratives often use cultural myths to inscribe their histories as new American subjects, *Soldier* is among a subset that also issues a social critique with "the autobiographical subject as interventionary social radical."[31] By placing this family drama within the global context of World War II, the narrative persona of the child-poet June becomes a figure for the world's dispossessed and a model of agency despite totalitarian circumstances, whatever they may be. In "Old Stories, New Lives," a 1978 keynote address for a child welfare convention, Jordan articulated the role children can play in transforming society: "To rescue our children we will have to let them save us from the power we embody: we will have to trust the very difference that they forever personify. And we will have to allow them the choice, without fear of death: that they may come and do likewise or that they may come and that we will follow them, that a little child will lead us back to the child we will always be, vulnerable and wanting and hurting for love and beauty."[32] *Soldier* emerges out of this lifelong preoccupation with the politics and poetics of childhood.

Though best known for poetry and political essays for adult audiences, Jordan's very first books were in the vanguard of the contemporary field of African American children's literature as it emerged from the civil rights and "black is beautiful" movements.[33] Her first volume, *Who Look at Me*, was a poetry project that she inherited upon the death of Langston Hughes. Set in conversation with twenty-seven paintings, the book evokes Du Boisian double consciousness as it asks readers to "look at me" in genuine, rather than stereotypical, modes of black experience.[34] The title's questioning mode will become a semantic hallmark of a dialogic writing style that frames *Soldier* as well: issuing a call to an implied reader in faithful anticipation of a response. In 1970, Jordan edited *Soulscript: Afro-American Poetry*, an anthology that introduced works by teenaged poets alongside the verse of established writers, such as Countee Cullen and Gwendolyn Brooks, in addition to *The Voice of the Children*, a representative sampling of prose and poetry by black and Puerto Rican students. A prominent theme in both poetry volumes—and one that is at the heart of *Soldier*—is young people's "sense of agency and unwillingness to wait on others, namely adults, to take action on their own behalf."[35] Jordan's most acclaimed and controversial work for children, *His Own Where* (1971), sought to interest black youth in social change through a teen love story written entirely in Black English.[36] Jordan argued that a person's native tongue, "as a carrier of consciousness and a conduit of power," could serve as a tool for change. Given that language was the "one currency common to all of us," despite differences of power and social identities, Jordan felt that it was the basis for political organizing and solidarity.[37] Consequently, creating literature accessible to all was essential to an activist pedagogy and writing style that she honed throughout her career. The poetry workshops she directed as a charter member of the Teachers and Writers Collaborative were staples of her tenure at institutions ranging from City College and SUNY Stony Brook to Yale and Sarah Lawrence. This approach to literature and activism had its most complete manifestation at the University of California, Berkeley, where Jordan founded Poetry for the People, a community-centered literary workshop where she nurtured a new generation of proletarian bards.

Many have noted that Jordan's workshop echoed Walt Whitman's literary philosophy about the civic role of the poet. Jordan considered Whitman the quintessential American poet, "as Shakespeare is to England, Dante to Italy, Tolstoy to Russia, Goethe to Germany, Aghostino Neto to Angola, Pablo Neruda to Chile, Mao-Tse-Tung to China, and Ho Chi Minh to Vietnam."[38] Her essay "For the Sake of a People's Poetry: Walt Whitman and the Rest of Us," the preface to her poetry collection *Passion: New Poems, 1977–1980*, evinces the way she emulated his democratic, didactic style. Its vision about the power of language to create an egalitarian society echoes Whitman's more famous preface to the 1855 edition of *Leaves of Grass*, another cultural manifesto regarding the role of the poet. Whitman declared that a national American idiom, or people's poetry, should be "clearness, simplicity, no twisted or foggy sentences, at all."[39] Jordan's formulation is a "traceable descendant": "In the first place, there is nothing obscure, nothing contrived, nothing an ordinary straphanger on the subway would be puzzled by. In the second place, the voice of those lines is intimate and direct at once: It is the voice of the poet who assumes that he speaks to an equal and that he need not fear that equality; on the contrary, the intimate distance between the poet and the reader is a distance that assumes there is everything important, between them, to be shared."[40] Jordan fashioned a decidedly democratic, dissident body of writing that "served an expressly moral purpose,"[41] what she called "acts of faith," cultural work whose moral witness might have political impact in the world.

This question of agency and its inextricable relationship to language animates the "working to win" ethic and global humanist vision that underwrite *Soldier*. There is therefore political import in remembering how she became a poet: the people, forces, and, as Phillis Wheatley would say, "intrinsic ardor" that shaped her art. To Lorde's question "to whom do I owe the strength of my voice?" in *Zami*, Jordan answers: her mother reciting nursery rhymes as she wiggled toes and tickled belly buttons; her father expecting her to recite Shakespeare and Dunbar on demand; using music to memorize poetry by meter if not by meaning, a trick she learned from her pianist cousin Valerie practicing Chopin in the parlor. As the narrative progresses, June's individual, interior thoughts are increasingly rendered in free verse, with her poetic voice emerging in moments of self-determination. Like Whitman's original 1855 folio, the memoir is a twelve-part narrative written in common, everyday language. When Jordan proclaims her childhood love of singing "at the top of my lungs!" so "everybody on the block could hear me!" (210), one can almost hear a "barbaric yawp from the rooftops." Where the two differ is in how they elicit reader engagement with their narrative and politics. Whitman's style sought to anticipate and "answer" an idealized reader:[42] "This hour I tell things in confidence, / I might not tell everybody but I will tell you," Whitman writes, appealing to readers' sense of exceptionalism.[43] Jordan's political essays issue a call to action. Their characteristically open-ended conclusions—for instance, "Can I Get a Witness?" and "I believe I am not alone. Please verify"—not only solicit readers' responses to her political vision but also cultivate a sense of their personal agency.[44]

Soldier has a deceptively simple, storybook quality, but its narrative strategies, from the episodic narrative to the representation of memory, develop readers' sense of agency and moral witness. On the one hand, *Soldier*'s episodic narrative evokes the free-flowing, though not necessarily carefree, days of childhood. In the course of a mere two pages, for instance, Jordan juxtaposes seemingly random experiences: eating mushrooms for the first time at a friend's house; wanting to have dimples like an upstairs neighbor; contemplating connections between men with moustaches, "Hitler, Charlie Chaplin, and my father"; loving the religious, children's magazine *Wee Wisdom* "because it was mine and because everything in it was orange"; sticking up for her cousin Valerie in a schoolyard fight (23–25). On the other hand, the fragmented framework creates temporal gaps that are literally marked by textual ones, line spaces between each scene, metaphorical ellipses that ask readers to literally read between the lines. In "Discourse and Human Agency," the political scientist Roland Bleiker explains how human agency can still exist in a world where identity is disciplined by discursive forces. Given that identity is temporal, fluid, and multiple, agency arises within the "discursive cracks." Rather than focusing on how the grid of discipline is becoming more extensive, Bleiker argues, one must pay attention to everyday practices—writing, talking, remembering—that "manipulate and evade the mechanism of discipline."[45] By highlighting the constructed nature of the text, its "discursive cracks," Jordan reminds readers of their agency, that their realities are constructions that they can question and change. Jordan models the ethical witnessing that *Soldier* demands through recounting her own childhood experience reading the *Ugly Duckling*, whose disturbing messages regarding loss and chrysalis she interrogated even as a very young girl:

> Why did the Ugly Duckling lose its mother?
> How could a duck turn into a swan?
> Why would that be a happy ending for a duck? . . .
> I thought I understood that story,
> and I didn't believe it,
> and I kept reading it to myself,
> over and over.
>
> (23)

The representation of memory also demands that readers pay attention and be ethical witnesses. For instance, calculated interruptions in the narrative mimic the act of retrieving lost memories suddenly recalled: "We must to remember *that*," her father reminds of their annual springtime ritual (xv); "I almost forgot," she says, thinking of how, when the family moved to Brooklyn, she became sickly and craved even her mother's clinical touch (54); "But I want to remember the roses!" she says while convalescing in the hospital after a bicycle crash (223). These disruptions of the linear narrative emphasize the elusiveness of memory, reminding readers that *Soldier* is a consciously crafted work and asking them to critically engage the gaps, that which is absent and unsaid. The interjections call attention to the fact that remembering is an active process of self-fashioning with both a politics and a context, that "the personal story of a remembered past is always in dialogue with cultural formations."[46]

Soldier's cover art is a case in point. A snapshot of "June & Spottie on the First Day of School" evokes the influences shaping her identity: the urban, black neighborhood in Brooklyn where she grew up; the indelible molding by her parents, for, presumably, one of them framed this shot and supplied its handwritten caption. However, the three personas mentioned on the cover—"June," the child-poet; "June Jordan," the adult autobiographer; and "Soldier," her nickname—challenge Philippe Lejeune's influential notion of an "autobiographical pact." According to Lejeune, the signature on a narrative's cover is a contract between reader and author affirming that the narrator is indeed the author. By having three names on the cover, Jordan acknowledges that identities are mutable and multiple, suggesting that a person is always more than the identity constructed for him or her. It is in the cracks and fissures of these myriad selves that resistance and agency can emerge. Given the other structural similarities with Whitman, it is intriguing to note that *Soldier*'s cover art recalls that of his 1855 edition of *Leaves of Grass*, one of the most famous in American literature. The engraved daguerreotype of a bearded "common man" with shirt open, hat cocked, arms akimbo, created the idealized figure of the "proletarian bard" whose "open yet self-contained stance invited communion with all comers."[47] *Soldier*'s idealized figure of a child, society's most vulnerable, speaks to the "emergent cultural formations" in the post-*Brown* era in which solidarity is determined, not from nationalist notions of a priori black unity but through like-minded publics acting in concert. On the cover, the child-poet stands on a series of thresholds, straddling planes and a host of identities. The traditionally feminine and masculine coexist in her attire of ruffled dress and Buster Brown boots. Her body is positioned in opposing planes as she stands in profile, on separate schoolhouse steps, in midstride, preparing to move through doors that will take her into another world quite different from the home of her immigrant parents.

Whereas the theme of the "Harlem" chapter is sowing seeds, Brooklyn is figured as the failed pursuit of "misbegotten American dreams." Soon enough, the run-down brownstone comes to feel like a "tombstone testimonial to a terrible mistake," despite "all the toil and shenanigans and fantasy and trust that went into the purchase of the deed to that house" (39). The child's judgment-free voice also invites readers to critique not her parents but the pieties of sacrifice and suffering that animated their striving: "I never heard the word *sacrifice* until we moved to Brooklyn. Suddenly I had to listen to my mother and father talking about sacrifice, day in and day out. I was told to remember sacrifice or to be grateful for sacrifice. And as far as I could see, sacrifice was not a good idea. . . . And the worst part about sacrifice was that it was supposed to be happening for my sake: My 'future'" (45–46). When her father moves the family to Brooklyn, the myth of the open frontier immediately seems suspect: "Brooklyn increased our living space 300 percent, but once we got there everything tightened up and felt crowded and jumpy and sounded like an argument to me" (46). And so her father's beatings begin, as do her mother's instruction in the ways of the cross.[48] In a chapter titled "More about My Father and Mother: Fighting," the two quarrel over whether to send June to boarding school. Her father aspires for her to "rub elbows with the best: The sons of bankers! The son of Captains of Industry!" like "the Rockafella children" (152–153). Her mother counters, "June is not a Rockefeller boy! She have to become a Black woman!" Tensions escalate to blows. In defense of her battered mother, June placates her father's fury with a recitation of Kipling's "If" ("You'll be a man my son!"). After he leaves for ice cream to reward his Rockefeller-in-training, her mother summons June to her knee:

> *This* day: I wan' that you learn
> something for me, June. And
> for all time . . .
> You repeat it after me:
> "Blessed are the poor in spirit" . . .
> "Blessed are those that mourn" . . .
> "Blessed are the meek" . . .

After a few lines of this lesson, June interrupts, in disobedience, to ask, *Why? Mommy? Why?* (157).

This Beatitudes scene evokes the turn-the-other-cheek Christian love ethic that animated the civil-rights movement philosophy of nonviolence to challenge traditional pieties of "struggle" and "suffering" that have long characterized black political progress. The child's confusion that such undeserved suffering could somehow be ennobling raises the question not only of *Why?* but also of the possibility of an alternative political ethic, a position Jordan took as an adult activist. When King said, during the Birmingham campaign, for instance, "'If any blood will flow in the streets of Birmingham let it be our blood and not the blood of our white brothers,'" Jordan countered, "then and there he lost me. Dr. King could not persuade me to adopt a posture that I felt was ignominious, abject, and suicidal. He was not a god. And, according to his terms, I was not even trying to be good."[49] Toward the end of her life, Jordan came to appreciate "that for Dr. King 'nonviolent' did not mean cowardly" or "yield and kneel,"[50] as her mother seemed to believe. Nonetheless, she was never a proponent of nonviolence, or even antiwar, despite raging against imperial aggression: "I came to understand that I am not against war," Jordan wrote in a 1981 essay linking the South African fight against apartheid to the domestic one against the Reagan revolution. "I am against losing the war."[51] Having fought bullies in the schoolyard and her father at home, Jordan as a child had learned that "a really excellent way to stop somebody from hitting you is to hit them back" (26). Joe Louis came to embody this alternative ethic to redemptive suffering ("Joe was better than Jesus" [198]), as he prevailed in the ring for black equality stateside and abroad:

> I thought, "This is the way to fight! This is the way to win! . . ."

> To me, Joe Louis was like the Bible, except Joe Louis was alive.
>   And fighting was a really good way to live.
>   There was nothing wrong about it.
>   Joe Louis made that obvious. (200–201)

The voice of the child thus challenges the prevailing pieties of the civil rights movement and offers a political alternative, what Jordan would later describe as "working to win" and "the good fight."

For Jordan, humanist solidarity with like-minded others, not identity-politics, to which she was famously opposed, animated this alternative, global politic. A 1989 essay originally titled "Beyond Gender, Race, and Class" (later renamed "Waiting for a Taxi") articulates her thinking: "I am wondering if those of us who began our lives in difficult conditions defined by our race or our class or our gender identities, I am wondering if we can become more carefully aware of limitations of race and class and gender analyses, for these yield only distorted and deeply inadequate images of ourselves. There is another realm of possibility, political unity and human community based upon concepts that underlie or supersede relatively immutable factors of race, class, and gender: the concept of justice, the concept of equality, the concept of tenderness."[52] The gender dynamics of this "Beatitudes" scene perhaps illuminate her political theorizing on the need for a secular humanist vision beyond the nationalist, liberationist theology her father represents and the mother's "strong black woman" ethic.

In some ways, of course, the question *Why? Mommy? Why?* speaks to the confusion of a child bewildered by the conflicting view of identities available to her: either the privileged white man or the accommodating black woman. It is reminiscent of the choice Douglass makes in his 1845 *Narrative* to align himself with traditional white masculinity as a "representative man" rather than Aunt Hester's dominated femininity. However, Jordan does not choose, identifying alternatively with both genders throughout the narrative and being equally attracted to boys and girls. The memoir's biconsciousness not only reflects Jordan's acknowledged bisexuality but also the narrative's humanist politic. As Adrienne Rich wrote, Jordan's life and writing were "directed by desire, moving between longings for a physical person and for a wider human solidarity."[53] In *Zami*, Lorde's androgynous desire brought her into a self-discovery rooted in the power of women. In *Soldier*, bisexuality and biconsciousness seemingly point to an alternate humanism beyond traditional politics—beyond nationalism and the strong black woman—and into an internationalist ethos that brings civil rights politics in conversation with the world.

The memoir's argument for the global nature of contemporary resistance is most evident as Jordan places her traumatic childhood into a broader historical context. The first scene of domestic violence in *Soldier*, included in the final six pages of the "Brooklyn" chapter, comes from her epic poem "War and Memory." Written as part of a public reading series, *War and Memory: In the Aftermath of Vietnam*, the poem opens with "Daddy at the sink or stove," emptying drawers onto the kitchen floor as he berates her mother for whatever stray item he cannot locate:

> open and shut/the spoons
> suddenly loud as the yelling . . .
> about: would he
> be late/had she
> hidden away the Chinese laundry shirts
> again/did she think
> it right that he (a man in his own house)
> should serve himself a cup of tea a plate
> of food/perhaps she thought he
> should cook the cabbage and the pot roast
> for himself
> as well?
>
> (70)

The jumbled structure of this verse—its midsentence punctuation, the litany of questions strung together as if uttered in one long breath—evokes not only the barrage of insults hurled but also the frequency with which such volatile scenes occurred. This revelation of domestic abuse takes on global significance in a subsequent scene about "life beyond our / neighborhood." As her father reads the *National Geographic*, Jordan "stare[s] at the front page / photo of the Daily News," asking, "What's this a picture of?" Her mother, ostensibly to protect a child's mythical innocence but also to avoid engaging the horrors of rape, says the picture is "about the Jews. In the war going on," with families forced to "march through the snow until they die!" Her father, always more concerned with the training of his daughter's mind than with the particulars of gender, opts for a factual rather than a fairy tale answer that also elides the issue of rape: "It's / not the snow. It's the Nazi camps: The concentration / camps!" Neither answer suffices, and June persists in wanting to know "what this is a picture of." After receiving yet another half truth—"'That's the trail of blood left by the Jewish girls / and women on the snow because the Germans / make them march so long'"—she nonetheless intimates the essence of the international situation, having witnessed the gendered violence of her household:

> and I remember
> wondering if my family was a war
> going on
> and if
> there would soon be blood
> someplace in the house
> and where
> the blood of my family would come from.
>
> (74–76)

Jane Creighton, the literary curator of the *War and Memory* exhibition and to whom "War and Memory" is dedicated, notes that, within the poem, "there is no castigation here, no final pinning of blame on the oppressor father, [or the victim mother]. Without, ever, excusing her father's violence, or her mother's passivity, Jordan brings forth elements of their lives that are the making of herself and the hugeness of her appetite for justice."[54] The final sections of "War and Memory" show the maturation of Jordan's activist sensibilities, as she identifies with Palestinians, challenges identity politics, emulates Chinese revolutionaries with nightly long walks, and advocates for the poor. The poem concludes with extensive anaphora that suggests "a person is always, necessarily, more than the identity constructed for her or him by a violating, oppressive system, and it is this excess, this excessive, unruly self, seeping out beyond borders, that is the subject of resistance":[55]

and I

thought I was a warrior growing up

and I

buried my father with all the ceremony all the music I

could piece together.

and I

lust for justice

and I

make that quest arthritic/pigeon-toed/however

and I

invent the mother of courage I require not to quit.

Although these lines of the poem are omitted in *Soldier*, the allusion to Bertolt Brecht's *Mother Courage and Her Children* becomes evident in their canny structural similarities. Set during the Thirty Years' War (1618–1648), Brecht's play is written in response to Germany's invasion of Poland in 1939 and the start of World War II, the memoir's global backdrop. The action takes place over the course of twelve years and is represented in twelve scenes, just as *Soldier* spans the first twelve years of Jordan's life and has twelve sections (a prologue and eleven chapters). Mother Courage, like her own mother, is an unsympathetic persona, whose negative example, losing her children to the war she sought to profit from, inspires a fight for justice."

Jordan has made it clear that *Soldier* honors her father. Despite her abusive, harrowing childhood at his hands, in countless interviews promoting the memoir Jordan spoke of his teaching as inspiring her political ethics: "Bottom line: My father made a fighter out of me. He taught me about looking the enemy in the eye—*never* take your eyes off the enemy—not to quit . . . That one lesson in itself has certainly governed my life."[56] But what of the despairing portrayal of her mother in *Soldier*? Given the dictates of the memoir's first epigraph to honor them both, how does *Soldier* honor her mother's memory to chart a new progressive politic? In the prologue, Jordan presents the annual spring ritual of putting up a clothesline as an intimate father-daughter project, but it is also a courtship ritual for her mother, "hidden away in her 'little room,' where she had probably gone to pray" (xviii). When her father instructs June to tell her mother, "She have herself a clothesline now. . . . why don' she wan' she try it out!" the little soldier gears up for the "second dangerous mission for the day, . . . squar[ing her] shoulders for the task ahead" (xix–xx). The memoir omits the scene of June's entreating her mother to come see "the gift" of a clothesline, but the text itself is Jordan's final confrontation with her mother and her difficult memory.

Moral Meaning of Memory

In 1966, Mildred Jordan committed suicide with a fatal overdose of prescription pills, finally succumbing to a protracted and debilitating depression. Jordan wrote about her mother's suicide "after swallowing fifteen/twenty/thirty-five pills" in the essay "Many Rivers to Cross" and the poem "Ghaflah." In *Soldier*, the still-palpable grief colors Jordan's representation of her mother, who is associated throughout the narrative with mortification and death. From the opening childbirth scene, Mildred Jordan is characterized as an abjectly pious woman who deemed suffering her due: "She was being blessed with a child . . . and she tried—she tried—to praise Jesus and his suffering as she suffered now, the curse of every woman. This, then, was her cross to bear. This giving birth to me" (3). This scene records a traumatic birth full of dissonance and alienation, creating a maternal longing that goes unmet and unresolved throughout the narrative—and seemingly throughout her life. Jordan's final directive regarding the music to be played at her memorial service, written just a few months before her death, requested Sweet Honey in the Rock's version of "Sometimes I Feel like a Motherless Child."[57]

Portrayals of her mother in earlier essays and poems suggest that Mildred Jordan lived as the proverbial "strong black woman." "Getting Down to Get Over," an early poem on the debilitating stereotypes attributed to black femininity, was dedicated to her mother. And in "On the Spirit of Mildred Jordan," Jordan writes that her mother "wasn't foxy, / she was *strong*." In *Soldier*, Jordan shows her mother grooming her daughter in the spirit-crushing beatitudes of strong black womanhood. "Be a big girl" is an oft-repeated admonition (166, 205), as well as "be fearless." This instruction reaches its peak, or perhaps better said its nadir, in two macabre scenes in which Mildred Jordan instructs her daughter in mortifying acts, one with the dead, another with human waste.

The first scene describes a distant family friend, Aunt Albee, who comes to visit one day and subsequently dies on the parlor-room couch. Summoning her daughter to this virtual stranger's deathbed, "she said she was going to fold Aunt Albee's arms over Aunt Albee's chest, and that while she was doing that I should reach up and shut Aunt Albee's eyes" (214). Why her mother felt the need to position the body in some customary pose of the dead, as if performing proper care, baffles. But since she herself was already attending the body, it seems gratuitous, if not psychotic, to solicit her child's help:

My mother asked me, "What is the matter?"
And I thought she was about to add on,

> "Are you afraid?"
> And so I reached out and put my index
> finger on Aunt Albee's left eyelid, and
> closed it, and then I used the same
> finger to shut the other eyelid,
> and then I wanted to cut off
> that finger: My own finger.
>
> (215)

The juxtaposition of the next scene suggests that her mother is descending into mental illness or some soul-crushing cruelty. Shortly after Aunt Albee's death, she became obsessed with matters scatological. On this occasion, she now needs June's help to have a bowel movement, guiding her daughter's hand in the mortifying task:

> She knew it was a lot to ask
> But she also knew how brave I was.
> So she was asking me.
> "Help me!," she said.
> I felt as stiff and heavy as lead.
>
> (217)

The fact that her mother then "scrubbed my fingertips" and "thanked me, again and again" (218) was not enough to nullify this soul-numbing act. Afterward, June is unable to return to her writing at the kitchen table, but she does summon the will to refuse tears and an overwhelming sense of powerlessness (218). Here, readers witness a metaphorical death by her mother's hand in troubling scenes that perversely mirror the account of Jordan's birth, and one may wonder why Jordan chooses to include them. Even if the circumstances of her mother's death and the portrayal of her family in print were not contested, as they are,[58] these scenes raise intriguing questions about the ethics of disclosure. What purpose does sharing these disturbing stories serve? They not only compromise Mildred Jordan, who is long dead and cannot speak on her own behalf; they also compromise June Jordan, for readers cannot help but wonder why she would talk about her dead mother, in public, this way. Why would she not let her mother's memory rest? Rather than take these stories to the grave with her, Jordan leaves them as her mother's legacy. Why?

There may be several readings, of course. In "My Monster/My Self," Barbara Johnson argues that women autobiographers metaphorically murder their mothers with "monstrous" representations in pursuit of a myth of self-invention.[59] However, from the cover art to the epigraphs framing this story of a daughter made a poet through her parents' indelible influence, the narrative argues for a notion of identity that is contextual and relational. It does not appear, then, that this is *Soldier*'s primary motive (although one might argue the memoir embraces the idea of the self as both contingent and autonomous). In the poem "One Minus One Minus One," Jordan suggests a therapeutic purpose for much of her autobiographical writings:

> (This is a first map of territory I will have to explore as poems, again and again)
> My mother murdering me
> to have a life of her own.
> What would I say
> (if I could speak about it?)
> My father raising me
> to be a life that he
> owns
> What can I say
> (in this loneliness?)[60]

The excerpt's allusion to repetition compulsion ("territory I will have to explore . . . again and again") conveys a sense of trauma, and, in a *New York Times* interview, Jordan acknowledges that the memoir has been a kind of working-through: "I hope in a way [*Soldier*] is very good news. I'm OK. One can reasonably say some very dire things about my parents. I'm here to say, I'm here. I'm OK."[61] However, given the anxieties about speaking in "One Minus One Minus One" ("What would I say?"; "What can I say?"), Jordan duly recognizes the ethical questions around revealing private details of family life, which suggests that these revelations are more than mere repetition compulsion of unresolved trauma. While many of the childhood memories in *Soldier* have iterations in earlier poems and essays, these two troubling stories that Jordan tells about her mother are peculiar in that this is the first time that Jordan shared them in print. I would argue, then, that these portrayals are conscious, deliberate acts of mourning with political import and intent.

In several political essays, Jordan expressed a desire to create a model of resistance that would honor the work and sacrifice of her mother's generation of black women, "to undertake, with pride, every transcendent dream of freedom made possible by the humility of their love."[62] For instance, in "Many Rivers to Cross," a 1981 essay read at a conference on women and work, Jordan recalls finding her mother sitting bedside just as rigor mortis set in, as if trying to get up. Building on Bertolt Brecht's saying that "it takes courage to say that the good were defeated not because they were good, but because they were weak," Jordan derives from her mother's sad example a model for "new women's work [that] will mean we will not die trying to stand up; we will live that way; standing up."[63] The essay "In Our Hands," which remembers her mother's drudgery doing laundry (also discussed in *Soldier*), suggests that creating a future progressive politic requires honoring the past: "Her woman's work never won permanent victories of any kind. . . . But she did raise me to respect her way of offering love and to believe that hard work is often the irreducible factor for survival, not something to avoid. . . . Her woman's work invented the potential for a completely different kind of work for us, the next generation of Black women: huge, rewarding hard work demanded by the huge, new ambitions that her perfect confidence in us engendered."[64] Patricia Hill Collins has argued that Jordan's representations of her mother and "woman's work" call for a new model of resistance that "honors our mothers' sacrifice" by debunking "superstrong Black mother" myths.[65] Black feminist thought often focuses on exceptional women of unparalleled strength—Sojourner Truth, Fannie Lou Hamer, Rosa Parks. But, as Melissa Harris-Perry writes in *Sister Citizen*, "for every Harriet Tubman there are hundreds of thousands of black women who died as slaves. For every Sojourner Truth there are hundreds of thousands who were never able to speak publicly about their experiences. For every black woman who remains an independent moral agent in the face of crumbling oppression, there are many who are, in fact, crushed."[66] In desanctifying motherhood by presenting Mildred Jordan in her complexities, and by mourning the loss of her life, Jordan creates a space for a different kind of resistance—beyond suffering, sacrifice, and pyrrhic moral victories. The poem "Ghaflah," from her last poetry volume, *Kissing God Goodbye*, explicitly explores the moral significance of honoring her mother's memory. The poem's persona pretends to have forgotten the "Be a big girl" admonitions; the clinical touch; the "lowered eyes / folded hands / withered limbs"; "finding her . . . / half seated half / almost standing up / just dead." Of course the "forgotten" memories named and listed emphasize the studied pretense: "I forget three or four other things / I cannot recall." The epigraph informs, "In Islam, *Ghaflah* refers to the sin of forgetfulness." In *Soldier*, the task, which Jordan emphasizes is indeed a moral one, is to remember rightly.

The title essay of *Some of Us Did Not Die*, a collection of political essays published posthumously, meditates on what Jordan calls "the moral meaning of memory":

> I got to thinking about how some of us choose to remember, and why, and how:
> why we do not forget.
>
> And I got to thinking about the moral meaning of memory, per se. And
> what it means to forget, what it means to fail to find and preserve the connection
> with the dead whose lives you, or I, want or need to honor with our own.[67]

Jordan writes these words in the wake of the attacks on the Twin Towers to
suggest a way of going forward after such a disaster. Such an ethic has been
posited about the Holocaust and the Truth and Reconciliation Commission.
In her study of Black Power memoirs, Margo Perkins notes that "given the
extent to which movement activists suffered massive repression at the hands of
the state, it is curious that the reality of death and loss is not explored more
extensively in their texts."[68] Indeed, Angela Davis recalls, "One of the things
that we didn't do is mourn. Our strength was often defined by our ability not to
allow the death of someone we loved to set us back."[69] I argue here that *Soldier*
models cultural mourning to show how activists use experiences of loss to
renew their commitment to revolutionary struggle.

The timing of *Soldier*'s publication—two years before Jordan died from
breast cancer, literally in the shadow of death—begs the question of whether
the narrative served as a kind of working through, a coming to terms with her
own impending mortality, and perhaps thoughts of death did indeed hasten its
publication. However, Jordan's archived papers at the Schlesinger Library reveal
that this story was first pitched to Harper & Row twenty years earlier, in 1979,
as *My Childhood*, a direct allusion to Russian writer Maxim Gorky's 1914 memoir
of the same title.[70] When Jordan returned to work on the text in 1996, the title
had been changed to "Portrait of the Artist as a Little Black Girl," an obvious
allusion to James Joyce's 1914 novel.

Both Gorky's and Joyce's texts are bildungsromans, and Jordan's deliberate
allusions to them make it clear she is engaging this literary tradition. The narrative form that modernist writers like Gorky and Joyce inherited from eighteenth-
and nineteenth-century originators had certain formal features: rebellion
against the father and the social values he represents, aesthetic education,
mentorship, marriage, self-sufficiency, before a final return to the father's home
and values. The traditional hero returns to the fold, older and wiser, closing the
narrative circle in symbolic acceptance of the social order; while a prodigal, an
artistic rebel, he is ultimately a good bourgeois, sustainer of the status quo.
Modernist bildungsromans dissent from this ideological function. By altering
the traditional structure, often through omitting the return, they register "dissent
from the social order" as they seek new ways to represent the relationships
among self, family, and society.[71]

Like *My Childhood* and *A Portrait of the Artist*, *Soldier* is an altered bildungsroman. It is a foreshortened work that moves sequentially from her birth in Harlem, to Brooklyn, and then finally, at age twelve, departure for boarding school in New England. Readers see only the aesthetic education element of the traditional narrative arc. The other elements of the traditional form—the stages of mentorship, marriage, self-sufficiency, and a final return to the father's home and values—are omitted. Rather, the narrative ends in a final departure:

> My mother didn't see me off.
> My father brought me to the railroad station by himself.
> Just outside Track 22 we faced each other:
> "Okay! Little Soldier! G'wan! G'wan!
> You gwine make me proud!"
> And I could hear nothing else.
> And I wondered who would meet my train.
>
> (261)

Like the modernist texts she alludes to, there is no return to the father's house, which I argue signals a dissent from the social order: the nationalist, patriarchal order that he represents. The prodigal daughter does not return to be a good bourgeois, upholder of the status quo. Instead, she breaks completely away from the father, charting her path as revolutionary poet, and those familiar with her actual life story know this to be true; the radical poet-activist that the narrative's logic suggests she will become is a well-known fact. However, Jordan's text brings yet another twist to the modernist innovation, because there is a return here, but with a difference. The return is not portrayed within the text at the end of the story. The text itself is the return. If we think of the bildungsroman in relationship to social context, then the signifying relationship of her text to modernist works makes *Soldier* a narrative that speaks to this post-*Brown* moment.

Whereas *Soldier*'s narrative arc and form suggest the historical moment to which her narrative is speaking, its representation of memory, particularly her mother's, signals the political ethic the book promotes. Far fewer scenes focus on Mildred Jordan, and they, by and large, figure in tropes of absence and loss, rendering her representation as yet another "gap" in the narrative that readers are asked to probe in relation to the memoir's larger political ethics. There are numerous scenes in which Jordan's mother retreats to her small room, to pray, or cowers in a fight with her husband, "hunching smaller than small bones should allow / silently beside the point"—sometimes of a knife and always of all household deliberations. But she is very much the point of the politic underwriting *Soldier*. The memoir's opening scene broadcasts the connection among memory, her mother, and ethics. The detailed account of her birth, which Jordan could not possibly have remembered, acknowledges the extent to which her identity is shaped by her parents, by what she has been told about who she is. And by having *Soldier*'s first line echo the "I was born" slave narrative convention situates the memoir within the slave narrative tradition and its legacy of social death.

In *Mourning Becomes the Law*, Gillian Rose argues that creating political alternatives that help modern societies move beyond unspeakable atrocities requires "workful beginnings." Rather than the Oedipal impulse of postmodern philosophers to kill off metaphysics in search of an uncontaminated ethics, one must delve into "the muck of mortal experience" to transcend it. Rose specifically refers to the horrors of the Holocaust, but Jordan would also include slavery, terrorism, breast cancer—all that seeks to destroy the sanctity of life. Jordan's physical, messy engagement with her mother's sad memory becomes a model of workful beginnings, what Jordan calls "working to win," and questions of death are at the heart of this model of resistance: "I have known and I have seen too many people dead, absolutely dead and gone, to settle for resistance or struggle. I am working to win. . . . Now whenever somebody dies in spirit or in flesh, I have learned to count that as an inconsolable, irreplaceable loss. I am fighting to enlighten and protect my life by joining with my students, my comrades, and my colleagues for the enlightenment and rescue of all sociable and tender qualities of human life everywhere."[72] The act of recalling an "irreplaceable loss" to inform a future politic speaks to how societies position themselves in relation to the past as they reconstitute themselves into a new public sphere.

Soldier's final chapter, titled "The Only Last Chapter of My Childhood," signals the theme of "irreplaceable loss," and the conclusion underscores how mourning can productively inform a twenty-first-century black politic. Now twelve years old, the child-poet June stands waiting for a train that will take her to boarding school. Her mother, who opposed the idea but held no sway in the decision, is absent from the platform, her disappearance into depression and pain, chronicled throughout the memoir, now complete. Marked as a moment of loss and perhaps even abandonment, the mother's absence raises the theme of death alluded to in the epigraph from the Gospel of Mark. In one of *Soldier*'s many narrative gaps, the epigraph omits the fact that the young girl has indeed been raised from the dead and that her resurrection is inextricably linked to the healing of the woman with the twelve-year hemorrhaging. Just as these intertwined parables are to be read as companion pieces, Jordan's representation of her mother informs the meaning of the child-poet's departure. In this final train scene, Jordan inscribes cultural memory and mourning onto the body of her mother to suggest how emergent publics orient themselves to the past, poised for "workful beginnings." Like the twelve-year-old girl raised from the dead and the proverbial blues figure at a crossroads, June stands on a threshold of change. In terms of the memoir's chronology, it is the early 1950s, the dawn of the civil rights movement. Considered in this light, the autobiography arguably provides insight into, and a critique of, the animating pieties that sustained the movement. However, given the post-*Brown* era in which the memoir arrives, *Soldier* can also be read as offering a recalibrated ethic of struggle for the contemporary period. In an interview, Jordan discussed how her terminal illness related to what she called "the good fight": "I call my own fight with breast cancer 'a good fight.' What I mean by that is that it is big. I feel the same way about it as I feel about justice, meaning that's a good fight, that's big. I might not win it, meaning we may not win it, but it's unimaginable to me that I wouldn't try to be a part of that fight." *Soldier*'s conclusion asks readers to make a similar promise. The memoir's final line—"And I wondered who would meet my train"—is written in the characteristically questioning style of her political essays. The child-poet does not say, for instance, "I wondered *if* someone would meet my train," but "I wondered *who*," in faithful anticipation that on the other side exists "a powerful company of others [who] would undertake collective action founded on admitted similarities and grateful connections among us."[73]

A pastiche of autobiographical writings that span almost forty years, *Soldier* can be read as a companion to Jordan's final work, *Some of Us Did Not Die*, published one month after her death. A collection of "greatest hits" from her previous four volumes of political essays, *Some of Us* was written in the wake of September 11, 2001. The forty essays are assembled in reverse chronological order, at least one for every year of her career, with the last essay in this volume being her first, the original introduction to *Civil Wars*, her first collection: "And then you know why one of the freedom fighters in the sixties, a young Black woman interviewed shortly after she was beaten up for riding near the front of an interstate bus—you know why she said, 'We are all so very happy.' It's because it's on. All of us and me by myself: we're on." This captures what Jordan felt was her mission: "to be a witness, to carry on, to let it be heard that there is no death for the ideals that shaped her fights—from youthful work against McCarthyism to a sane response to 9-11."[74] In Jordan's dialogic style, the title is a rallying cry to those who not only survived the terrorist attacks but also will survive her. The collection's title performs the ethics of moving forward, the "righteous certainty that resistance requires that would explode paralysis and bring [one] to an 'over my dead body determination.'"[75] Jordan outlived her mother and picked up the mantle. Readers outlived Jordan and must do the same.

4

Storytelling as Diasporic Consciousness
Edwidge Danticat's *Brother, I'm Dying*

To the journeywoman pieces of myself.
Becoming.
Afrekete.

Audre Lorde,
Zami: A New Spelling of My Name

While second-generation immigrant writers such as June Jordan and Audre Lorde have contributed to black politics and culture primarily as African Americans, Edwidge Danticat is among a growing contingent of first-generation immigrant writers with a longing for native lands. Forty years ago, critics viewed immigrant narrative as a subgenre of American autobiography with a singular arc: a protagonist leaves the Old World for the New but, upon arrival, must confront hardscrabble realities and relinquish utopian dreams even while embracing the culture.[1] Jordan's *Soldier*, in portraying a harrowing childhood as a result of her immigrant parents' "misbegotten American dreams," their longed-for Brooklyn brownstone becoming a "tombstone testimonial to a terrible mistake" (39), draws on this convention. Today, however, a generation of immigrant American authors has developed a body of literature distinct from canonical U.S. immigrant literature: Edwidge Danticat, Junot Díaz, Cristina García, Oscar Hijuelos, Jhumpa Lahiri, Chang-rae Lee. In what Bharati Mukherjee calls this "Literature of New Arrival," contemporary immigrant writers have a sense of exile but little desire to erase their "premigration . . . historical inheritance."[2] The Immigration and Nationality Act of 1965 facilitated this shift in the literary landscape, as well as a shift in black America from a domestic to an increasingly diasporic consciousness. In abolishing national quotas and restrictions that earlier twentieth-century immigration policies established, the act allowed for a rate of immigration from the African diaspora that surpassed that of the transatlantic slave trade. When considering the exigencies and concerns of the post-*Brown* era, traditional civil-rights cultural memory rarely considers the 1965 immigration act as part of the narrative frame, even though it bookends the civil rights movement alongside the more celebrated Voting Rights Act. Yet the resulting influx from the African diaspora has been as transformative of today's evolving questions of cultural formation and politics as it was four hundred years ago.

Complicating concepts of "blackness," and even "nationality" and "citizenship," beyond U.S. borders has been a theme of African American studies (the "transnational turn") since Paul Gilroy's *The Black Atlantic* (1993). Recent catastrophes—natural, terroristic, political—have made the discussion less academic as traditional notions of nation collapse in the face of disaster. America's relative geographic isolation has protected its borders from the wars and geopolitical dynamics that have challenged other nations, but climate change and the looming menace of terrorism now erode its sense of exceptionalism. In the essay "Another Country," Danticat explores how these changing geopolitics have forced a reconsideration of "facile allegiances." On the one hand, the 9/11 terrorist attacks elicited worldwide sympathies and solidarities, rendering the globe, however briefly, "American." On the other, the devastation of Hurricane Katrina recalled the tsunami in Thailand a year earlier and the floods in Mozambique in 2000, exposing the structural inequalities that do the demolition work of natural disasters and create a "third world" America inside the first.[3] At the time, media commentators noted with surprise and seeming disgust that "Katrina-ravaged New Orleans" looked like Haiti, buffeted century after century by disasters natural and political.[4] Danticat argues that a diasporic consciousness would have made the Bush administration's unconscionably slow response entirely predictable. A year earlier, Tropical Storm Jeanne hit Haiti and "blanketed an entire city in water the way Hurricane Katrina did parts of New Orleans," killing three thousand and leaving a quarter million homeless. Just as with Katrina, "patients drowned in hospital beds. Children watched as parents were washed away. Survivors sought shelters in trees and on rooftops while corpses floated in the muddy, contaminated waters." The Bush administration sent "sixty thousand dollars in aid and the repatriation of Haitian refugees from the United States back to the devastated region even before the waters had subsided. New Orleans' horrific tragedy had been foreshadowed in America's so-called backyard."[5]

With this critique, Danticat joins scholars who cite Katrina as a signal moment that exposed the shortsightedness and inadequacy of traditional black political discourses.[6] Once again, "race language" failed to describe the complex causes and impact of the devastation, to discuss the structural realities and the malign neglect that ensured those who lived in the poorest areas and were the most vulnerable to natural disaster were primarily black. As Eddie Glaude writes in *A Shade of Blue*, "The structural dimensions of racism that revealed themselves in the very material conditions of poor black New Orleanians could not be captured in a sound bite or in the traditional language of the civil rights establishment."[7] The "refugee" rhetoric used to describe people displaced from their homes, within their own country, conveyed how very tenuous claims to citizenship continue to be for black Americans. No wonder appeals to rights and the politics of respectability—for instance, "We are from here. Law-abiding. Tax-paying"—failed to counter the marginalization or to garner prompt government response.[8]

The cultural studies scholar Richard Iton argues that continually resorting to bankrupt politics reflects a lack of political imagination and a misunderstanding of the inherent limitations of the nation-state. Like theorists of Afropessimism who believe that the structural relation between blacks and the state is always already antagonistic,[9] Iton argues that colonial and racist structures will persist despite the independence of former colonies or the success of the civil rights movement, because the nation-state as a Western political construct inherently excludes nonwhites. As with the international group of black vagabonds in Claude McKay's Harlem Renaissance novel *Banjo*, the political status for nonwhites "and all others *nous sommes tous de sans-papiers*" is always "nationality doubtful . . . with no place to go."[10] But unlike Afro-pessimists, Iton does not believe such statelessness necessarily means social death. Rather, the limbo reality provides an opportunity for artists and cultural workers to draw outside of the lines, to "disorganize the sign of the nation and the citizen."[11] Iton's theorizing about the "anticolonial labor" of cultural actors who "disassemble, re/present, and reimagine"[12] in a postrevolutionary, or post-*Brown*, era resonates with Danticat's essay collection *Create Dangerously: The Immigrant Artist at Work* (2010), where she outlines her own philosophy of the artist's social role. In this chapter, I argue that her memoir, *Brother, I'm Dying*, performs this cultural and political work of storytelling in service of social justice as it explores the diasporic dimensions of contemporary black cultural formation. The traditional way of thinking about diaspora centers on the dislocations and dispersals associated with the slave trade and the Middle Passage, alongside notions of redeeming "'Africa,' . . . figured as a home that does not allow easy return."[13] Scholars such as Paul Gilroy (1993) and Carol Boyce Davies (1994) have troubled this concept of redeeming pure roots with the idea of "diaspora space," where the movement between homeland and diaspora is not one of uneasy, incomplete return, "but a web of possible journeys" in between.[14] Iton's formulation of diaspora, "the impossibility of settlement," embraces a similar idea in which those of the African diaspora are forever displaced. Within this "modern matrix of strange spaces—outside the state but within empire"—writers and artists can facilitate "deliberation, and the interpellation of subjects, and the representation of a community that might claim priority over or alongside state identifications."[15] *Brother, I'm Dying*'s storytelling ethic forges such diasporic consciousness and transnational citizenship.

The autobiography chronicles a triad of events occurring in 2004: the author's unexpected pregnancy; her father's terminal diagnosis; her uncle's tragic death while in U.S. Customs. On the one hand, *Brother, I'm Dying* is a *testimonio*, a collective story that speaks out against injustice to gain agency through narration and to inspire reader activism,[16] as her uncle's death in detention provided the original catalyst for this protest against imperialism. But the memoir is also a creation myth, a myth of origins, in which Danticat contemplates the influence of her uncle and father, her "two papas," on her formation as an immigrant writer. This chapter demonstrates that, as much as this memoir is about mourning her father's and uncle's deaths, and Haiti's travails since independence, it also revisits Danticat's own immigrant odyssey and the very personal consequence of diaspora. The story of the black nation and subjectivity has traditionally been the story of men, with women serving only as mothers and mates who created male heirs.[17] In creating subjectivity through nonlinear, dialogic structures in the vein of black feminists writers, such as Mae G. Henderson and Audre Lorde, *Brother, I'm Dying* joins an intellectual tradition of black feminist writing on diaspora. Chronicling her subject formation at the hands of her father and uncle, all the while positioning herself as a mother-to-be, Danticat creates a black diasporic identity beyond gender and nation.

The Immigrant Writer at Work

One significant paradigm shift since the passage of the Immigration and Nationality Act of 1965 has been the creation of "a broader space" for artists to articulate cultural memories "not directly connected to the concerns of the 'movement.'"[18] Danticat is among an influx of contemporary immigrant writers introducing cultural memories whose histories and perspectives serve to expand the black political imagination in the post-*Brown* era. In *Create Dangerously: The Immigrant Artist at Work*, an essay collection adapted from her 2008 Toni Morrison lecture at Princeton, Danticat engages the question of the social role of the artist. Combining memoir and essay, the volume "tells the stories of artists, including herself, who create despite, or because of, the horrors that drove them from their homelands and that continue to haunt them."[19] The title essay, taken from an Albert Camus lecture, opens with the executions of Marcel Numa and Louis Drouin, two guerrilla fighters with Jeune Haiti, a group of thirteen men plotting to overthrow dictator François "Papa Doc" Duvalier. When Papa Doc came to power in 1957, Numa and Drouin immigrated to the United States, escaping the ensuing reign of terror and establishing comfortable lives. The rebels nonetheless chose to return in 1964 to liberate their country from Duvalier and his paramilitary force, the notoriously savage Tonton Macoutes. After months of guerrilla warfare, Numa and Drouin were the only survivors of the thirteen. Once caught, Papa Doc made spectacles of them, rebroadcasting their executions on state television for a week. The story of the Numa/Drouin executions, like that of the civil rights movement, has become a cultural memory passed down through generations and various media. "I don't even remember when I first heard about it," Danticat writes in *Create Dangerously*. "I feel as though I have always known it, having filled in the curiosity-driven details through photographs, newspaper and magazine articles, books, and films as I have gotten older."[20] Danticat recounts the executions, which occurred years before her birth, from old documentary footage, yet she claims this Haitian cultural memory of "a disobeyed directive from a higher authority" as her own personal "creation myth"—like Adam and Eve in Eden, like Antigone defying Creon in Thebes—helping to define her identity and social role as an immigrant writer:

> Their death is possibly among the shocking incidents that eventually motivated so many others, like my parents, for example, to leave. This may be one of the reasons I live in the United States of America today, writing in this language that is not mine. This could possibly be why I am an immigrant and hopefully an artist, an immigrant artist at work. Even though there is probably no such thing as an immigrant artist in this globalized age, when Algeria and Haiti and even ancient Greece and Egypt are only a virtual visit away. Even without globalization, the writer bound to the reader, under diabolic, or even joyful, circumstances inevitably becomes a loyal citizen of the country of his readers.[21]

In evoking Antigone as a model of political work, Danticat reflects what political theorist Bonnie Honig calls a millennial revival of Sophocles's *Antigone*, a classical drama that has been central to feminist studies, political theory, and philosophy since G. W. F. Hegel first canonized it for modern philosophy in the early nineteenth century. In the ancient myth, Antigone's father, Oedipus, has been exiled, his tragic failings having corrupted the city of Thebes. Her two brothers, Eteocles and Polynices, have slain each other in civil war, vying for their father's crown. When her uncle Creon ascends the throne, he allows Eteocles to be buried with full honor but decrees that Polynices must be left in the elements to rot, his state law violating the humanist one of dignity in death for all. In the dead of night, Antigone defies Creon's decree, as Numa and Drouin defy Duvalier and Adam and Eve, God. Such scholars as Jacques Lacan, Jacques Derrida, and Judith Butler have interpreted the heroine primarily in three models of citizenship: as a martyred, conscientious objector, a grieving sister honoring universal human dignity, a mad woman whose political passions are as excessive as the state power she laments. Honig argues that the contemporary turn to Antigone, both play and heroine, reflects a humanist resurgence in reaction to the twentieth-century horrors, such as the Holocaust. Enlightenment humanism defined reason and rationality as the basis for what makes us all human. The new millennial humanism finds universalism in suffering and mortality, what Honig calls "mortalist humanism," with the hope that mourning might provide a new universalism to replace the discredited others. The impetus for the shift from rationality, often associated with Oedipus, to mortality as humanity's defining trait, defined by Antigone, has been a desire among intellectuals and activists to protest state power without replicating the autocratic forces they challenge. A worthy goal, of course, but this "Antigone effect," Honig argues, has transformed political resistance into resignation and malaise, the "lamentation of politics." In *Antigone, Interrupted*, Honig tries to bring back a resistant politic to humanism by offering a fourth interpretation of Antigone: a political actor who is a symbol of principled civil disobedience and humane grief, yes, but also who strives for power, who models "agonistic humanism," a cultivation of power to implement "democratic or redistributive agendas." *Brother, I'm Dying* asserts such an agonistic politic as it protests U.S. imperialism while advancing new notions of nationality and citizenship, new forms of resistance.

When asked about the political implications of her writing, Danticat has demurred: "I am not well versed in theory." Rather, she writes "opinion pieces to purge the preaching from my work" so that her creative writing might be "an engaging story that then leads people to think and question and possibly act for change."[22] Despite Danticat's disclaimers, I claim her memoir as a work of black feminist thought engaged with political theory. Contemporary black feminist criticism argues that black women's cultural productions, in creating "intersectional" works that are conscious of power dynamics, construct their own theory, their own "guiding principles of the subject's becoming and un-doing."[23] A central argument in *Words of Witness* is that storytelling, in its rejection of rigid ideology and political schema, offers radical insights for addressing contemporary issues in that it demands critical engagement from an audience, ethical witnessing, encouraging the deliberative space necessary for creating post-*Brown* politics.[24] Danticat's philosophy of storytelling in fact echoes political theories about storytelling as a mode of political thinking: "Storytellers initiate political reconciliation. Their work is to tell stories that accord permanence to fleeting actions, crafting them into events whose meaning can be opened to public disputation. This reconciliation is neither retrospective nor passive, but the quintessential realization of natality, the condition that makes way for new beginnings."[25] This storytelling function is what makes the genre of autobiography and memoir conducive to political theorizing in general and particularly useful for crafting progressive politics.

Danticat has said that all her fiction up to this point—from the semiautobiographical debut novel, *Breath, Eyes, Memory* (1994), and short-story collection *Krik? Krak!* (1996), to the American Book Award–winning *The Farming of Bones* (1998) and *The Dew Breaker* (2004)—prepared her to write this memoir.[26] One hallmark of her fiction that she brings to *Brother, I'm Dying* is mapping individual stories onto national history. The three familial moments that precipitate this memoir—Danticat's unexpected pregnancy, her father's terminal diagnosis, her uncle's tragic death—coincide with corresponding national crises: President Jean-Bertrand Aristede's second ouster, thirteen years after the first; Tropical Storm Jeanne; fire fights between United Nations "peacekeepers" and Haitian police against neighborhood gangs that left "a generation of young people, some violent, some bystanders, [all] in the line of fire, dying."[27] The dying "I" of the memoir's title is thus a collective one, at once referring to her uncle and father, Haitian brothers who die within months of each other on the soil of the imperial regime that occupied their country at their births, as well as to Haiti's twentieth-century travails. Through this memoir, like Antigone, Danticat ensures that her uncle and father receive dignity in death:

> I write these things now, some as I witnessed them and today remember them, others from official documents, as well as the borrowed recollections of family members. But the gist of them was told to me over the years, in part by my uncle Joseph, in part by my father. Some were told offhand, quickly. Others, in greater detail. What I learned from my father and uncle, I learned out of sequence and in fragments. This is an attempt at cohesiveness, and at re-creating a few wondrous and terrible months when their lives and mine intersected in

startling ways, forcing me to look forward and back in both celebration and despair. I am writing this only because they can't. (25)

Brother, I'm Dying is indeed a collaborative text in which Danticat stitches together scraps of diaries and letters, along with overheard conversations, with her own memories and novelistic voice. In speaking out against U.S. imperialism, just as Antigone speaks out against Creon, Numa and Drouin against Duvalier, she uses the memoir to pursue justice for her uncle, for Haiti, and "on behalf of collective life."

The agonistic politics that animates Danticat's portrait of her "two papas," their deaths, and, more importantly, their lives can first be seen in the mortalist humanism that infuses the memoir's structure, from the title and epigraphs to its narrative arc. The title comes from a conversation in which her uncle Joseph, fearful that a throat tumor will suffocate him, calls his brother in New York to say, "Frè, map mouri" (40). At memoir's end, as Danticat reassembles the circumstances surrounding his tragic death in U.S. Customs, one wonders if these poignant words were among her uncle's last thoughts. However, the title could just as easily refer to Danticat's father, Mira, who is dying throughout the novel, his robust frame thinning as her belly swells with new life. Linking mortality and natality, death and birth, evokes the human lifecycle, universalizing her father's suffering. Upon hearing of his terminal diagnosis, one friend replies, "We are all dying" (59). If there is one progressive plotline in this nonlinear narrative, whose chapters alternate between the past and present, from an array of perspectives, it is the pervasiveness and inevitability of death. Just as Danticat relays one of her minister uncle Joseph's sermons describing birth as the beginning of dying (72), news of her pregnancy brings thoughts of death: "Would I die? Would the baby die? Would the baby and I both die? Would my father die before we died? Or would we all die at the same time?" (14). From that early moment in the memoir, the losses unfold one after the other. In the chapter "Good-bye," Joseph loses his ability to speak because of throat cancer, and her Granmè Mèlina dies, leaving the children "the task of identifying [a corpse], recognizing the transition from the living to the dead" (71). This is followed by the story of how a stray bullet, lodged between opposing military factions in 1986, kills her cousin Marie Micheline, "a reflection of Haiti and its potential, a flicker of light frustrated in its attempt to shine" (133). Then Aunt Denise, Joseph's wife, dies of a stroke, with the story of her death and funeral intertwined with that of an attempted assassination, as well as the escalating violence among the street gangs, police, and UN "peacekeepers." Recounting familial deaths alongside national losses bolsters the idea that this memoir is a *testimonio*,

collective story, the voice of contemporary Haiti suffering disaster upon catas-
trophe. Danticat's description of the coup-ravaged landscape upon her first
return to Haiti at age twenty-five conveys the widespread devastation: "There
were also monuments to losses everywhere: the charred shantytowns of La
Saline and Cité Soleil, the busts and frieze of the murdered: a justice minister, a
campaign financier and a beloved priest among thousands of others. Piles of
brick and ashes stood where homes and offices had been, places that had been
both constructed and destroyed in the time I'd been gone. Chunks of Port-au-
Prince, I realized, had been wholly assembled and disassembled in my absence"
(139). This portrait of pervasive death establishes a mortalist humanism that
serves to underwrite the memoir's philosophy about the social role of the artist.

In *Create Dangerously*, Danticat reminds that a line in the Haitian national
anthem is *Mourir est beau* (To die is beautiful). She evokes the anthem in tribute
to Numa and Drouin, national heroes who "abandoned comfortable lives in
the United States and sacrificed themselves for the homeland," but questions
whether "writing could [even] attain that kind of beauty."[28] The essay collection
meditates on the social role of the artist, with Danticat ultimately concluding
that writing becomes subversive when audiences "read dangerously," that is,
pick up challenging texts the way writers pick up their pens in "a revolt against
silence."[29] During the Duvalier regimes, possessing certain texts could be a
death sentence, as Haitian writers considered polemical had been banned or
exiled. Because foreign or long-dead authors could not be tortured or killed or
banished, people gravitated to classics, going underground to stage works such
as Albert Camus's *Caligula* and Sophocles's *Antigone*. Their politically subversive
messages provided reassurance "that words could still be spoken, that stories
could still be told and passed on."[30] Despite her doubts about writing's impact,
Brother, I'm Dying serves, first and foremost, as a protest, a cry, an Antigonean wail
against her uncle's tragic, needless death in U.S. Customs. The opening epigraph
telegraphs not only the narrative arc but the ethos of creating dangerously:

> To begin with death. To work my way back into life,
> and then, finally, to return to death.
> Or else: the vanity of trying to say anything about anyone.

The opening phrase, "To begin with death," perhaps refers to the story's
precipitating tragedy, with "To work my way back into life" suggesting the
work of mourning and the memoir's theme of moving beyond mortality to
natality, from death to life. The fact that the arc necessarily must "return to
death" suggests a certain futility: "The vanity of trying to say anything about

anyone." Which is not to suggest the work should not be undertaken but speaks, perhaps, to Danticat's nagging self-doubt about the artist's social role and utility: "As immigrant artists for whom so much has been sacrificed, so many dreams have been deferred, we already doubt so much. It might have been simpler, safer, to have become the more helpful doctors, lawyers, engineers our parents wanted us to be. When our worlds are literally crumbling, we tell ourselves how right they may have been, our elders, about our passive careers as distant witnesses."[31] The epigraph's "all is vanity" theme recalls the Book of Ecclesiastes and sets a fitting biblical tone, given that her uncle Joseph was a minister and that scriptural epigraphs frame the memoir's two sections. The epigraph for part one, "He Is My Brother," comes from Genesis 20:13: "This is how you can show your love to me: Everywhere we go, say of me, 'He is my brother.'" The epigraph for part two, "For Adversity," comes from Proverbs 17:17: "A friend loves at all times, and a brother is born for adversity." The themes of brotherhood in the scriptural epigraphs, first articulated in the title, once again universalize this story of suffering, with the linked-fate echoes of "Am I My Brothers' Keeper?" fashioning a mortalist humanism.

While themes of death and dying, mourning and loss frame the memoir, these tropes underwrite more than lamentation. Honig argues that it is natality—the possibilities of life, pleasure, and new beginning—that animates agonistic humanism, and, indeed, Danticat's focus on natality within the memoir undergirds its challenge to empire and imperialism. The memoir refuses to allow the tragedy surrounding Joseph's death to define his life. Readers learn, instead, of the loving man who raised her. Who settled his family in the neighborhood of Bel Air, a seat of resistance to the U.S. occupation that began in 1934. Who married a beautiful woman first glimpsed riverside one morning and who then built a pink house whose rooms expanded to accommodate all their children, biological and chosen. As a young man, the pink house held rallies supporting Daniel Fignolé, who was elected president and held power for nineteen days before François "Papa Doc" Duvalier overthrew him. In later life, after the Duvalier regime dashed his political hopes, Joseph turned to religion, building a church, L'Eglise Chretienne de la Redemption, then a clinic, across the street from the pink house.

Throughout the narrative, Danticat consciously aligns her uncle's life with a resistant political ethos. For instance, when Jean-Claude "Baby Doc" Duvalier fled Haiti on February 7, 1986, her uncle's birthday became the official date for Haitian presidential inaugurations, marking the various coups and elections of Haiti's fledgling democracy (131). By the end of the Duvalier dictatorships, Joseph had become a preacher, disillusioned with formal politics: "He's certainly the best man," he said when the young radical priest Jean-Bertrand Aristide won his first election in 1991. "But in my old age, I'm no longer interested in best men. I'm interested in the people around me and what he can do for them" (136). Though the model had changed, the ethos of resistance remained the same as his church became a focal point for resistance activity. In subsequent years, whenever a political murder occurred, artists and intellectuals remembered the underground productions of *Antigone* and *Caligula* after the Numa-Drouin executions and suggested putting on a play, occasionally staged in the backyard of Joseph's church (8). He avoided overt political activity such as mass demonstrations and refrained from using his pulpit to speak out against the military. Yet, every morning after the fire fights between the protesters and police, the UN "peacekeepers" and neighborhood gangs,

> he got up to count the many bloody corpses that dotted the street corners and alleys of Bel Air. During the years when he couldn't speak, he had developed a habit of jotting things down, so he kept track of the cadavers in the small notepads he always carried in his jacket pocket. In his notebooks, he wrote the names of the victims, when he knew them, the condition of their bodies and the times they were picked up, either by family members or by the sanitation service, to be transported to the morgue or dumped in mass graves:
>
> Jonas, pt. 20 ans, main droite absent, 11:35 a.m.
>
> Gladys, pt. 35 ans, nue, 3:09 p.m.
>
> Samuel, Personage, 75 ans, chany, 5:42 p.m.
>
> Male Inconnu, pt. 25 ans, visage mutilée, 9:17 p.m.

This work of mourning certainly recalls the classical story of Antigone, who attempts to give a proper burial to her brother despite Creon's decree against it. Joseph attempts to dignify these deaths through narrative, taking the blown bits of body and sinew and reassembling them on the page. In *The Work of Mourning*, Jacques Derrida describes how modern eulogizing replaces the ancient rites. Joseph recalls Antigone here, yet Danticat seems to suggest that, despite his efforts, the deaths remain unavenged: "Yet, when he showed me his list of casualties . . . all I could see was Jonas, Gladys, Samuel and the hundreds of men and women who'd died, their mutilated bodies eternally rotting under the boiling sun" (139). The sense of futility recalls the "all is vanity" theme of the memoir's epigraph, Danticat's doubt about whether writing makes an impact. But like Joseph who rises every day to list the lives lost; like his neighbor's *bat ténéb* (beating the darkness), pounding on pots and pans to protest street violence; the social role of the writer, Danticat argues, is to bear witness and break silence, to reassemble losses and tragedy through narrative for the sake of justice.[32]

The memoir honors this political ethos as it details how her uncle Joseph died at the hands of the imperial regime that ruled Haiti at his birth. As Mukherjee writes, "Danticat's fury at America's original sin—because of its own slave-holding past—of shunning Toussaint L'Ouverture's successful slave revolt against the French, its later invasion and occupation, and its reflexive habit of backing ruthless dictators, is palpable."[33] Danticat stresses that the 2004 unrest that exiled her uncle, sending him to seek asylum, had its roots in the 1915–1934 U.S. occupation. A United Nations operation made the situation all the more volatile as "peacekeepers" indiscriminately sprayed her uncle's neighborhood of Bel Air with bullets to kill gang members, with the innocent bystanders considered collateral damage. The roving gangs, descendants of Duvalier's Tonton Macoutes, think Joseph has allowed U.N. troops to use his church roof to fire into the streets, so they burn down the church, school, and pink house. They promise to kill him if he ever returns. When he arrives in the United States, Joseph requests asylum, although he had in his possession a valid visa that should have allowed legal entry into the country. That he requested asylum, Danticat argues, indicates that he planned and wanted to return home.

Joseph reflects those contemporary immigrant writers for whom exile and longing for a native land are still palpable. He had never planned to migrate, become American. Except for occasional visits to the United States for a life-saving operation to remove a cancerous throat tumor and to see relatives, Joseph lived in Bel Air despite the worsening of events, the increasing criminality, the rise of the Tonton Macoutes. He stayed even as Danticat's parents fled the reign of terror. He had been many times to the United States in the previous thirty years and had ample opportunity to immigrate—when his brother Mira left for the United States, when his son Maxo followed—if that is what he wanted: "Exile is not for everyone," he told Danticat when she wondered why he never immigrated to the United States like her parents. "Someone has to stay behind, to receive the letters and greet family members when they come back" (138).

Joseph's tragic experiences in U.S. Customs speak bitterly to the tension of the immigrant in exile. Danticat imagines that perhaps he sought asylum because he knew he would need to stay in the United States longer than the visa-approved thirty days and wanted to be truthful. Or perhaps he was simply traumatized and disoriented. Whatever the reason, his request for asylum ensnared him in a racist immigration policy: "[I] suspect that my uncle was treated according to a biased immigration policy dating back from the early 1980s when Haitians began arriving in Florida in large numbers by boat. In Florida, where Cuban refugees are, as long as they are able to step foot on dry land, immediately processed and released to their families, Haitian asylum seekers are disproportionately detained, then deported. For instance, while Hondurans and Nicaraguans have continued to receive protected status for nearly ten years after Hurricane Mitch struck their homelands, Haitians were deported to the flood zones weeks after Tropical Storm Jeanne" (220). These catastrophes are linked to the twentieth century's greatest horror, the Holocaust, when, upon arrival in this country, Joseph received Alien # 27041999, a dehumanizing brand reminiscent of the concentration camps. During his credible-fear interview, custom officials accused him of faking illness, despite his vomiting throughout the proceedings. Danticat stresses that her uncle's death in U.S. Customs, where he was denied medications, entry, and human dignity, is an extension of a U.S. occupation that began in his youth. She recalls his "most haunting childhood memory": being sent on a rare errand to the market, during the U.S. occupation in Haiti, where he saw marines, bored, kicking a man's head like a soccer ball, for sport: "Suddenly my uncle realized why [his parents] wanted him to stay home. Then, as now, the world outside Beauséjour was treacherous indeed." The "world" refers to U.S. imperialist presence: ubiquitous, sovereign, the state power she protests and critiques in this memoir. Of course the gross irony that "he would soon be the dead prisoner of the same government that had been occupying his country when he was born" does not escape Danticat: "In essence he was entering and exiting the world under the same flag" (248). Joseph spent his life in Haiti, determined not to be driven out by the Duvaliers and then the gangs. He died completely exiled and almost forcibly American, "becom[ing] part of the soil of a country that had not wanted him" (249). Consistent with the contemporary literature of new arrivals, *Brother, I'm Dying* inverts the traditional immigrant arc, challenging this notion of America as the great melting pot where all immigrants would like to come. As Danticat's father says after the uncle's funeral, had Haiti after independence been "given a chance and allowed to be a country like any other, none of us would live or die here" (249). This sense of exile, of "nationality doubtful . . . with no place to go," prefigures Danticat's own personal immigrant odyssey in diaspora.

Myths of Origins

While *testimonios* such as *Brother, I'm Dying* bear witness to injustice on behalf of others, they ultimately are about "affirming the individual in a collective mode."[34] Immigrant autobiographies also use myths and stories from a writer's place of origin as a way to tell her own story, with the autobiography itself becoming a myth of origin, a re-creation of the forces that shaped the writer.[35] In writing of the Numa-Drouin executions, which Danticat claims as her own personal creation myth, she asserts that all creation myths represent a clash in dualities: homeland and exile, life and death. Dualities structure *Brother, I'm Dying*, which opens with an impending birth *and* an impending death: "I found out I was pregnant the same day that my father's rapid weight loss and chronic shortness of breath were positively diagnosed as end-stage pulmonary fibrosis" (3). This contrasts with Jordan's immigrant narrative *Soldier*, which begins with the "I was born" trope of the slave narratives and invokes the social death often associated with black life in America. This domestic focus is arguably characteristic of second-generation immigrants like Jordan, the self-proclaimed "dissident American poet," who identified primarily as black American. *Brother, I'm Dying* dramatizes dualities that illustrate the double-consciousness characteristic of contemporary immigrant writers, of being suspended between two countries, in the story of her "two papas" who are separated for the majority of their lives, with one living in Haiti, the other in the United States.

According to Honig, balancing life and death, natality and mortality, is what animates a resistant humanist ethos, and we see that in the portrayal of her uncle and father. Certainly Danticat shows her own humanist commitment to the value of "dignity in death." Neither of her paternal figures has what can be called "a good death": Joseph is chased from his home in Port au Prince and then dies tragically, unnecessarily, in U.S. Customs. State law requires paramedics to pound her father's seventy-eight-pound frame, fruitlessly, for an hour, for lack of a DNR directive on file, despite his expressed desire to die peacefully at home. "Even if they had succeeded in resuscitating him, he probably would have had a couple of broken ribs," Danticat writes of the excessive force. In fact, a policeman, the state's representative, "the distant outside authority figure," was on the scene to ensure that there had been "no foul play or euthanasia" (262). It is ironic that the law against euthanasia, meant to protect life, actually dehumanizes it by disregarding suffering and causing more pain, preventing the peaceful, "good death" her father hoped to have. Despite the memoir's sorrow and anger, however, it chooses to pay tribute to the essence of their lives and legacies. For instance, the opening chapter orients readers to the question of natality, not only in the birth announcement but also in its title: "Have You Enjoyed Your Life?" the question posed during the family meeting to announce the father's terminal illness. Remembering life's hardships and disappointments, Mira hesitates to answer. In fact, later in the memoir, he tells his children that, as he declines, he does not want to be kept alive on machines, as "there's already been too much suffering." But in this moment, the question challenges him to look past suffering, to remember life's pleasures, even in dying. Of course then Mira thinks of his children: "Edwidge and Bob, your mother and I left you behind for eight years in Haiti. Kelly and Karl, you grew up here, in a country your mother and I didn't know very well when we had you. You all could have turned bad, but you didn't. I thank God for that. . . . Yes, you can say I have enjoyed my life" (21). Haitian custom believes that people are alive as long as you can call their names. The daughter that Danticat learns she is carrying the day her father is diagnosed becomes a repository of his legacy, for she will inherit his name, Mira. "Now even when I'm gone—and we can all say that, even those of us who are not sick—even when I'm gone, the name will stay behind" (255).

The memoir honors these two brothers, who live on not only through their progeny but also through the text itself. At memoir's end, they are "sharing a gravesite and tombstone in Queens, New York, after living apart for more than thirty years" (266). Like Antigone, Danticat, through narrative, effectively ensures their dignity in death. When she learns of her uncle's death, she holds mortality and natality together: "We spent most of the night awake, cradling along with my large belly this horrendous news" (240). The chapter after her uncle dies, "Transition," recounts her daughter's birth and her father's death. As he lies dying, he dreams of long dead relatives standing at his bedside: "His mother in a red dress. His father singing. His sister laughing" (255), as if already the customary "jubilant country wake," where Haitian cultural tradition directs, "We will eat. We will sing. We will dance and tell stories. . . . For it is not our way to let our grief silence us" (265).

Carol Boyce Davies has argued that immigrant narratives often have a mythic element as they draw on others' personal stories and cultural myths to tell their own. Audre Lorde's *Zami: A New Spelling of My Name* is a prime example. The title itself, *Zami*, a Carriacou name for women who work together as friends and lovers, derives from a mythic past, and the memoir's narrator is "a persona that Lorde creates out of the realities and imaginings of lived experiences."[36] In a classic interview with Claudia Tate, Lorde defines "biomythography" as essentially "fiction [with] the elements of biography and the history of myth."[37] Lorde creates for herself a personal myth of origin, connecting herself to Caribbean ancestry, especially her "root-woman grandmother" Ma Mariah; to West Indian and black American communities in Harlem; to a mythical precolonial West Africa that is home to goddesses and amazons, forming a mythic "matrilineal diaspora." In a sense, Danticat's *Brother, I'm Dying* is also a biomythography. The author has described the book as a "we-moir," given that it is largely comprised of biographies of extended family members, including their personal memories, official documents, and "borrowed recollections" (25).[38] But there is also folklore and fiction, lending the memoir a mythic quality. For instance, Granmè Melina's story about the Angel of Death who "doesn't play favorites," who "takes us all" (140–142), and Marie Micheline's bedtime fables to comfort orphaned children (55) establish how oral traditions construct our sense of identity within community. And the novelist's voice emerges repeatedly in scenes that she could not have possibly witnessed, as in the one of her uncle fleeing Bel Air but feeling buoyed by the neighbors' *bat tenéb* to protest gang violence (170). I argue here that the mythical space Danticat creates in *Brother, I'm Dying* through storytelling is also a diasporic one in which she reimagines herself, as both immigrant writer and world citizen.

In the aftermath of the Numa-Drouin executions, Duvalier tried to kill the two freedom fighters a second time by taking away "the mythic elements of their story,"[39] calling them *blans*, foreigners. A naturalized U.S. citizen, Danticat grapples with a similar sense of exile and dislocation. On return trips to Haiti, customs officials now issue her the form designated for foreigners, making her feel "a bit traitorous" (144). And Haitian readers' negative reception of her work has only heightened the sense of alienation. When Oprah selected *Breath, Eyes, Memory* for her televised book club, Danticat received backlash for her representation of "testing," the practice of obsessively probing a daughter to ascertain virginity. In the years since, Danticat has become more sensitive to reader critique. In "Daughters of Memory," for example, an essay within the *Create Dangerously* collection, she assumes a defensive posture in relation to her Haitian readers. The essay discusses the rote memorization used to teach Haitian children and the fact that, while growing up, she knew of no one who read Haitian writers. Danticat anticipates the objections to this assessment and representation of Haitian education: "I can hear now as I write this cries of protest from other Haitians my age (and younger and older, too) shouting from the space above my shoulders, the bleachers above every writer's shoulders where readers cheer or hiss and boo in advance."[40] To deflect the anticipated criticism, Danticat insists that she is speaking only for herself, her own personal experience, despite beginning the essay with broad cultural and national claims about the state of education. The contradictory impulses reflect a kind of immigrant double consciousness: wanting to speak for Haiti, for the collective, but fearing that those she claims will reject her voice as alien and perhaps even hostile. In creating her own myth of origins, Danticat demonstrates that this limbo space, "outside of homeland but within empire," can be a space of progressive political possibility and vision. When Haitians smuggled those underground classics after the Numa-Drouin executions, daring to read subversive texts during the Duvalier regimes, in that moment, Danticat argues, Camus and Sophocles became Haitian writers, their nationalities defined by their readers. Similarly, the immigrant writer belongs to all, not just her homeland. Danticat calls both Haiti and the United States home, refusing to "fetishize a particular national citizenship."[41] Rather, she argues, the immigrant writer resides in a limbo space of diaspora that is almost its own national identity,[42] "another country," for in this "illusory but meaningful space between the national and the imperial"[43] diasporic black subjects are made.

In *Becoming Black: Creating Identity in the African Diaspora*, Michelle Wright argues that exploring black female identity and agency through collective, dialogic narratives is an established tradition in black feminist writing about the diaspora.[44] Wright is among contemporary scholars of diaspora studies who define diaspora not only as movement and space but also as intellectual tradition, as a set of aesthetic and interpretive strategies and methodologies.[45] She argues that, given the range of histories and geographies, racial discourses and resistance strategies experienced by people of African descent through the world, there is no commonly shared history that can link everyone, like the civil rights movement for a certain generation of black Americans. Rather, there is a shared intellectual tradition through which writers and intellectuals have developed models of African diasporic identity and politics. Black theorists such as W. E. B. Du Bois, Aimé Césaire, Leopold Senghor, and Frantz Fanon sought to counter Western discourses that, in the tradition of philosophers such as Hegel and Thomas Jefferson, rendered people of African descent as Other—without history, without progress, without humanity. Their dialectical, linear narratives created an illusion of progressive time, even though the narratives were simply a random ordering of events, "incidents," as Harriet Jacobs would say. This manipulation of time and space, what Mikhail Bakhtin called "adventure-time," legitimated philosophies of an enlightened male subject anchored in notions of a black Other. While twentieth-century black male writers such as Du Bois, Césaire, and Fanon produced counterdiscourses to these Western theories of the subject and the nation, their writings, in the dialectical, "adventure-time" tradition of Hegel and Jefferson, negated the subjectivity of black women just as the earlier works negated black people. In traditional political discourses on the nation and the subject, black women became "the Other of the Other," as Michele Wallace has written.

According to Wright, creating an inclusive black diasporic identity requires a nonlinear, dialogic narrative that challenges the adventure-time chronotype. *Brother, I'm Dying* duly eschews the pretense of linear progression. Throughout the memoir, there is no precise beginning or end, as the chapter sequence alternates between borrowed memories from the past and Danticat's personal story in the present. It also embodies Mae Gwendolyn Henderson's theory of black female diasporic subjectivity formed through Bakhtian dialogic principles. In "Speaking in Tongues," Henderson famously argued that black women realize their singular subjectivity through "heterogeneity" and "omnivocality," the diverse voices of others. The memoir's dialogic structure develops such a collective consciousness, with the titles of most chapters in fact taken from conversations with others. The book's title, *Brother, I'm Dying*, for instance, comes from a conversation her uncle had with her father. The opening chapter's title, "Have You Enjoyed Your Life?," comes, as noted above, from a family meeting about her father's terminal diagnosis when the oldest son asks his father, who is now nearing the end of his life, if he has enjoyed it. The chapter title "What Did the White Man Say?" echoes Danticat's mother, chiding her only daughter for the mumbled announcement of her pregnancy, with the teasing challenge introducing a theme of anxiety around cultural belonging. In telling the experiences of her larger family, Danticat's *testimonio* breaks from the established mold of the enlightenment subject as she creates a diasporic one.

Within this dialogic structure, Danticat emphasizes the story of her own immigrant experience. Amid these chapters detailing the lives of her family, alternating between past and present, are three consecutive chapters focused on her arrival in the United States. Singling out her personal immigrant experience emphasizes that it is central to the memoir, that the "I" in the title is both individual and collective. The chapter "Gypsy" develops the idea of the social role of the artist. The morning after her arrival in New York, her father presents her with a gift that she had longed for while in Haiti: a typewriter. She wanted it to help her uncle with his church and school, as well to help him write letters. Now, living in New York with her birth family, apart from the beloved uncle who raised her, she could not imagine how she might use it. Danticat and her father shared a similarly illegible script; a typewriter, he thought, might help her to better "measure your words . . . to line them up neatly." Thirty years and several novels later prove the prescience of the gift, "this typewriter and his desire, very early on, to see me properly assemble my words" (118). The typewriter becomes a link between her father, as well as the uncle who first inspired her desire for it, and her identity as a writer. The father's influence is made more explicit as she compares their chosen careers. "Gypsy" refers to an unauthorized taxi driver without official affiliation to the Taxi Authority: "*My father's cab is named for wanderers, drifters, nomads. It's called a gypsy cab.*" The parallels between the nomadic existence of the immigrant writer and her father as gypsy cab driver are apparent. "Unlike a yellow cab, a gypsy has no medallions or affiliations. It belongs entirely to the driver, who roams the streets all day looking for fares" (119). Like her father looking for fares, Danticat looks for readers who might step into this limbo space of political possibility with her.

In showing how her father and uncle shaped her identity as a writer, *Brother, I'm Dying* recalls June Jordan's *Soldier*, another self-conscious meditation on identity formation. In the "Daughters of Memory" essay from the *Create Dangerously* collection, Danticat shares that she modeled her collage style of writing on literary mentors, novelists Jan J. Dominque and Jacques Domain, whom she encountered as a teenager in "the Livres Haitiens section" of the Brooklyn Public Library. However, the memoir makes clear that her collective narrative style could just as well have been inherited from listening to her father and uncle speak together. A few months after her father's diagnosis, her uncle Joseph comes to New York for a visit. The two brothers would pray together for Mira's healing, "their combined voices, my father's low, winded, my uncle's loud, mechanical, yet both equally urgent in their supplications" (157). Afterward, they would reminisce about some mutual friend or some event in Danticat's childhood, as she sat listening, absorbing: "*More please*, I wanted to say. *Please tell me more. Both of you, together, tell me more. About you. About me. About all of us*" (159).

The father-daughter relationships in *Brother, I'm Dying* fashion a new diasporic and dialogic subjectivity in black women's life writing. In *Becoming Black*, Wright argues that writers such as Black Arts poets Carolyn Rodgers and Audre Lorde have created diasporic consciousness through tropes of motherhood. Since her debut novel, *Breath, Eyes, Memory*, Danticat has been known for exploring relationships between women: mothers and daughters, grandmothers, aunts, and sisters, "celebrating the strength of the matrilineal Haitian family." As Mukherjee notes, in Danticat novels, "It is the storytelling passion of grandmothers, mothers, and aunts that transforms individual acts of failed political resistance into inspiring acts of political martyrdom."[46] Danticat first shifts to exploring father-daughter relationships in *The Dew Breaker* (2004), a collection of linked short stories that explore the Duvalier reign of terror but eerily prefigure themes and plotlines in *Brother, I'm Dying* (2007). In the collection, a former Tonton Macoute (a "Dew Breaker") is assigned to kill a preacher whose popularity threatens Papa Doc's power, just as the roving gangs threaten to kill her preacher uncle if he should ever return to Bel Air. Thirty years later, the Dew Breaker is a Brooklyn barber dying of pulmonary fibrosis, his life trajectory and fate recalling that of Danticat's father, a Brooklyn cab driver dying of the same disease. And like Danticat, the Dew Breaker's daughter is an artist, in this case a sculptor, who creates a work to honor her father's life. Perhaps the major difference between the two works is that the scope of *Brother I'm Dying* is both more personal and broad, as she contemplates how imperialism and excessive state power affected her relationships with her two father figures.

Danticat's shift to fatherhood represents a departure or development in her writing, as well as in the larger field of black feminist diasporic discourse. Wright argues that writers such as Lorde have used tropes of motherhood to counter erasure of women in traditional black political discourse on the nation and the subject. While that strategic essentialism serves to critique a sexist nationalist discourse, omitting men simply repeats the erasure.[47] *Brother, I'm Dying* makes an important intervention by positioning both mothers and fathers as generative beings in her theorizing of black diasporic subjectivity. Her myth of origins begins with her two papas, but it is not the founding-father trope in traditional narratives regarding the nation and subject. Rather, she complicates the trope with overlapping and conflated lines of ancestry. For instance, she portrays herself as shaped indelibly by a patriarchal lineage, but it is a diverse one, with "two papas," and their legacy is a daughter, who by memoir's end has yet another daughter, Mira. Named for Danticat's father, baby Mira embodies the memoir's theorizing about contemporary black diasporic consciousness. On the day of her birth, a moment readers have been anticipating since the memoir began, Danticat thinks, "Today is not just her day, but all of ours. And we're not the only ones who will cradle and protect her. She will also hold and comfort us. She too will be our repozwa, our sacred place to rest" (253). Like Afrekete in Lorde's *Zami*, Mira becomes a mythic figure who reflects what Wright calls a "truly diasporic structure" as a black subject united across national boundaries and across genders.[48]

5

Cultivating Liberatory Joy
Eisa Davis's *Angela's Mixtape*

I wish to live because life has within it that
which is good, that which is beautiful, and that
which is love. Therefore, since I have known
all of these things, I have found them to be
reason enough and—I wish to live.

Lorraine Hansberry,
To Be Young, Gifted and Black

$\mathbf{H}$ip-hop culture emerged as changes in immigration law in 1965 facilitated an influx of immigrants of African descent in U.S. cities. The encounter between American-born blacks and those from throughout the diaspora created a new generation faced with the question of negotiating and defining an increasingly diasporic identity.[1] The burgeoning generation, in turn, developed artistic expressions that collectively became known as hip-hop. Rapping, or MCing, is the most well known, but there are three other traditional elements: DJing, break dancing, and graffiti writing. In the midseventies, when hip-hop was born, black social movements were in collapse and urban blight on the rise. Funding for youth services and arts programs was cut while prisons grew. But, in the tradition of creating "something outta nothing," black and largely immigrant youth fashioned cultural practices to help them negotiate this alienated reality. DJs and MCs "took two turntables and a microphone," as the story has come to be told— borrowing beats from soul and funk, disco and reggae, overlaying them, initially, with lighthearted, playful lyrics. In parks and on city streets, or, in the parlance of the culture, "the boulevard," crews staged freestyle rap competitions and break-dancing battles. Throughout cities, graffiti writers sprayed their tags on crumbling infrastructure to ensure a forgotten generation would still be seen.[2]

Much has been written about rap as an extension of the black musical tradition, but it is part of the black autobiographical tradition as well, serving as a forum for self-assertion and social commentary. A primarily masculine aesthetic characterizes hip-hop culture, with many of the coming-of-age tales in rap lyrics echoing the life trajectory in *The Autobiography of Malcolm X*.[3] Given the prevalence of the autobiographical mode in rap, for many hip-hop artists, the transition from writing lyrics to writing autobiographies was only a matter of time. Black women's hip-hop life narratives often introduce a counternarrative through an examination of the unique perspective of women in the culture, much as Harriet Jacobs's *Incidents in the Life of a Slave Girl* offers a different perspective on slavery from the one found in Frederick Douglass's 1845 *Narrative*. As Gwendolyn Pough argues, several black women's hip-hop autobiographies can be likened to manifestoes in the ways that they use lived experience to critique the culture or advise young women within it. For instance, Sistah Souljah's *No Disrespect* (1996) and Queen Latifah's *Ladies First* (1998) recall nineteenth-century clubwomen as they challenge stereotypes that demean black women.[4] And Joan Morgan's *When Chickenheads Come Home to Roost: My Life as a Hip-Hop Feminist* (1999) explores feminism's "gray areas," the space between equality and equity, objectification and desire, sexism and complicity, as it seeks to empower a generation averse to the "f-word." Playwright Eisa Davis's personal essay "Sexism and the Art of Feminist Hip-Hop Maintenance," collected in Rebecca Walker's Third Wave anthology, *To Be Real: Telling the Truth and Changing the Face of Feminism*, is among this genre of black women's life narratives musing on the paradox of being a feminist in the misogynistic culture that can be hip-hop. Davis's essay describes a crisis of feminist faith that ensues when Queen Latifah's righteous *Black Reign* album was released the same day as Snoop Dogg's infectiously buoyant but sexist *Doggystyle*. Within this feminist "gray area," Davis, a self-proclaimed "hip-hop head" who studied political science at Harvard, sought to create both a black-feminist theory that would push against ideologies that "incarcerate individuality" and a political practice that might make space for joy within revolutionary struggle.[5] In her play *Angela's Mixtape*, Davis takes up her own charge.

Mixtape is a coming-of-age tale that is as much about the political awakening of the hip-hop generation as it is about growing up the niece of radical icon Angela Davis, the Marxist philosophy professor and political activist. From the beginning their lives were intertwined. The younger Davis was conceived the night of August 7, 1970, the same day seventeen-year-old Jonathan Jackson took hostages in a Marin County courthouse in frustration that his brother George had been imprisoned for ten years in San Quentin for aiding a seventy-dollar theft. In the shootout, Jonathan and hostages were killed, and Angela, the registered gun owner, was charged as an accomplice. After being a fugitive for two months and spending eighteen months in jail before being acquitted, the elder Davis became the face of black radicalism with a worldwide "Free Angela" campaign touting her cause. As Farah Griffin writes in an essay on black feminism in the Black Power era, "Those photographic images of Angela and Kathleen [Cleaver] were [the] iconography for what it means to be a revolutionary black woman."[6] *Angela's Mixtape* seeks to find a twenty-first-century answer for that question. A central motif in the play is that Eisa, whose first name is also Angela, is often jokingly "mistaken" for her famous aunt because they share the same name: Angela Davis. In some ways, the play enacts a classic adolescent search for identity that is doubly troublesome because the playwright's name is not her own. But given the symbolic weight of the name, the play also arguably explores generational shifts regarding contemporary notions of black identity and politics.

In "Restaging Revolution: Black Power, *Vibe* Magazine, and Photographic Memory," Leigh Raiford examines how Black Power–era iconography "has moved through time," tracking the ways those images continue to shape current memory of Black Power culture and politics. Raiford outlines four distinct periods between the Black Power movement and the millennium. Initially, she asserts, Black Power photography was used in service of the movement, helping to reenvision revolutionary possibilities for black politics and identity. Then, as the Black Power movement collapsed in the early 1970s, both from within and without, Hollywood summoned its iconography in the Blaxploitation film cycle that both championed and caricatured the movement, enshrining its militant aesthetics while prematurely evacuating the substances of any radical politics.[7] In the 1990s, these images became part of popular commodity culture. For instance, fashion spreads that hip-hop magazine *Vibe* called "docufashion" used contemporary clothing to mimic 1970s style and commissioned hip-hop celebrities to restage the era's iconic imagery: Angela Davis's FBI wanted posters; leather-jacketed, black-bereted Panthers on the steps of the California state capitol; the 1967 poster of Huey Newton in a wicker fan chair, holding a rifle and spear in each hand.[8] Angela Davis has understandably challenged the use of her image and history as a "commodified backdrop for advertising."[9] Raiford, however, allows that it may "be entirely too easy to dismiss these images out of hand for their almost complete commodification of 1960s radicalism." Rather, she suggests that these revisionist images enlist Black Power iconography in a way that is aware of the tensions between differing historical periods and contexts.[10] Raiford asks whether, at the millennium, it is "possible to infer a kind of performative dialogue" between the contemporary figures and the icons they attempt to impersonate. In "Restaging Revolution," Raiford specifically considers the role of photography in shaping memories of the Black Power era; however, her essay is helpful in thinking about how popular culture in general continues to use these images to stage intergenerational dialogues, and to what end.

This chapter considers the way Eisa Davis's *Angela's Mixtape* stages such a performative dialogue between the playwright and her (in)famous aunt, raising a question at the heart of Raiford's study of social-movement iconography: "What happens when these images travel through time?"[11] A time-travel motif borrowed from the film *Back to the Future* structures *Mixtape*, with the two Angela Davises, the senior and the younger, metaphorically representing the past and present converging in the same dimension. The play engages the iconography of the Black Power era to image a post-*Brown* politic, for in reshaping how we think of the past, we change our understanding of the present moment and future politics. I draw on various contexts to demonstrate how the play seeks to "Free Angela" from the nostalgia of the movement's iconography and, in turn, free her namesake, as well as the hip-hop generation Eisa Davis symbolizes, from narrow nationalism and joyless politics. First, I examine the rise of the hip-hop theater movement, of which Eisa Davis is both a practitioner and theorist, as a cultural space that facilitates the democratic deliberation from which new politics arise, what Richard Iton calls "the black fantastic." I then discuss how the play engages with Black Power playwrights, such as Adrienne Kennedy, Ntozake Shange, Amiri Baraka, and Lorraine Hansberry, in addition to contemporary writers, such as the novelist Eisa Ulen and the scholar Joan Morgan, to develop its perspective on the social role of the artist. Finally, I demonstrate that *Mixtape* repurposes Angela Davis's iconic history to imagine a post-*Brown* politic animated by an infectious sense of joy and a renewed sense of solidarity. Here, I refer specifically to Cornel West's political distinctions between pleasure and joy: "Joy forces you to look out and make connections so that there's the possibility of collective engagement, whereas pleasure, under commodified conditions, tends to be inward. You take it with you, it's a highly individuated unit. . . . But joy tries to cut across that. Joy tries to get at those non-market values — love, care, kindness, service, solidarity, the struggle for justice — values that provide the possibility of people coming together."[12] This position counters the Afro-pessimist theorists who assert that the black condition in the West is always already one of disenfranchisement and subjugation, or social death. Davis's vision in *Angela's Mixtape*, a work of political theory posing as a lighthearted, whimsical production, acknowledges those structural realities while maintaining a belief in the transcendent power of imagination.

The Emergence of Hip-Hop Theater

Many have described the post-*Brown* era as characterized by a "rupture with politics," in that, for almost forty years, until the Black Lives Matter campaign of 2014 launched police brutality protests nationwide, there had been no visible social movement. In identifying politics with events, such as demonstrations and elections, this view overlooks the processes and energies that must necessarily precipitate them. The real rupture in the post-*Brown* era, Richard Iton argues in *In Search of the Black Fantastic*, has been between *culture* and the larger political economy as an array of impulses have sought to separate the roles of creative artist and political activist since the Cold War.[13] In "Black Youth Black Art Black Face—An Address," Ras Baraka, son of Black Arts Movement co-founder Amiri Baraka, describes the impact of this paradigm shift on the hip-hop generation. Baraka pinpoints, for instance, a top-down education system focused more on the history of government and laws rather than actual people: If students are ever introduced to a black author, he writes, "the social and material forces behind them, or the political movements that ushered them into existence," are never discussed. The paradigm shift has left a generation floundering: "So many of us today are grasping for straws, guessing. You found an old record that moves you: James Brown, Curtis Mayfield, John Coltrane, Nina Simone, you tape it, you sample it. You found an old book. You read a beautiful poem. Someone told you about Paul Robeson and Du Bois. You read *The Autobiography of Malcolm X*, or just went to see the Malcolm X movie, and then 'Panther,' but no real education or preparation."[14] There is no lack of material that might stir political consciousness as Malcolm X's nationalist oratory once did for Angela Davis in the early stages of the formation of her radical subjectivity.[15] The difference is that there is no organization or network through which to channel that political consciousness. According to Baraka, the rupture between culture and politics has resulted in a culture of death in which black history and culture are being controlled, revised, and told by people who were once deeply opposed to it. Hollywood and the hip-hop industry's (from music to journalism to fashion) subsequent commodification of culture is a loss as devastating as the deaths of charismatic figures, from activists Malcolm and Martin to rap artists Tupac and Biggie.[16] Like many political scientists, Baraka, who is now the mayor of Newark, New Jersey, has joined the call to rebuild black public spheres, cultural spaces where political deliberation and debate might occur: "Our response to this should be the re-creation and re-development of our own institutions. We need writers' guilds, community theater, film production groups, artist collectives. We have to find ways to reach and teach masses of people who are being controlled by international multimedia conglomerates."[17] Some have looked to translate the culture into formal politics, from expecting rappers to assume roles as political leaders and activists to Russell Simmons's Hip Hop Summit Action Network establishing the first hip-hop convention, in 2001. However, the emergence of hip-hop theater is a testament to the political power of culture alone.

Eisa Davis has been a major architect of this burgeoning theater movement, a network of performance artists merging hip-hop's four foundational elements with traditional theater practices and bringing the boulevard's beats to Broadway. In an influential article in *Source* (March 2000), she described how, simultaneously, all over the world, theater-loving hip-hop heads began incorporating elements of the culture into their productions, creating "a syncretic art form that, in combining two genres, was actually revitalizing the aesthetics of each." Davis did not coin the term *hip-hop theater*; it had first appeared a few months earlier in an *American Theatre* article by Holly Bass, who would later curate the Hip-Hop Theater Festival. But because Davis's article was in *Source*, the bible of hip-hop culture at the time, the term *hip-hop theater* was able to galvanize a community of artists already developing the form. Naming the practice revealed a burgeoning community, an evolving public sphere: "We had crew, comrades, an umbrella 501(c)3," Davis writes. The hope was that this theater movement would defy the death-culture Baraka describes in his address and be "a clarion call to artists who want to resurrect American hip-hop by siphoning the formaldehyde out of its commodified veins, and to infuse theatre with bright, fresh blood."[18] That same year, Danny Hoch, Kamilah Forbes, and Clyde Valentin founded the New York Hip-Hop Theater Festival, featuring the works of Will Power and Sarah Jones.[19] Since then, hip-hop theater has appeared in more traditional venues, with playwrights such as Lin-Manuel Miranda revolutionizing musical theater with the hip-hop-infused productions *In the Heights* and *Hamilton*; and foundations convening artist retreats to consider "Future Aesthetics." The enormously talented Davis is also a celebrated practitioner of the genre. In 2007, her play *Bulrusher* was named a finalist for the Pulitzer Prize. In 2008, she won an Obie for her work in the musical *Passing Strange*. *Angela's Mixtape* debuted in 2009 at the Ohio Theater as part of the New Georges and Hip-Hop Theater Festival.[20] By year's end, both the *New Yorker* and the *Village Voice* had named it among the best New York theater in what critic Michael Feingold called a decade "of freewheeling joy" that saw new work by celebrated black women playwrights, such as Lynn Nottage (*Intimate Apparel, Ruined*, and *Fabulation*), Suzan-Lori Parks (*In the Blood, Top Dog/Underdog*, and *365 Days/365 Plays*), Tracey Scott Wilson (*The Good Negro*), and Adrienne

Kennedy (*The Ohio State Murders*).[21] In 2012, Davis was among five recipients of the prestigious Herb Alpert Award, a $75,000 prize for "risk-taking mid-career artists," and in 2013 she won yet another Obie—for Sustained Excellence in Performance.[22]

In "Found in Translation: The Emergence of Hip-Hop Theater," Davis theorizes how various narrative forms and structures within hip-hop theater make it a cultural space that nurtures the kind of deliberation and debate out of which a joyful politic and praxis might arise. She notes that, just as hip-hop theater incorporates the foundational elements of the culture, it also draws on traditional theater. Davis builds on the work of director-actor Stuart Vaughan to situate hip-hop within the "two major epochs" of drama history: William Shakespeare's theater of the articulate, where each character eventually says what s/he feels, and Sam Shepard's theater of the inarticulate, "where much of the play's meaning takes place in the subtext, in what is not being said or is unable to be said." Davis asserts that hip-hop theater combines both: "The lyrics provide the articulation of intellect, the need to speak plainly or with complexity, with irony, local and personal specificity, satire, longing—and the beat brings the inarticulate release of pure music, of the drum, of our primal rhythm. And we can flip it. The lyrics can be inarticulate, the pure feeling evoked by a curse word, a nonsense rhyme—and the beat can be intellectual, not danceable, just something to contemplate, to analyze. When hip-hop moves from the corner and into a theatre, you get the one-two punch. Articulate inarticulateness. Restoring theatre to its full power."[23] These ideas about how the form of hip-hop theater works to express the ineffable recalls Richard Iton's notion of "the black fantastic": the way popular culture freely engages time, space, and modes of agency outside the parameters of traditional politics to imagine new possibilities.[24] Davis invokes the playwright and poet Cornelius Eady to argue that creative works always contain instructions for how the work should be read to ensure every audience member or reader has a way to understand it.[25] Davis embeds several narrative devices—the mixtape form, the time-travel motif, the hip-hop "breaks"—to conjure the inarticulate spaces in which new identities emerge and new politics can be practiced.

The first and most immediate interpretative cue, of course, is the title, which telegraphs that the play's narrative structure is like that of a mixtape, a compilation of songs that the compiler usually shares with someone as a gift. On a basic narrative level, the play is Davis's gift to her aunt. At the outset, the Eisa character says, "This mixtape th-th-this mixtape th-th this mixtape is for her,"[26] enacting this ritual of exchange. In scratching her line like a DJ on a turntable, Davis signals that the line also gestures to hip-hop's storied history:

before the Sugar Hill Gang's "Rapper's Delight" was first played on the radio and brought hip-hop to the mainstream, the music traveled underground, hand-to-hand, on mixtapes. The opening stage notes make even more explicit the play's debt to hip-hop forms that conjure the ineffable. "Rhythm or melody," rather than words or themes, drive the play's scenes, which are episodic and frenetic, the pace never "[dropping] below 100 beats per minute" (2). Jive Rhythm Trax's hip-hop song "122 BPM" opens and closes the play, establishing the hip-hop aesthetic and providing the play's overarching narrative frame. The play's episodic, mixtape form—with short scenes sliding into new ones, themes and motifs recurring like sampled tracks in a rap song[27]—facilitates the dialogue between Black Power–past and post-*Brown* present. The time-travel motif structuring the play reveals how these seemingly oppositional eras are in fact contemporaneous as the play skips back and forth between the 1970s and the 1980s and beyond. An embedded reference to the film *Back to the Future* illustrates how the play's restaging of Black Power cultural memory recalls the return of Michael J. Fox's character to the past, changing his parents before they ever meet and conceive him. In changing them, he changes who he eventually becomes. As Davis restages her own life story and revisits her aunt's history, she alters understanding of the past and, thereby, understanding of herself in the present and any future possibilities. By play's end, it becomes clear that *Angela's Mixtape* refers to Eisa herself: she is her aunt's "mixtape," Black Power iconography and politics reconfigured and reimagined.

Given that the play is a metaphorical mixtape, one expects music to be a significant structuring device—to cue narrative details, convey moods, provide an interpretative lens: "I'll find tunes to play the part / Of my memories, linked up reveries" (13), the Eisa character states in the play's opening lines. For a play so deeply indebted to the hip-hop aesthetic, the soundtrack is surprisingly diverse, with styles ranging from pop and calypso to gospel and rock. Traditionally, a mixtape's song selection and sequence reflect the giver, in this case Davis, and creates an overarching message greater than any one song. Davis has argued that hip-hop theater reflects the "multiness" of identity that is characteristic of the post-*Brown* era, the ways contemporary black subjectivity pushes beyond traditional "boundaries of blackness."[28] On the one hand, the wide range of musical genres reflects this broadened identity; arguably, the black musical voice in literature supplants the notion of writing as the visible sign of humanity, with music reflecting a desire to express humanity in all its complexity rather than to prove it. On the other, the musical diversity provides a point of entry into the play for multiple audiences through what is known in hip-hop as the "break," the instrumental or percussive interlude within songs that allows listeners to add their own voices and movement—to sing or hum or dance along with the author's lyrics. As Joan Morgan writes in the introduction to *When Chickenheads Come Home to Roost*, "Truth is what happens when your voice fills in the breaks, provides the remixes, and reworks the chorus."[29] In this instance, Morgan is inviting readers to join their voices with hers to create a message larger than both. While it is important to note that my analysis derives from my experience of the play as a *reader* versus as a viewer of a live production, I argue that the music in *Angela's Mixtape* serves a similar function: bringing readers' voices into the play by eliciting knowledge of the songs, whose lyrics readers themselves provide as they read the script and hum the words in their minds. Readers become a sort of chorus that, throughout the play, is singing songs and chanting slogans. With this polyglot of voices filling the "breaks," tensions and arguments inevitably happen, creating the intergenerational dialogue that hip-hop theater seeks to stage. As Davis writes in "Found in Translation," "Sometimes it's a screaming match, sometimes it's a passing of the torch, sometimes it's an active collaboration. But it's a dialogue that is entirely welcome, and it has to do with the conscious relationship that hip-hop has always had to the past. When you sample old records and quote lyrics, you're not just stealing: you're showing respect. A DJ is doing her job if she generates nostalgia for music itself. And tradition is strengthened—our parents may not know their parents' songs, but we know our parents' songs like they're ours."[30]

Intergenerational Dialogues

According to Kevin Powell in *Step into a World: A Global Anthology of the New Black Literature*, the intergenerational dialogue is an emergent genre "as more traditional modes of writing become too time-consuming for our cellular sensibilities."[31] Written by "children of the dream" who are both beneficiaries of the movement's gains and now custodians of all its failed promise, these dialogues reflect what Mark Anthony Neal calls a "post-soul aesthetic," a postmodern self-consciousness about the historical tensions as their contemporary works repurpose civil rights–Black Power iconography and styles.[32] For instance, Morgan's *Chickenheads* self-consciously positions itself as a black-feminist manifesto in the vein of Michele Wallace's *Black Macho* and Ntozake Shange's *for colored girls*, drawing on hip-hop aesthetics and pieties to create a "remixed feminist agenda" for her generation that resonates outside of the academy. And Rebecca Walker's anthology of third-wave feminist thought, which included Eisa Davis's personal essay on being a feminist within hip-hop, indirectly engages second-wavers Gloria Steinem, who pens the foreword, and Angela Davis, who writes the afterword.

Mixtape brings that indirect intergenerational dialogue between the Black Power–era icon and her post-*Brown* descendant literally center stage. The play's opening sequence establishes "post-soul" reflexivity through its self-conscious awareness about the constructed nature of performance: the idea that personas, even autobiographical ones, are fictions. With the chorus singing the bass line to George Benson's jazz classic "On Broadway," Eisa Davis describes arriving in New York City at age nineteen and reading her famous aunt's autobiography for the first time (4). In content, Benson's "On Broadway" cues the scene's New York City location, while gesturing to the performative nature of autobiography. The moment reminds both spectators and readers that they are engaging a fiction whose protagonist is also a construction, in essence, demanding they be ethical witnesses of the story that unfolds. Throughout the play, the events of her aunt's famous case frame Eisa's life: she is conceived the night of the shootout in the Marin County courtroom. Her first day of life is spent visiting her aunt in prison. She shares a birthdate with Karl Marx, whose ideology fueled the Communist Party affiliation that rendered Angela Davis suspect to the state. Her college graduation is on the twentieth anniversary of Angela's acquittal. At the outset, when Mommy and Grandma shout "Free Angela," raising their fists in a Black Power salute, the slogan refers as much to freeing Angela Davis's cultural memory from this incarcerating iconography as to Angela Eisa Davis's fight for individuality.

The iconic Angela Davis's life is so central to this work that the play is not only a relational autobiography, structured around a central figure, but also an auto/biography, a combination of Eisa's personal memoir and her aunt's famous history. Davis accomplishes this split narrative with an ensemble of actors. Having starred on Broadway (*Passing Strange*) and in HBO's *The Wire*, Davis plays herself, from girlhood to present, while four other actresses are cast as her aunt Angela, mother Fania, and a host of subsidiary roles. As the stage directions indicate, "CHORUS = multiple voices, sometimes all, sometimes some" (2). The ensemble approach of one actor playing several characters, or other characters transforming into new roles, recalls Adrienne Kennedy's *Funnyhouse of the Negro*, a one-act drama set inside the head of Sarah, a troubled young woman obsessed with whiteness in the age of "black is beautiful." But whereas Kennedy's various characters often represent Sarah's other, dissociated selves, in *Mixtape* the ensemble represents not Eisa herself but the people and stories from her coming-of-age—a kaleidoscopic collage that was purposely designed to evoke the sound and sensibility of a hip-hop mixtape. When *Funnyhouse* debuted in 1964, the now-cult classic won the Obie Award for Distinguished Play and profoundly influenced theater as its fantastical staging demonstrated "the political potential of abstract theoretical language."[33] Kennedy's impact on Davis and her work is unmistakable. The two collaborated on *June and Jean in Concert*, a play based on Kennedy's autobiography in scrapbook form, *People Who Led to My Plays*. And the senior playwright has been a longtime mentor, encouraging Davis to mine the personal history that informs *Mixtape*. Many official histories mark hip-hop theater's beginnings in 1992, when GhettOriginal Production Dance Company staged *So What Happens Now?* about the rise and fall of break dancing, at PS 122 in New York City. However, Davis's artistic debt to Kennedy, as well as the influence of Amiri Baraka and Ntozake Shange, suggests that hip-hop theater has its roots in the Black Arts Movement.

Davis's debt to movement progenitors can be seen in her poem "will poetry be enuf?," included in Powell's *Step into a World* anthology. The conversation that the verse initiates with Shange and Baraka about the social role of the artist infuses the ethos of *Mixtape*,[34] anticipating the dialogue the play conducts not only with Davis's famous aunt but also with her like-minded contemporaries. The poem's complete title, "if we've gotta live underground and everybody's got cancer/will poetry be enuf?" riffs off the title of Shange's famous choreopoem, *for colored girls who have considered suicide when the rainbow was enuf*. Shange emerged from the 1970s women's theater movement in San Francisco, responding to the sexist energies of the Black Arts Movement that Amiri Baraka helped launch in the mid-1960s. In "Revolutionary Theater," Baraka wrote that plays should be "a political theater, a weapon to be a help in the slaughter of these dimwitted fatbellied white guys," to "teach them their deaths."[35] His Obie Award–winning *Dutchman*, a cautionary tale, exemplified the Black Aesthetic of "killing" white culture's death grip on black life, as the play's protagonist, Clay, an aspiring "black Baudelaire," fails to create revolutionary art, what Baraka once called "poems that kill,"[36] resulting in his murder on a New York City subway. Shange's choreopoem challenges the Black Aesthetic through a more life-affirming ethos as it sought to bring in a woman's perspective on the black experience. From the outset, the seven women actors, known by their color of dress, evoke the image of a young girl who has "been dead so long / closed in silence so long / she doesn't know the sound / of her own voice / her infinite beauty." The actors imagine the play as a gift or song designed to restore her to life: "sing her sighs / sing the song of her possibilities / sing a righteous gospel / the makin of a melody / let her be born / let her be born / & handled warmly."[37] Since its publication, the choreopoem has remained a black feminist touchstone across generations: part of a controversial textual trinity in the '70s and

'80s, alongside Michele Wallace's *Black Macho and the Superwoman* and Alice Walker's *The Color Purple*, as well as the inspiration for Morgan's 1990s *Chickenheads*. The poster for the play's 1976 Broadway debut became as iconographic as Angela Davis's FBI wanted posters. Morgan writes that, even as a young girl, she had been "transfixed by the poster": "Afro-puffed and arms-akimbo, I'd stare at it every day, struck by the poster-woman's sad, sad eyes and the eeriness of the title scribbled in child-like graffiti across an imaginary tenement wall."[38] The play ultimately captivated audiences, not for its troubling specter of death, "since departed colored girls are part of the ghetto's given," but because it seemed that "the play had something to do with being black, female, and surviving."[39]

The life-affirming outlook evokes another Black Arts–era play, Lorraine Hansberry's *To Be Young, Gifted and Black*, which influenced the Black Aesthetic and, consequently, the dialogue Davis is having with Black Arts elders such as Shange and Baraka in *Mixtape*. *To Be Young* is a representative sampling of select Hansberry works: excerpts from her plays, essays, and speeches, but also letters, journal entries, and interviews. This postmodern pastiche sought to put the artist's career of words in relation to each other so that the parts in context of the whole might reflect the playwright as persona, just one of many characters who join her on stage. The self-portrait that emerges is of a "rebel who celebrated the human spirit."[40] Produced posthumously, *To Be Young* toured college campuses at the height of the Black Power movement and expressed solidarity with the generation's growing militancy in response to the civil rights movement's mounting pyrrhic victories. An April 1964 letter to the editor of the *New York Times* describes the bitter frustration of watching her father "win" a housing-discrimination case in the Supreme Court, only to have "hellishly hostile" neighbors throw a brick through the Hansberrys' window that barely missed an eight-year-old Lorraine: "That is the reality that I am faced with when I now read some Negroes my own age and younger say that we must now lie down in the streets, tie up traffic, do whatever we can—take to the hills with guns if necessary—and fight back. Fatuous people remark these days on our 'bitterness.' Why, of course we are bitter." She ends the letter suggesting the nation remember Langston Hughes's "Harlem," an excerpt of which she used as preface for her most famous play, *A Raisin in the Sun*: "What happens to a dream deferred? / Does it dry up / Like a raisin in the sun? / Or fester like a sore—/ And then run? / Does it stink like rotten meat? / Or crust and sugar over / Like a syrupy sweet? / Maybe it sags / Like a heavy load. / *Or does it explode?*"[41]

In this 1964 letter, the Hughes reference speaks to the movement's increasing radicalism and cities on the verge of riots. But in 1959, when *Raisin* had its historic run on Broadway, few recognized the play's militant strains. Many audiences interpreted the Younger family's move into a new home in a white neighborhood as a "happy ending," as a confirmation of, rather than a challenge to, the American dream.[42] The playwright, however, knew that their troubles were only beginning, having barely missed that brick after the court "win" and watching her father succumb to "an early death as a permanently embittered exile in a foreign country when he saw that after such sacrificial efforts the Negroes of Chicago were as ghetto-locked as ever."[43] The critique of traditional civil rights discourse and strategy recalls Beals's *Warriors Don't Cry* without the ambivalence about the direction of a future politic. Whereas Baraka's "Revolutionary Theatre" called for "Black Art" that "killed" white culture, Hansberry's *To Be Young* focused on affirming life. Nemiroff writes in the play's foreword, "The view of life which permeates these pages was inextricably rooted in the collective history of a people with a special vantage point on life, a vantage point that made it difficult—in her eyes, unseemly and impossible—to take refuge in the comforting illusions—or underlying assumptions—of our society. But if blackness brought pain, it was also a source of strength, renewal and inspiration."[44] *To Be Young* invokes this ethos in its inclusion of a speech (an excerpt serves as preface to this chapter) that Hansberry gave at a conference on the "Negro Writer and His Roots" two weeks before the Broadway debut of *A Raisin in the Sun*. In it, she challenged young black writers to have "sighted eyes" but a "feeling heart." Despite the reality of racism and sexism, poverty and war, cancer and disease, and all the "indescribable displays of man's very real inhumanity to man," their task was always to "impose the reason for life on life."[45] Like Danticat in *Brother, I'm Dying*, Hansberry argues for a revolutionary politic that promotes life and natality.

It is this revolutionary quality focused on living, found in Hansberry's *To Be Young*, as well as Shange's *for colored girls*, that Eisa Davis seemingly engages most in asking, "will poetry be enuf?" Certainly, Davis positions Shange in the poem as an elder and literary mentor from whom she is seeking wisdom and direction: "just tell me how / to feed this light / to my responsibilities" (ll. 178–180). She acknowledges that she "found a groove" (l. 51), that is, found her voice, while memorizing *for colored girls* monologues. In an homage to Shange, her poem mimics the play's unconventional spelling and grammar, replete with lowercase letters, most notably "I," and the unconventional contractions such as *wd* for *would* and *cd* for *could*. As Davis grapples with the question of the artist's social role, her literary mentor's books are "open like fans" all around her (l. 168). Here, it seems less that Davis is falling into what Morgan has decried in *Chicken-heads* as the "complacency . . . typical of my generation" in looking to make an

old movement fit new issues. Rather, Davis seems to be engaging the earlier
assumptions of what constitutes "revolutionary" art and theater as she grapples
with the question of whether culture can create and be a progressive politic that
makes an impact on material realities. For instance, the poem opens with the
sense of loss characteristic of post-*Brown* intergenerational dialogues:

> i wear corrective lenses that feature
> high definition tragedy.
> baby in the dumpster   ethnic cleansing
> assassinations   multinational mergers
> (ll. 7–10)

What follows is doubt about both the ethics and practicality of responding to
social inequity with poetry:

> i'm supposed to shake my head
> write a poem
> believe in the ripples
> (ll. 11–13)

The line "i'm supposed to shake my head" suggests a perfunctory, routine
sense of social outrage that is dutifully channeled into a poem through a thin
faith in the social "ripples" of one voice singing, one hand clapping, one poem
speaking truth. Laying out the crisis of the social artist, Davis poses the pivotal
question to Shange: "so when . . . / . . . the world ain't so cool / do you write a
poem / or a will?" (ll. 94–97). The binary is one that the Black Aesthetic of the
1960s promotes: revolutionary art or death. Writing a will seems to suggest a
resignation to the world's troubles and the inevitability of death. Writing a
poem, then, suggests choosing life. Davis further interrogates the binary's assumptions with an allusion to Amiri Baraka's *The Dutchman*:

> like leroi jones said   if bessie smith had killed some white people
> she wouldn't have needed that music
> so do we all write like amiri baraka does
> or do we all get our nat turner on?
> (ll. 98–101)

For Baraka, like Ishmael Reed, "writin' is fightin,'" but the binary that Davis
establishes — "do we all write like amiri baraka" or "get our nat turner on?" —

asks a more existential question: "What does it mean to choose life even when the fight is not yet won?" The great irony, of course, is that "if bessie smith had killed some white people," she might have killed off white supremacy but also the source of her signifying musical genius. This irony gestures toward the karmic consequence of a killing ethos. Davis's poetic persona pursues the point, as she insistently repeats the phrase "i beg the question":

> . . . cuz I wanna get my life right
> do some real work
> and I really don't want to kill any white folk
> i mean   can we talk abt this
> maybe it's just my red diaper that's itchin
> but I still got that will to uplift the race
> sans bootstraps or talented tenths or paper bag tests
> this time we uplift the human race
> and I know the rainbow might be
> but is poetry enuf?
>
> (ll. 102–111)

In the religious idioms of black vernacular, the phrase "get your life right" is to "get right with God," to experience a spiritual conversion, or *metanoia*. In this context, "getting my life right" refers to embracing righteous, "uplift the race" politics. Despite interrogating the nationalist and masculinist assumptions of the 1960s Black Aesthetic, Davis still wants to be a "race woman." In the 1960s, the embrace of the "gospel of blackness," that cultural and psychological conversion from Negro to Black to Afro-American, what Eddie Glaude has called the "politics of transvaluation," also altered black communities' sense of their relation to the state; there was a shift from being a subordinate people to a self-determining nation.

In the post-*Brown* era, Davis has "still got the will to uplift the race," but she is looking to go beyond traditional models of Booker T. Washington's "bootstrap" conservatism and Du Boisian "talented tenth" elitism, beyond domestic civil rights to global human rights. "This time we uplift the human race," she writes. The question is, "is poetry enuf?" of a praxis to accomplish these political goals, especially when market values and logic dictate the politics of publishing, reception, and reading:

> if we finally do unload the canon
> clean it out

> stock up on some more colorful balls
> ain't we only getting the ones that are available at a store near you?
> doesn't the market end up setting the new standards anyway?
> is poetry enuf if it ain't sellin?
> if ain't nobody reading it?
>
> (ll. 113–116)

The pun on "canon" evokes late twentieth-century literary canon wars, when establishment traditionalists like Harold Bloom and Helen Vendler scoffed at "political" poetry as writers of color stormed ivory-tower gates, their works filling university curricula and bookstore shelves like cannon balls ready for launch. Davis wonders, even if we succeed in diversifying the literary canon, "stock up on some more colorful balls," will market dynamics keep conscious art—poetry and novels and plays—off bookshelves and out of readers' hands? The poem ends with the question unresolved, as Davis calls on icon and mentor Shange to "just tell me how / to feed this light / to my responsibilities" (ll. 178–180). It is a somewhat rhetorical request, for with *Angela's Mixtape*, she answers herself.

In some ways it is unsurprising that the intergenerational dialogues that Davis has been staging in earlier work, from her essay in Rebecca Walker's anthology to "will poetry be enuf?," crystallize into the fullest expression of her political theorizing in *Angela's Mixtape*. Besides the fraught family history, public dialogues with Angela Davis have become a staple of progressive politics, with the open letter to the radical icon almost constituting a literary genre unto itself. Perhaps the first was an open letter that James Baldwin penned just a month after the professor-activist was captured and imprisoned in October 1970.[46] The letter praises "the enormous revolution in black consciousness which has occurred in your generation, my dear sister." After an almost half century's remove, with the lack of a viable political movement before the Black Lives Matter campaign, what many call the "postmodern malaise," his assessment seems premature: "In considering you, and Huey, and George and (especially) Jonathan Jackson, I began to apprehend what you may have had in mind when you spoke of the uses to which we could put the experience of the slave. What has happened, it seems to me, and to put it far too simply, is that a whole new generation of people have assessed and absorbed their history, and, in that tremendous action, have freed themselves of it and will never be victims again." For Baldwin, the pivotal moment in consciousness between the two generations occurred when "Cassius Clay became Muhammad Ali and refused to put on that uniform (and sacrificed all that money!)[—] a very different impact was made on the people and a very different kind of instruction had begun." In the

Black Power era, this spiritual coming of age, proclaimed in "Black and Proud" and "black is beautiful" sloganeering, can arguably be said to have ushered in the era of the New Black. In *Is It Nation Time?* Eddie Glaude describes this "politics of transvaluation," when black Americans underwent "a fundamental psychological and cultural conversion from their socialization as a subordinate people to a self-determining nation."[47]

In the intervening thirty years, the novelist Eisa Ulen wrote "What Happened to Your Generation's Promise of 'Love and Revolution'? A Letter to Angela Davis." Eisa Ulen is Eisa Davis's other namesake, and she begins her letter by detailing their extended-family ties with the playwright's famous aunt and mother, Fania: "Dear Ms. Davis, You know my father. You know my mother. They know you. And your sister Fania." Ulen's father was one of many aiding Angela Davis's flight when she went underground. When she was caught, Ulen's mother provided refuge and respite for the pregnant Fania, who would name the baby she was carrying first after her sister, Angela, and then her friend's two-year-old daughter, Eisa. "Mommy kept your niece's birth announcement. It is taped, next to pictures of people sporting Afros, in my baby book: 'Born of the bloodfire of struggle for the people. I honor my child with your daughter's name. May they both be strong forces of love and revolution.'"[48] The reassertion of fictive-kin ties serves to re-create the familial structures that she considers lost for so many in her generation in the post-*Brown* era. Given that the trope of family often serves as a symbol for the nation in nationalist rhetoric, reordering those extended-family ties also revives the nationalist hopes that the Black Power movement inspired. Amid the nostalgia for nuclear family and nation, Ulen acknowledges a paralyzing paradox that is characteristic of the post-*Brown* era: "I feel the lost potential [of family]—at times feel imprisoned by it. . . . I think we, now, are feeling the same way, imprisoned by the past. The Black Nation's hip-hop generation has been looking back at itself."[49]

The rest of Ulen's open letter to Angela Davis describes the hip-hop generation's revisiting of Black Power iconography as an attempt to break free from the paralysis of paradox. The appropriation that Raiford describes in hip-hop "docufashion" Ulen sees happening in her generation's reliving the seventies in parties, film, and on wax: "A few of the best in the rap music industry can take and twist 1970s sound with 1990s image through old sampled beats and new spoken works."[50] The fear is that these samplings and restagings, this "looking back at itself," reflects the uncritical nostalgia that so many scholars warn about when repurposing civil rights and Black Power cultural memory,[51] rather than the self-awareness about time and space that is characteristic of a post-soul aesthetic. Like Raiford, Ulen frets that this "retro movement in Black cultural expression" reflects a preoccupation with return without any future vision,[52] divorced from Sankofa, the African principle of looking backward to see the future more clearly. The hip-hop generation compulsively recasts itself into the past, Ulen argues, conveying stagnant "messages of return" and consuming an earlier generation's music and ideals, because the present looks so bleak. Films from *Crooklyn* to *The Inkwell* to *Boyz n the Hood* to *Dead Presidents* to *Jason's Lyric* to *Panther* to *Set It Off* reflect a desire to return to a time before AIDS, Reaganomics, and crack. The litany of statistics documenting ongoing black misery—"racism, sexism, poverty, inadequate education, escalating rates of incarceration, piss-poor health conditions, drugs, and violence"[53]—has become a cultural narrative almost as ubiquitous as the movement's cultural memory. Trapped between lost promise and looming disaster, the hip-hop generation seems unable to imagine other forms of family, community, and revolution.

The great irony of Ulen's open letter is that, in her own nostalgia for an earlier ideal of "love and revolution," she fails to exhibit the critical self-reflexivity about her own retro repurposing of Black Power iconography and seems equally unable to imagine new forms of family or politics. In *The Wretched of the Earth*, Frantz Fanon famously said, "Each generation out of relative obscurity must discover their mission, fulfill or betray it."[54] But many children of the Black Power generation charge their elders with failure to parent, guide, and mentor: "I know each generation struggles, Ms. Davis," Ulen writes. "But I'm asking you to help me come to terms with these losses. . . . Where are our leaders? Where are our parents? . . . We have come of age without the wisdom of the earlier generation. We have your style, but we don't have your substance. Tupac was just a symbol of our murdered potential. A future so lost, so gone, that sometimes, just sometimes, Ms. Davis, it seems gone for good."[55] In these passages, Ulen, in some respects, represents those whom Morgan critiques for looking to "older heads to redefine the struggle to encompass our generation's issues."[56] Rather than looking to elders for solutions, Davis engages her aunt's memory, history, and example to offer a way to revive love and revolution, her own notions of black political thought and praxis.

"A Feeling Heart"

The new politic that the play promotes can be seen in its deployment of hip-hop aesthetics. Davis refers to the late film critic James Snead to explain hip-hop theater's aim and ability to express feelings and thoughts beyond words, the ineffable. Snead argues that the "black experience was simply untranslatable to" linear, rational narratives of the Hollywood film formula. Building on Snead, Davis argues that "for colored folks, music has been the most direct form of expression because it isn't necessarily about the passing of time and all that prickly cause and effect. It can be about holding a single moment and its emotion up to the light, and in the rhythm, the trance of that, the plight and joy of a people can be felt. Fully. In all its contradictions. What hip-hop theatre is up to is bringing the bittersweet complexity of music out and into narratives that never expected us to visit."[57] In other words, the play's underwriting ethic can be found within its music.

Take a scene when an adolescent Eisa, practicing for an end-of-year piano recital, begins to play Claude Debussy's "La cathédrale engloutie." Known for their musical impressionism, Debussy's compositions evoke an idea through repeating motifs and chord sequences rather than thematic variations.[58] On a narrative level in the play, Debussy's musical impressionism cues the ambience of moody adolescence. But his impressionistic style is also meant to be an interpretative lens for reading the play. "La cathédrale engloutie" refers to a legend about a submerged cathedral that rises out of the sea on a clear day; the piece depicts the cathedral's rise and fall with ascending chords that reach a fortissimo before descending slowly, softly, like distant, fading church bells. The motif of ascending and descending chords mimics the cathedral's movement, just as the play's fast pace and pastiche of songs re-create the feel of a mixtape. But in "holding a single moment and its emotion up to the light," the Debussy piece highlights the post-*Brown* politic that Davis's theatrical memoir underscores. It opens a section titled "Grenada," in which the Davis family travels to the Caribbean island nation to celebrate "the first peaceful social revolution in a black country—it's a beacon of hope for all of us" (34). The trip conflicts with Eisa's final school concert, where she is to play Debussy alongside her new crush, a chubby Filipino oboe player. Her mother insists she bear witness to this "once in a lifetime opportunity to see the revolution in action," and the love-struck Eisa expends her thwarted passion in an anguished rendition of an original love song. It is a lighthearted scene meant to suggest that our young protagonist is in the melodramatic throes of her first school-girl crush: "Eisa (stops playing; to audience): But what about my oboe player? He has big feelings. Sometimes he gets so frustrated with playing a piece in concert, he just walks off the stage. He *crescendoes* and *decrescendoes* real well. And his tone is so sweet and pure. Lionel Ritchie and Diana Ross have an oboe on 'Endless Love.' I['ll] write him a song." Given the scene's positioning in the play, however, as a culmination of a series of moments that emphasize the importance of feelings and emotions, the fortissimo, if you will, of the song that is *Angela's Mixtape*, I argue that Davis is engaging contemporary debates about the role of affect in the public sphere, what the political theorist Martha Nussbaum calls "political emotions."[59] After her song, Mommy asks, "Are you trying to have a conversation with me?" (35). Here, the idea of the music staging an intergenerational dialogue, a conversation, within hip-hop theater's "breaks" becomes explicit.

Indeed, as the play interrogates civil rights–Black Power aesthetics and politics, it is the figure of Mommy, the character representing Eisa Davis's mother, Fania, who most symbolizes this bygone ethos of politics without affect: "Well, it was the movement. The struggle," Mommy concedes, when challenged about the absence of feelings in the house. "No one ever laughed. We were at war" (75–76). Throughout the play, Mommy's commitment to "the struggle" blinds her to the childhood issues, from the routine to the rocky, that her daughter faces. Shola Lynch's documentary *Free Angela* (2012) reveals the truth of the portrayal. Fania presents as intensely committed to her sister's fight for freedom as she takes the Free Angela campaign all over the world. These moments of maternal alienation engage debates about political children seen earlier in Melba Beals's *Warriors Don't Cry*, for which Davis wrote a stage adaptation that premiered in 2007.[60] For instance, in *Mixtape*, a school-aged Eisa, having overheard that her dance teacher at the Oakland Creative Arts Center had once been raped, asks her mother for a definition. The uncomprehending child receives a brutally matter-of-fact explanation of sexual trauma that she is expected to absorb as blithely as ballet lessons: "It's when a man takes sexual advantage of a woman by force. White slave masters did this to our ancestors daily. Keep your shoulders down! And chassé" (14). It is not that the play challenges the idea of political children. Like June Jordan's *Soldier* (as discussed in chapter 3) and Ralph Ellison's articles on Little Rock (as discussed in chapter 1), *Angela's Mixtape* acknowledges that childhood is always political, the first political experience that any of us ever has to negotiate. Rather, the play asks readers to sympathize with their feelings, the traumatic toll that resistance struggles exact. For instance, Angela shares a story about Eisa running in the house after playing outside as a child, crying, "He hurt me, he hurt me." Her family searched frantically for "bruises or blood." After all, they had grown up in Birmingham, better known as Bombingham, where their neighborhood was nicknamed Dynamite Hill for the houses racists bombed to stop integration; where they were not just contemporaries but also neighbors of the four little girls killed at the Sixteenth Street Baptist Church in 1963. To be "hurt" in that time was to be maimed or murdered. So when Eisa wails, "He hurt *my feelings*" (23, emphasis added), everyone laughs, at first in relief, then mockery—and a teasing moment subsequently turns poignant. The audience at once sympathizes, and empathizes, with the uncomforted child (who does not know the loneliness of being dismissed?), even as understanding about the numbing effects of trauma on an older generation become apparent. Reading or watching the scene, one asks, what must they have endured to become so dismissive of feelings? A subsequent section called "KKK" makes this point. A hysterical woman screams, "They burned a cross on our lawn," as Mommy, a lawyer, records the details of a 1990s KKK attack in Contra Costa, California. Thirty years after Birmingham, racial violence is as virulent as ever, if more widespread, and Mommy appears almost numb as she "coolly, calmly"—as the stage directions instruct—administers a hate-crime questionnaire, again. At the end of the scene, Eisa has fallen asleep on her homework while her mother works with this client. In this moment, the audience feels for the lonely child, as well as the committed activist still fighting the good fight, and losing.

This "affective turn" is a prominent feature of contemporary black feminist thought.[61] For instance, Joan Morgan describes working with a young acting student on Shange's "somebody almost walked wid alla my stuff" monologue from *for colored girls*. The student's first rendition simply parroted the tough "eye-rollin,' smart-talkin,' finger-snappin'" voice immortalized in the original play. Morgan suggests that what the hip-hop generation brings to black politics is a return to feeling, tenderness, and vulnerability:

> What I wanted in lieu of the black girl attitude was her truth. [This student] was raised on hip-hop, not jazz or the blues, and she didn't know nothing about Sun-Ra, Dew City, or Mr. Louisiana Hot Link. In order for her to possess the piece and make it hers she was going to have to infuse it with her own voice and experiences. . . . After a few difficult and teary-eyed attempts, Mr. Louisiana Hot Link became the rapper D-nice; the neck-rollin,' finger-snappin' anger gave way to the soft-spoken, vulnerable, fearful sound of a sixteen-year-old heart breaking for the very first time. It was both fantastic and powerful.[62]

Morgan goes on to discuss how this experience with her student represents an entire generation's attempt to free itself from the constricting notions of blackness and femaleness, much of it handed down to them from civil rights and Black Power–era cultural memory and iconography, as well as contemporary cultural stereotypes. "In a society of ever-shifting identity politics, I was asking the sixteen-year-old to sift through so many conflicting interpretations of femaleness and blackness and free her voice. In order to do this she was going to have to liberate it from the stranglehold of media stereotypes—the pathetic SheNayNay impersonations of black male comedians, the talk-to-the-hand

Superwomen, the video-hoes, crackheads, and lazy welfare queens—that obscure so much of who we are. And she was going to have to push her foremothers' voices far enough away to discover her own."[63] It is interesting that it is through performance, in embodying a scripted character as if for the first time, that Morgan enables her student to drop the masks and free her voice. In *Angela's Mixtape*, Davis similarly deconstructs notions of black identity through performance, both as genre and as trope.

In *Mixtape*, Davis plays with the idea of fictive personas several times when Eisa encounters an airport porter who asks for her ID. During the first of three encounters, Eisa gets the customary ribbing when her driver's license lists the iconic name "Angela Davis." Upon learning that Eisa is in fact Angela Davis's niece, the porter reveals that his memories have been invariably shaped by Black Power iconography. Davis takes pains to show that it is the icon, not the actual person, whom he is recalling: "I had a crush on her when I was a kid. That FBI Ten Most Wanted poster, mm. And you know they showed that photo on TV all the time. Wow. What's she doing now?" The porter's memory fuses imagery from the time of the Free Angela campaign with that of the Blaxploitation films *Foxy Brown* and *Cleopatra Jones*, whose Afros and sexualized personae evoked Angela Davis's image. Part of this deconstruction, of course, serves to humanize the aunt whom iconography has frozen in memory. Several times in this first sequence the character Eisa makes a distinction between the Black Power icon and "the Angela I know . . ." (8, 16), who french-braids hair, pegs pants in the latest fashion on her sewing machine, and makes her niece mixtapes with Keith Jarrett and Billie Holiday. In this way, *Angela's Mixtape* is like other contemporary black popular culture that uses civil rights and Black Power memory to humanize mythic figures who are often presented as "warriors who don't cry," as Melba Beals might say—for example, Martin Luther King Jr., as portrayed in Katori Hall's *The Mountaintop* (2011), Tracey Scott Wilson's *The Good Negro* (2009), and Clark Johnson's TV movie *Boycott* (2001), cultural productions that remind us that King "was not a god" but a man trying "to be and do good."[64]

The play's efforts to humanize Angela Davis are evident in an early scene, as Eisa stands at the corner of Greenwich and Sixth Avenues, where her aunt was imprisoned at the Women's House of Detention for eighteen months. The prison was demolished shortly after, in 1973, and replaced with a library and a garden. In this scene, the present and past run on parallel tracks. The Angela persona reads from her autobiography about how, as a student in New York, she would walk by the prison, long before she was ever incarcerated there, pretending not to hear "the terrible noises spilling from the windows, . . . from the women locked behind bars, screaming incomprehensible words" (4). As Angela sorts through feelings of fear and doubt about her own fate, Eisa sings a freedom song: "It is for freedom that we gladly go / Oh we don't care if we go to jail / It is for freedom that we gladly go." Stalwart, unwavering, the song captures the courage of activists who literally faced down death in pursuit of justice. As Angela finishes her monologue, the chorus picks up the verse along with Eisa, who alters the last two lines:

Chorus	Eisa
It is for freedom that we gladly go	It is for freedom that we gladly go
Oh we don't care if we go to jail	Oh we don't care if we go to jail
It is for freedom that we gladly go	A heavy load, a heavy load
Oh we don't care if we go to jail	And it will take some real strength

At this point, Eisa is the only person on stage singing these two lines against the chorus's collective proclamation of commitment. The solo reveals the cost of such courage for young activists—much like the humanizing portraits of King—who were full of doubt and fear as they forged ahead. The temporal juxtaposition provides new insights into the movement, not so much of its factual history, but of its human history, the emotional cost and toll. "No knowledge, no gratitude," Eisa says, echoing the social-activist slogan "No justice, no peace." In revising the activist chant, Davis suggests a new politic infused with emotion, a sense of justice animated by human feeling.

This notion of activism contrasts to that of her childhood, figured in the play as demonstrations and marches that had become, to her girlish eyes, another part of the Berkeley aesthetic, alongside the free love ethos, holistic diets, and VW vans for trips to Zihuatenejo. An early dance-studio sequence illustrates the idea of an affectless politic as the dance teacher leads warm-up exercises, while "carrying a picket sign" and chanting "5-6-7-and I-so-LA-TIONS" (14). At these various demonstrations and political meetings, Mommy trots Eisa out to read excerpts from Angela Davis's political autobiography, a series of "monologues" that she dutifully recites without much comprehension or connection. But stepping into her aunt's life story through *Mixtape*, truly embodying that scripted persona for the first time, finally allows Davis, like Morgan's drama student, to "drop the masks," to break free from narrow notions of black identity and politics.

A section called "Egypt" most vividly unpacks this idea. The title alludes to the single "Egypt, Egypt" by the Los Angeles–based DJ Egyptian Lover, but it also has intriguing resonances with the biblical Exodus narrative that has framed black liberation struggles since the nineteenth century. The section opens with a "You've got to" list of hip-hop cultural commandments (". . . be hard / . . . boast your crew / . . . talk about beating up people with your flow") that of course recalls the "Thou shall not" anaphora of the Ten Commandments (20). The religious idioms within the section build as Grandma invokes God to forbid cursing, developing the sense that Eisa has been immersed within a long-standing cultural tradition. Therefore, when she cannot sing a gospel song, Walter Hawkins's "Changed," with the melisma characteristic of the black church, the moment suggests a subtle but distinct break with inherited tradition. As the song lyrics state, "a change has come over me." The difference between her vision of black politics and that of an earlier generation is developed in a scene with her stepfather, Larry, who puts her through a rigid "Slavery? Or death?" catechism: "If you were put in that position like our ancestors were, what would you do?" (26). The choices echo the quandary in her poem "will poetry be enuf?" where the alternatives are "write like Baraka or get our nat turner on?" While mulling the options, Angela, in an aside, proposes a third way: "In *Back to the Future*, Michael J. Fox is in two places at once: the past and the future." Invocation of the play's time-travel conceit inspires Eisa to step outside of the binary, outside the dimensions of this political framework, to enter what Iton calls "the black fantastic": "Right! To fix things! (to self) *I guess I would want to live. Then I could learn to read and escape like Frederick Douglass. I could be a stop on the Underground Railroad! I could be like Harriet Tubman and lead people to freedom through the woods!* (to Larry) Be a slave?" (27, emphasis added). The language and sentiment of this passage echo the ethos animating Lorraine Hansberry's *To Be Young, Gifted and Black*: "I wish to live because life has within it that which is good, that which is beautiful and that which is love. Therefore, since I have known all of these things, I have found them to be reason enough and—I wish to live."[65] Of course, according to the logic of the proposed, untenable binary, a revolutionary ethos would choose death: Larry thunders, "NO!!! No. You should DIE. You should choose death instead of slavery."

This moment in the play echoes "Lecture on Liberation," Angela Davis's first lecture as a professor at UCLA before the Marin courthouse shootout sent her underground and launched the Free Angela campaign. Acknowledging the autobiographical tradition as a foundation of black political thought, Professor Davis draws on *The Life and Times of Frederick Douglass* to discuss the concept of freedom, what she deems a static principle, and liberation, what she calls active struggle. Methodically illustrating Hegel's "master-slave dialectic," the lecture asks: Is freedom internal, one's thoughts, or external experience, the freedom to act? Can one be free in human bondage? Davis notes that the existentialist Jean-Paul Sartre argued that even a man in chains remains free because he always has the option of death:

> That is, his freedom is narrowly defined as the freedom to choose between his state of captivity or his death. This is extreme. But we have to decide whether or not this is the way in which we are going to define that concept. Certainly, this would not be compatible with the notion of liberation, for when the slave opts for death, he does much more than obliterate his conditions of enslavement, for at the same time he is abolishing the very condition of freedom, life. Yet there is more to be said, when we take the decision to die out of an abstract context and examine the dynamics of a real situation in which a slave meets his death in the fight for concrete freedom. This is to say, the choice, slavery or death, could either mean slavery or suicide, or on the other hand, slavery or liberation at all costs. (48–49)

The character Larry occupies the existentialist Sartrean position on freedom. *Mixtape* works to expand the idea toward the concept of liberation. Eisa tells the audience, "I don't tell anyone, but I'm also trying to come up with an alternative utopic society. . . . I want to create something important, a *new* ideology" (50–51), a revolutionary ethos in which one might live in order to one day laugh and love. At the play's conclusion, a dialogue between aunt and niece reveals that the thoughts interrogated in *Angela's Mixtape* began in an "undergraduate thesis paper . . . about *In Living Color* . . . and the role of laughter in resistance." Angela says, "I liked it. You told me you didn't, that it wasn't exactly how you wanted to do it. I told you to revise it, to keep working" (79). And it seems that she did, with *Angela's Mixtape* as the result, a work of creative theorizing about cultivating joy in revolution. This whimsical, lighthearted play, in its enactment of Iton's "black fantastic"—popular culture's "willingness to engage time, space, and other modalities outside of the given parameters" of traditional politics and identity to imagine new possibilities"[66]—serves as political philosophy. It has been the hip-hop version of "Lecture on Liberation," linking "philosophical understandings of freedom with histories of black political struggle and cultural production as they resonated with contemporary efforts to extend and enlarge the meaning of freedom."[67] The playwright Davis has drawn on foremothers Ntozake Shange and Lorraine Hansberry, in addition to her famous aunt, staging intergenerational dialogues that imagine a post-*Brown* politic animated by life and liberatory joy. The realization of her project, using literature to craft political theory, using her art for social change, finally resolves a question that has been anxiously coursing throughout the play: "Am I living up to my name?" (3, 79).

Three times in *Mixtape* Eisa is called "Angela," with each successive occurrence revealing political maturation, a generation coming of age. When Eisa decides to pass as mixed to escape the stultifying "boundaries of blackness," she declares, "I am Angela Davis." During the Free Angela campaign in 1970, supporters possibly chanted such a slogan in solidarity with the imprisoned Black Power activist. However, when Eisa says it, the slogan conveys how fixed notions of black identity inherited from the Black Power era "incarcerate individuality." The second moment occurs during an encounter with the porter as she prepares to board a plane to Senegal for her first trip to the motherland. This time Eisa volunteers that her name is Angela, welcoming association with her iconic aunt. She has converted to what Eddie Glaude has called "the gospel of blackness" and donned the "Angela" of the romanticized, nostalgic notion of Black Power (73). The moment is in dialogue with "Black Nationalism," an essay in which the elder Davis charts her journey toward what bell hooks calls "radical black subjectivity." For Angela Davis it begins with first hearing Malcolm X speak at her college. Malcolm's oratory stirred a "naïve nationalist consciousness" that, through fits and starts with organizations of varying nationalist politics, ended with membership in the Che Lumumba chapter of the Communist Party. In the play, Eisa's radicalization begins when her aunt comes to Harvard to speak. To give a sense of that speech, Davis uses a verbatim excerpt from the "Black Nationalism" essay. Eisa's subsequent visit to the motherland and her conversion to "the gospel of blackness" reflects the "naïve nationalist consciousness" described in "Black Nationalism." The final instance occurs at play's end. Angela calls Eisa "Angela," as she repeats advice first heard in "will poetry be enuf?": "Just do one thing to keep the struggle going. Just one. Why don't you sing to keep me moving while I get prepared for my lecture" (79). As Eisa sings, Angela, still the philosophy professor she was before the Marin County shootout made her a fugitive and an icon, discovers that her lecture notes have been lost and asks her niece to fill in for her. It then dawns on the audience that this whimsical performance has been a lesson in political philosophy, a post-*Brown* "Lecture on Liberation," all along.

The transformations of character reveal the impact of cultivating joy in service of liberation. Eisa has become a performance artist—actress, singer, playwright—committed to social consciousness, clear that art can be praxis, that writing is fightin.' Angela has been released from stultifying Black Power iconography and cultural memory: "I'm not a tape you can play / I'm live, live, all the way live," she says. Even Mommy has a new playlist: "I have the same intentions but / I'm not playing the same set I used to." All then joyously "slide, slide, slippity slide" into a larger chorus singing, "I wonder if you can see that I am *soft* / Black steel in the hour of chaos" (83). Their insertion of "soft" within Public Enemy's anthem about a prison break underscores the play's ultimate message about embedding joy, and black feminism's "tender side," within post-*Brown* political discourse and praxis.

Epilogue

Bodies, Material Histories, and Black Women's Autobiography

A defining tenet of black feminist thought has been "intersectionality," the idea that "systems of oppression" are "interlocking." To teach this intellectual history, we usually begin with the Combahee River Collective from the 1970s, working our way up to the present with thinkers such as Kimberlé Crenshaw and Valerie Smith, then, increasingly, back to the past with nineteenth-century foremothers such as Harriet Tubman and Anna Julia Cooper, whose writings and activism prefigured the concept.[1] Lately, our increased awareness of the prison industrial complex has revived some interest in Ida B. Wells's analyses of carceral politics and myths of black male criminality.[2] Otherwise, however, scholars have not identified the interpretative categories, the analytics and ethics, that define black women's conceptual contributions to black political thought. We associate Du Bois, of course, with "double consciousness"; Washington with "accommodation"; Garvey with "black nationalism." But, as Brittney Cooper has observed, we tend to regard black feminists simply as those "who made race interventions in feminism and gender interventions in national-ism."[3] A major objective of *Words of Witness* is to help build the burgeoning field of black women's intellectual history by moving beyond rote gender politics to put black feminist thought in conversation with broader political thought. In capturing how select black women's autobiographies published in the last two decades act as counternarratives to official and often nostalgic representations of the civil rights and Black Power movements, which is still the dominant template for contemporary black identity and activism, the study has sought to outline critical interventions black women intellectuals are making to shape a progressive post-*Brown* politic.

By chance, all five texts featured here are childhood memoirs—three from the mid-twentieth century, two from the 1980s—that memorialize literal mothers while extending the intellectual genealogies of literary ones. In *Warriors*

Don't Cry, Beals portrays her mother through discourses of protection, invoking Abbey Lincoln's classic essay "Who Will Revere the Black Woman?" to decry the unshared sacrifices traditional civil-rights discourse demands. Her simultaneous critique of the "strong black woman," or warriors who don't cry, joins a large body of black feminist thought, from Michele Wallace's *Black Macho and the Myth of the Superwoman* and Melissa Harris-Perry's *Sister Citizen* to Tamara Winfrey Harris's *The Sisters Are Alright: Changing the Broken Narrative of Black Women in America*. Beals's portrayal offers an alternate model of political action that reclaims vulnerability while eschewing victimhood, reflecting the "affective turn" of contemporary black feminism. In *Unafraid of the Dark*, Bray's mother represents the everyday women who revolutionized the welfare system of the 1960s, such as the National Welfare Rights Organization (NWRO) executive director Johnnie Tillmon, a mother of six who founded a Los Angeles–based welfare-advocacy group before leading the NWRO. With her mother modeling the ethic of social interdependence that the memoir promotes, Bray recovers the welfare-rights movement's argument about the radical politics that emanate from care in the public sphere. Like the priest-poet, lawyer-activist Pauli Murray, Bray utilizes theologies of love to broaden our understanding of the civil rights movement's breadth, scope, and radicalism.

Alienated motherhood grounds the ethics that underwrite Jordan's *Soldier*, Danticat's *Brother, I'm Dying*, and Davis's *Angela's Mixtape*. The silent, fading presence of Jordan's mother in *Soldier* is central to the ethic of resistance and agency that the memoir promotes. Jordan suggests that the only way to move forward in progressive struggle, to create a politic that refuses to settle for pyrrhic, moral victories, is to mourn our "irreplaceable losses," to remember that for every Harriet Tubman and Sojourner Turth, for every Fannie Lou Hamer and Rosa Parks, there are hundreds of thousands of black women like Mildred Jordan who were crushed under the weight of oppression. Honoring that painful past is to remember rightly, honestly, freeing us for future victories. In *Brother, I'm Dying*, Danticat's mother is also a faint presence floating on the periphery of this memoir focused on her "two papas." Danticat's exploration of father-daughter relationships not only reflects a shift from her early fiction, which was deeply invested in the mother-daughter dyad, but also fashions a new diasporic subjectivity in black women's life writing. Writers such as Audre Lorde have used tropes of motherhood to counter the erasure of women in traditional black political discourse on the nation and the subject, with the omission of men simply repeating the erasure they sought to critique. Danticat, however, positions both mothers and fathers as generative beings in her text, making an important intervention in the larger field of black feminist diasporic discourse.

Similarly generative and life-affirming philosophies transform maternal alien-
ation in Davis's *Angela's Mixtape*. In the play, her mother, Fania, symbolizes
Black Power–era politics, full of righteous commitment but little joy. Building
on the works of literary foremothers such as Adrienne Kennedy, Ntozake
Shange, and Lorraine Hansberry, as well as contemporaries Eisa Ulen and
Joan Morgan, Davis repurposes her family's iconic history to imagine a post-
Brown politic animated by an infectious sense of joy and a renewed sense of solidarity. May this spirit continue to guide and sustain the young women activists
leading the current movements for social justice, from #BlackLivesMatter to
#SayHerName.

While the autobiographies featured in *Words of Witness* seek to place black
feminist thought in conversation with modern political theory, there are many
other contemporary texts, including those by men, that employ a variety of
narrative strategies to engage readers, not only with the story but also with the
larger world.

In terms of "movement memoirs," those written by people who grew up
during the civil rights movement, a spate of such first-hand accounts immediately
followed the social movements of the 1960s and 1970s: among them, Daisy
Bates's *The Long Shadow of Little Rock* (1962); Anne Moody's *Coming of Age in
Mississippi* (1968); Eldridge Cleaver's *Soul on Ice* (1968); Gwendolyn Brooks's *Report
from Part One* (1972); Huey P. Newton's *Revolutionary Suicide* (1973); and *Angela
Davis: An Autobiography* (1974). But the memoir boom beginning in the 1980s
witnessed a cavalcade of texts that are significant, at thirty and forty years remove, as "countercultural memory" to recover lost people and politics that the
dominant narrative has obscured. One of the major objectives of these works is
to profile everyday people who made the movement possible, often relegating
well-known leaders to the periphery of the narrative, as in Beals's *Warriors Don't
Cry*. Jo Ann Gibson Robinson's *The Montgomery Bus Boycott and the Women Who
Started It* (1987), for example, provides a countercultural memory that recovers
the role of women in the milestone mobilization celebrated for igniting the
movement of the 1950s and 1960s. And *Freedom in the Family: A Mother-Daughter
Memoir of the Fight for Civil Rights* (2003), by the Florida activist Patricia Stephens
Due and her novelist daughter Tananarive Due, uses alternating chapters to
highlight local and intergenerational protest traditions, as well as the behind-
the-scenes organizing of high-profile actions. Like *Warriors*, movement memoirs
also frequently note the passing of a bygone era and what was lost with integration: Henry Louis Gates Jr.'s *Colored People: A Memoir* (1995), Clifton Taulbert's
Once upon a Time When We Were Colored (1989), and Carlotta Walls LaNier's *A
Mighty Long Way: My Journey to Justice at Little Rock Central High School* (2009) come

to mind. Deborah McDowell's *Leaving Pipe Shop: Memories of Kin* (1996) is also a nostalgic remembrance of a southern girlhood, but, in her retelling, it is the civil rights movement that is on the periphery of everyday people who tell of "missing a protest rally because of a flat tire, or being tempted to break a bus boycott because it was freezing and they were human."[4]

Closely linked to movement memoirs are narratives by the "children of the Dream," beneficiaries of movement gains who found the uncharted territory of integration surprisingly treacherous, as suggested by the title of Lorene Cary's *Black Ice* (1991), which chronicles her two years at the formerly all-white, all-male Saint Paul's School in New Hampshire. Jennifer Baszile's *The Black Girl Next Door* (2009) elaborates on how being "the only" or "the first" to integrate an affluent suburb or Ivy League department can be as damaging and enraging as outright discrimination. Veronica Chambers's *Mama's Girl* (1996) explores generational tensions when children embody the civil-rights movement triumphs and gains that their parents never expected for themselves and are sometimes frightened to see in their progeny.[5]

The structural changes since the fall of Jim Crow allowed subjectivities beyond race to come to the fore, prompting works on class and sexuality, about immigration and prison. The growing class divide in black America has been explored in narratives structured around the trope of "contrasting destinies" introduced by the novelist John Edgar Wideman's *Brothers and Keepers: A Memoir* (1984), about two brothers, one an award-winning novelist, the other a fugitive wanted for robbery and murder. The editorial writer Brent Staples uses the trope to similar effect in *Parallel Time: Growing Up in Black and White* (1995), and Wes Moore's *The Other Wes Moore: One Name, Two Fates* (2010) extends the linked-fates metaphor as it meditates on diverging trajectories, not of two brothers but of two black men with the same name, born blocks apart in the same Baltimore neighborhood. Audre Lorde's biomythography, *Zami: A New Spelling of My Name* (1982), is the forerunner for contemporary "coming-out" stories, such as the Jamaican American performance artist Staceyann Chin's *The Other Side of Paradise: A Memoir* (2009) and Janet Mock's *Redefining Realness: My Path to Womanhood, Identity, Love and So Much More* (2014), an exploration of transgender issues that is helping to shape the evolution of women's, gender, and sexuality studies.[6] As the scholar Brittney Cooper has noted, Mock's memoir is "a gift to our intellectual and cultural traditions of how we think about Black womanhood."[7] Lorde's *Zami* also paved the way for narratives exploring the diasporic dimensions of black identity, such as Danticat's *Brother, I'm Dying*. Chin's *The Other Side of Paradise* fits into this category, as does Barack Obama's *Dreams from My Father*, a meditation on African American cultural formation, as the son of "a mother from Kansas and a father from Kenya," as the story has come to be told; and Elizabeth Alexander's *The Light of the World* (2015), a poignant memoir about love and loss between an East African son born in Asmara, Eritrea, and an American girl child from Harlem, New York.

With the incarceration epidemic, there has been a resurgence in prison memoirs. R. Dwayne Betts's *A Question of Freedom: A Memoir of Survival, Learning, and Coming of Age in Prison* (2009) recalls Douglass's 1845 slave narrative and *The Autobiography of Malcolm X* in its description of literacy as the route to spiritual and physical freedom. And in *The Prisoner's Wife: A Memoir* (1999), Asha Bandele recounts the difficulty of sustaining family under state surveillance.

In terms of hip-hop, despite the prevalence of life stories in rap lyrics, complete memoirs on wax have been rare. In this regard, *The Miseducation of Lauryn Hill* (1998) is truly groundbreaking, winning the multitalented rapper an unprecedented five Grammy awards. For many hip-hop artists, the transition from writing lyrics to writing memoirs was only a matter of time. In 2010, Jay-Z, a.k.a. Shawn Carter, released *Decoded* with ghostwriter dream hampton. A rags-to-riches tale, *Decoded*'s redemptive arc structures several recent memoirs by male hip-hop artists: *One Day It'll All Make Sense* (2011) by Common with Adam Bradley; *Ice: A Memoir of Gangster Life and Redemption—from South Central to Hollywood* (2011) by Ice-T with Douglas Century; and *My Infamous Life: The Autobiography of Mobb Deep's Prodigy* (2011) by Albert "Prodigy" Johnson with Laura Checkoway. That many hip-hop memoirs are ghostwritten, that they voluntarily relinquish the hard-won authorial voice that early slave narrators insisted upon, raises questions about self-mastery, market influence, and authenticity. However, these texts also provide intriguing studies for literary scholars interested in evolving representations of the collective, contingent self in contemporary African American memoir.

Along with studying these texts for the past few years, I have taught them in several classes at Southern Methodist University (SMU) in my hometown of Dallas and have observed their impact on my students.[8] In general, the SMU student body is as socially connected and pop-culture savvy as their national peers, if less diverse and more conservative. For instance, millennials were among Barack Obama's strongest supporters in the 2008 presidential campaign, but SMU is Bush country: home to the George W. Bush Presidential Library and alma mater of former First Lady Laura Bush. Conservatives have long held that universities are liberal bastions that undermine their own principles of diversity by discriminating against minority political opinion.[9] Full disclosure: a student recently described my course on contemporary memoir and autobiography as "*very* liberal" (emphasis hers). While I strive to create a space where all feel comfortable voicing their views, political and otherwise, I do feel as the Warren court ruled in *Brown* that education "is the very foundation of good citizenship" in a democratic society. During the Little Rock campaign that Melba Beals's *Warriors Don't Cry* recounts, Hannah Arendt's great fear about "political children" was that, if they were prematurely politicized, they might become indoctrinated zealots unable to be the freethinking citizens that democracy requires. I would argue that it is in fact a lack of exposure to ideas different from those experienced in their homes or among their peers that ensures homogeneity and the status quo; of course, Beals was referring to schoolchildren but the point pertains to those in college as well, perhaps even more so, as they are on the cusps of first jobs and new families. Students have the choice of entering formal politics. But, as Ralph Ellison countered Arendt, they will have no choice about the inherently political nature of our society, and their educations must prepare them to engage in an increasingly global world, to think critically and ethically about the nature of the human experience. In *Create Dangerously*, Edwidge Danticat asks how writers and readers find each other in a hostile environment, one in which it is dangerous to go against authority or prevailing opinion. She was speaking, of course, of dictatorial regimes like the Duvaliers in Haiti. But it seems that her question could be asked in a neoliberal moment when corporations are deemed people and actual people are treated like machines made increasingly obsolete. Often it is in a humanities classroom when students encounter "dangerous" texts that challenge that status quo. Just as public spheres have gathered and formed in salons, coffee shops, juke joints, churches, in magazines, blogs, hip-hop ciphers, and social-media platforms, classrooms can be considered public spheres, or "locations," as Richard Iton puts it, for the debate and discussions at the heart of any democratic politic. Indeed, "a politicized space" is any one in which ordinary people through shared words and deeds appear to each other as citizens and continue to plan extraordinary acts.[10]

In one of his last interviews, Stuart Hall, a founder of cultural studies, lamented that contemporary politics has lost its "sense of politics being educative, of . . . changing the way people see things." The idea recalls Cornel West's argument that the polity must turn from market values to human ones to revive civil society, a spiritual shift that he likens to conversion, or *metanoia*. *Words of Witness* subscribes to the idea that storytelling has a better chance of converting minds and hearts than polemics. It has been my experience that these texts, even in a neoliberal age of individualism, facilitate the development of a people-centered ethos, Howard Thurman's "radical reorientation of personality," which Rosemary Bray's *Unafraid of the Dark* dramatizes. During office hours a student once said, "This is the first English class I have ever taken that has focused on the people." Her quizzical look suggested that she appreciated the perspective but did not know what to make of an English class that privileged the bodies in the text, and the material realities their stories represent, over bodies of theory, critical and otherwise. In that moment I thought of June Jordan, who called her teaching an "act of faith," moral witness that dares to inspire people to social consciousness and engagement.

In many ways, teaching autobiography reminds me of working with Lisa Sullivan in the 1990s. Sullivan's worry then was that the hip-hop generation, born between 1965 and 1984,[11] did not have the language to articulate a set of values, without which transformative organizing was impossible. In recent years, scholars within the field of African American studies have debated whether to stop using *slavery* and *race* as organizing terms in literary and cultural studies.[12] Teaching these texts to millennials, the first generation to come of age in the new millennium, reveals how limited the national education and conversation about race, privilege, and inequity already are, for there is an emerging generation without sufficient history to talk about the issues of our time.

Some students are swayed by the seductive rationale that the way to end racial discrimination is to stop talking about racial discrimination. Supreme Court Justice John Roberts's arguments that the way to end racism is to stop talking about race has become the base argument for the Supreme Court as it systematically dismantles legislative gains made during the civil rights movement, even though recent incidents make it clear that there is nothing post-racial about the post-*Brown* era. Some are weary of movement history and talk of race. "Here we go again" thought bubbles appear over their heads when anything related to the civil rights movement appears on the syllabus. Unlike the proverbial lightbulbs, these "aha" moments are full of dread and weariness. Many white students seem to fear that the memoirs will have a bitter, angry tone that might challenge them to "check their privilege," in today's post–New Left political vocabulary.[13] And they in fact know that it is privilege that allows them to demand how others voice justifiable grievances, but they are also honest/realistic/entitled enough to say dialogue will not happen otherwise. Black students worry that protest politics will be the only politics, without regard that the increasing variation in black life demands a shift in the political lexicon: new vocabularies for conceptualizing black identity, new strategies for constructing progressive black politics. (It is other students of color who most appreciate these traditional narratives of the civil rights movement. American students of Pakistani, Mexican, Ethiopian, Egyptian, Guatemalan, and

Honduran descent often find language for their experiences with race through these texts.)

To complicate the old civil rights narrative for everyone, I draw on the work of Sidonie Smith and Julia Watson to teach autobiography as a performance situated within historical and literary mise-en-scènes. This requires acquiring knowledge of classical and canonical texts, "authors you've heard of," as one student put it: Sophocles's *Antigone* to Augustine's *Confessions*; the Bible to Shakespeare. Foundational American texts range from John Bunyan's *Pilgrim's Progress* and Benjamin Franklin's autobiography to Walt Whitman and Phillis Wheatley. Modernist writers are a major influence, such as novelists James Joyce and Maxim Gorky, as is the entire African American canon, from the slave narratives to the Black Arts Movement: Douglass, Jacobs, Du Bois, James Weldon Johnson, Hughes, Hurston, Wright, Ellison, Hansberry, Malcolm X, Baraka, and Shange. Grounding the contemporary within the classics and the canonical immersed us within a humanist project that Patricia Hill Collins has argued is at the very heart of black feminist thought.

The great irony is that students often have little knowledge of the history they instinctively resist or embrace. I often rely on documentaries like *Eyes on the Prize* to provide historical narratives of the Little Rock campaign, and *The Black Power Mixtape* and Shola Lynch's *Free Angela* to provide context for Angela Davis's story. In future iterations of this course I imagine using Freida Mock's documentary, *Anita: Speaking Truth to Power* (2014), in teaching Rosemary Bray's *Unafraid of the Dark* and the Clarence Thomas–Anita Hill hearings. Jordan's *Soldier* provides an opportunity to extend the story of the Great Migration to include Caribbeans, and Joshua Guild's forthcoming *Shadows of the Metropolis*, a comparative examination of diasporic black communities in central Brooklyn and Notting Hill, will help contextualize that history. Grounding the texts within actual history made students see these authors as people in a shared world to be negotiated and engaged.

During my last class on memoirs and essays, *Atlantic* senior editor Ta-Nehisi Coates ignited a public debate about race, politics, and academia when he called then Tulane University political science professor and MSNBC cable news host Melissa Harris-Perry "America's foremost intellectual." The observation was met with incredulity and ridicule within mainstream media. *Politico*'s Dylan Byers argued Coates's belief that a black woman and cable news pundit might be the most influential public intellectual reflected "inferior thinking." Byers's assessment seemed to come from as much a belief that black women are not intellectuals as a tradition that deems accessible thought insufficiently rigorous. Columnists and pundits weighed in, critiquing contemporary intellectual thought without awareness of black women's intellectual tradition even though a black woman's intellectual work launched the entire conversation. It is such a familiar moment when national issues are played out on a black woman's body: Anita Hill, Lani Guinier, Joycelyn Elders, even Michelle Obama; so very characteristic of what Harris-Perry in *Sister Citizen* describes as black women's utter invisibility alongside hypervisibility in America.

Some discounted Harris-Perry's credentials because of sexist and racist notions about who can be an intellectual. Others dismissed her because there are scholars who have written tomes with bigger words and fewer readers. Then the debate shifted to the academic enterprise itself. Nicholas Kristof in the *New York Times* argued that academic writing is too jargon-laced and theoretical to be useful. Jonathan Rotham in the *New Yorker* suggested that it was the academic enterprise that actually required scholars to write in arcane jargon for tenure and promotion. Both overlooked a contemporary generation of scholars committed to engagement with the world in both trenchant and beautiful prose. Emily Lordi in *The Feminist Wire* website named them: Cheryl Wall, Hazel Carby, Valerie Smith, Farah Griffin. Brittney Cooper in her Salon.com column reminded that, a generation earlier, Barbara Christian's "Race for Theory" had already opened a conversation mainstream pundits thought new.

I left graduate school for journalism seeking answers to the questions Barbara Christian raised in "The Race for Theory": *What are we doing, and whom are we doing it for?* Now as a professor in the classroom, I return to it when thinking about black women's literature and intellectual traditions as a way to bridge the empathy gap and connect the historical dots—to give students a language and a moral vision to engage the world with full deliberation.

Notes

Introduction

1. See Eddie S. Glaude Jr., *In a Shade of Blue: Pragmatism and the Politics of Black America* (Chicago: University of Chicago Press, 2002), 129.

2. See Cornel West, *Race Matters* (Boston: Beacon Press, 1993).

3. For instance, see Valerie Smith, *Self-Discovery and Authority in Afro-American Narrative* (Cambridge, MA: Harvard University Press, 1987); and Craig Werner, "On the Ends of Afro-American 'Modernist' Autobiography," *Black American Literature Forum* 24, no. 2 (Summer 1990).

4. See Barbara Rodriguez, *Autobiographical Inscriptions: Form, Personhood, and the American Woman Writer of Color* (New York: Oxford University Press, 1999), which builds on the work of scholars such as Sidonie Smith, Francoise Lionnet, Barbara Johnson, Leigh Gilmore, and Paul de Man.

5. Robert Stepto, *From Behind the Veil: A Study of Afro-American Narrative* (Urbana: University of Illinois Press, 1979); Charles T. Davis and Henry Louis Gates Jr., eds., *The Slave's Narrative* (New York: Oxford University Press, 1985); William Andrews, *To Tell a Free Story: The First Century of Afro-American Autobiography, 1760–1865* (Urbana: University of Illinois Press, 1986).

6. For a discussion of autobiography, specifically the emancipation narrative, as the foundation of modern black political thought, see Robert Gooding-Williams, *In the Shadow of Du Bois: Afro-Modern Political Thought in America* (Cambridge, MA: Harvard University Press, 2009). For a discussion of "the self-consciously politicized autobiography" as the founding motif of black literary history, see Paul Gilroy, *The Black Atlantic: Modernity and Double Consciousness* (Cambridge, MA: Harvard University Press, 1993), 7; Andrews, *To Tell a Free Story*; Joanne Braxton, *Black Women Writing Autobiography: A Tradition within a Tradition* (Philadelphia: Temple University Press, 1989); and V. Smith, *Self-Discovery*. For a discussion of the ideological origins of the black literary tradition, see Henry Louis Gates Jr., *Figures in Black: Words, Signs, and the "Racial" Self* (New York: Oxford University Press, 1987), 25–26.

7. Sidonie Smith, guest editor, "Autobiographical Discourse in the Theaters of Politics," special issue, *Biography* 33, no. 1 (Winter 2010); James Kloppenberg, *Reading Obama: Dreams, Hope, and the American Political Tradition* (Princeton, NJ: Princeton University Press, 2011); Stephanie Li, guest editor, "Writing the Presidency," special issue, *American Literary History* 24, no. 3 (Fall 2012); "New Radical Subjectivities: Rethinking Agency for the 21st Century," University of Nottingham, UK, September 19, 2008; "Life Writing and Intimate Publics," 7th Biennial International Auto/Biography Association Conference, University of Sussex, June 29–July 2, 2010.

8. Mia Bay et al., eds., *Toward an Intellectual History of Black Women* (Chapel Hill: University of North Carolina Press, 2015). The burgeoning field builds on the early work of scholars such as Carol Boyce Davies (*Black Women, Writing, and Identity: Migrations of the Subject* [New York: Routledge, 1994]) and Hazel Carby (*Reconstructing Womanhood: The Emergence of the Afro-American Woman Novelist* [New York: Oxford University Press, 1987] and *Race Men* [Cambridge, MA: Harvard University Press, 2000]). Other projects that are helping to build this burgeoning field include Deborah Gray White, ed., *Telling Histories: Black Women Historians in the Ivory Tower* (Chapel Hill: University of North Carolina Press, 2008); Mia Bay, *To Tell the Truth Freely: The Life of Ida B. Wells* (New York: Hill and Wang, 2010); Paula Giddings, *Ida: A Sword among Lions; Ida B. Wells and the Campaign against Lynching* (New York: Amistad, 2009); Ula Taylor, *The Veiled Garvey: The Life and Times of Amy Jacques Garvey* (Chapel Hill: University of North Carolina Press, 2001); and Brittney Cooper, *Race Women: Gender and the Making of a Black Public Intellectual Tradition* (forthcoming).

9. Farah Jasmine Griffin, "Introduction" (Toward an Intellectual History of Black Women: An International Conference, Columbia University, April 28, 2011).

10. Braxton, *Black Women Writing Autobiography*.

11. Margo Perkins, *Autobiography as Activism: Three Black Women of the Sixties* (Jackson: University Press of Mississippi, 2000); Johnnie M. Stover, *Rhetoric and Resistance in Black Women's Autobiography* (Tallahassee: University Press of Florida, 2003); Stephanie Li, *Something Akin to Freedom: The Choice of Bondage in Narratives by African American Women* (Albany: State University of New York Press, 2010); Kenneth Mostern, *Autobiography and Black Identity Politics: Racialization in Twentieth-Century America* (Cambridge: Cambridge University Press, 1999); Katherine Clay Bassard, "Gender and Genre: Black Women's Autobiography and the Ideology of Literacy," *African American Review* 26 (1992).

12. See Manning Marable, *Race, Reform and Rebellion: The Second Reconstruction in Black America, 1945–1982* (Jackson: University Press of Mississippi, 1984); and Eddie Glaude, "Black Intellectuals Have Sold Their Souls," *New York Times*, April 10, 2013.

13. Catherine R. Squires, "Rethinking the Black Public Sphere: An Alternative Vocabulary for Multiple Public Spheres," *Communication Theory* 12, no. 4 (November 2002): 446–468.

14. Albert E. Stone, "Modern American Autobiography: Texts and Transactions," in *American Autobiography: Retrospect and Prospect*, ed. John Paul Eakin (Madison: University of Wisconsin Press, 1991).

15. Johnnie M. Stover, "Nineteenth-Century African American Women's Autobiography as Social Discourse: The Example of Harriet Jacobs," *College English* 66, no. 2 (November 2003): 134.

16. William L. Andrews, "African American Autobiography Criticism: Retrospect and Prospect," in Eakin, *American Autobiography*.

17. Martha Nussbaum, *Political Emotions: Why Love Matters for Justice* (Cambridge, MA: Harvard University Press, 2013), 2–8.

18. Griffin, "Introduction." See also Melissa V. Harris-Perry, *Sister Citizen: Shame, Stereotypes, and Black Women in America* (New Haven, CT: Yale University Press, 2011); and Nussbaum, *Political Emotions*.

19. Allison Berg, "Trauma and Testimony in Black Women's Civil Rights Memoirs: *The Montgomery Bus Boycott and the Women Who Started It*, *Warriors Don't Cry*, and *From the Mississippi Delta*," *Journal of Women's History* 21, no. 3 (2009).

20. Robin D. G. Kelley, "Stormy Weather: Reconstructing Black (Inter)Nationalism in the Cold War Era," in *Is It Nation Time? Contemporary Essays on Black Power and Nationalism*, ed. Eddie S. Glaude Jr. (Chicago: University of Chicago Press, 2002), 67–68. The original citation transposed the chronology of *Brown* and Emmett Till's murder.

21. Renee Romano and Leigh Raiford, eds., *The Civil Rights Movement in American Memory* (Athens: University of Georgia Press, 2006); Jacquelyn Dowd Hall, "The Long Civil Rights Movement and the Political Uses of the Past," *Journal of American History* 91, no. 4 (March 2005); Glaude, *In a Shade of Blue*.

22. Glaude, *In a Shade of Blue*, 130.

23. Houston A. Baker Jr., "Critical Memory and the Black Public Sphere," in *The Black Public Sphere: A Public Culture Book*, ed. Black Public Sphere Collective (Chicago: University of Chicago Press, 1995), 7.

24. Gooding-Williams, *In the Shadow of Du Bois*, 240–241; Cathy J. Cohen, "Deviance as Resistance: A New Research Agenda for the Study of Black Politics," *Du Bois Review* 1, no. 1 (2004): 31–32.

25. See Kenneth W. Warren, *What Was African American Literature?*, W.E.B. Du Bois Lectures (Cambridge, MA: Harvard University Press, 2012); Charles R. Johnson, "The End of Black American Narrative," in *Best African American Essays 2010*, ed. Gerald Early (New York: Ballantine Books, 2009); Touré, *Who's Afraid of Post-Blackness: What It Means to Be Black Now* (New York: Free Press, 2011).

26. Cathy J. Cohen, *The Boundaries of Blackness: AIDS and the Breakdown of Black Politics* (Chicago: University of Chicago Press, 1999).

27. Carby, *Race Men*, 5.

28. Toni Morrison, "Introduction: Friday on the Potomac," in *Race-ing Justice, Engendering Power: Essays on Anita Hill, Clarence Thomas, and the Construction of Social Reality*, ed. Toni Morrison (New York: Pantheon Books, 1992).

29. Manning Marable, "Race, Identity, and Political Culture," in *Black Popular Culture*, ed. Gina Dent (Seattle: Bay Press, 1992), 296.

30. For a discussion of how the devastation of Hurricane Katrina, as well as all the disastrous aftershocks, challenged black Americans' assumptions about the country's ideals and their own sense of nationality, see Clyde Woods, "Katrina's World: Blues, Bourbon, and the Return to the Source," in *In the Wake of Hurricane Katrina: Paradigms and Social Visions*, ed. Clyde Woods (Baltimore: Johns Hopkins Press, 2010).

31. Richard Iton, *In Search of the Black Fantastic: Politics and Popular Culture in the Post-Civil Rights Era* (New York: Oxford University Press, 2008), 286.

32. Ibid., 287.

33. Glaude, *In a Shade of Blue*, 129.

34. Iton, *In Search of the Black Fantastic*, 285–286.

35. Eddie S. Glaude Jr., *Exodus! Religion, Race, and Nation in Early Nineteenth-Century Black America* (Chicago: University of Chicago Press, 2000).

36. Kevin Powell, "Black Leadership Is Dead," *Huffington Post*, September 29, 2010.

37. David Remnick, *The Bridge: The Life and Rise of Barack Obama* (New York: Knopf, 2010).

38. Martin Luther King Jr., "I See the Promised Land," in *I Have a Dream: Writings and Speeches That Changed the World*, ed. James M. Washington (New York: HarperSan-Francisco, 1986), 203.

39. Quoted in William Jelani Cobb, "The Joshua Generation: The Age Divide and Obama," in *The Substance of Hope: Barack Obama and the Paradox of Progress* (New York: Walker, 2010), 99–100.

40. Angela Ards, "Organizing the Hip-Hop Generation," in *That's the Joint: The Hip-Hop Studies Reader*, ed. Mark Anthony Neal and Murray Forman (New York: Routledge, 2004).

41. Michael C. Dawson, "The Future of Black Politics," *Boston Review*, January 1, 2012. Other calls for the re-creation of a black public sphere include Glaude, *In a Shade of Blue*, 147–148; Marable, "Race, Identity, and Political Culture," 300; Ras Baraka, "Black Youth Black Art Black Face—An Address," in *Step into a World: A Global Anthology of the New Black Literature*, ed. Kevin Powell (New York: Wiley, 2000). Rather than speak of one black public sphere or counterpublic, some scholars embrace the notion of micropublics as a more sophisticated and nuanced way to think about the various collectivities and subjectivities within black America. Michael Dawson, "A Black Counterpublic? Economic Earthquakes, Racial Agenda(s) and Black Politics," *Public Culture* 7 (1994).

42. See Jürgen Habermas, *The Structural Transformation of the Public Sphere: An Inquiry into a Category of Bourgeois Society*, trans. Thomas Burger (Cambridge, MA: MIT Press, 1991); Jürgen Habermas, "Further Reflections on the Public Sphere," in *Habermas and the Public Sphere*, ed. Craig Calhoun (Cambridge, MA: MIT Press, 1996).

43. See Dawson, "Black Counterpublic?"

44. Michelle Alexander, *The New Jim Crow: Mass Incarceration in the Age of Colorblindness* (New York: New Press, 2010). See also Randall Kennedy, *The Persistence of the Color Line: Racial Politics and the Obama Presidency* (New York: Pantheon, 2011); Iton, *In Search of the Black Fantastic*, 26–27.

45. See Gilroy, *Black Atlantic*.

46. For discussion of the political significance of black Twitter, see Mark Anthony Neal, "A History of Black Folk on Twitter," TEDxDuke, April 19, 2011. Neal argues that Twitter reflects black Americans' relationship to technology and social media since slavery (drums, sorrow songs, sit-in networks, et cetera). He argues that black Americans have always used technology in very intimate ways to communicate with each other. According to Neal, two things compel the constant contact. One is the sense of being fictive kin who have a responsibility to acknowledge one another and who share a social reality. The other is that Twitter allows black Americans to introduce discourse into the public sphere—Twitter trending topics often originate with black users—that mainstream media often ignore.

47. Partha Chatterjee, "Whose Imagined Community?," in *The Nation and Its Fragments* (Princeton, NJ: Princeton University Press, 1993), 6. See also Jeff Chang, *Who We Be: The Colorization of America* (New York: St. Martin's, 2014).

48. Iton, *In Search of the Black Fantastic*, 4.

49. Ibid., 11.

50. Lisa Jane Disch, *Hannah Arendt and the Limits of Philosophy* (Ithaca, NY: Cornell University Press, 1994), 142. For a discussion of the ways traditional political discourse and practice, fixed by ideology, rules, and norms, attempt to "escape from the frailty of human affairs into the solidity of quiet and order," see Hannah Arendt, *The Human Condition* (Chicago: University of Chicago Press, 1958), 222.

51. See Michael Dawson, *Black Visions: The Roots of Contemporary African-American Ideologies* (Chicago: University of Chicago Press, 2003), where he offers an alternative political scheme that includes disillusioned liberalism, black Marxism, black conservatism, black nationalism, and radical egalitarianism; and Gooding-Williams, *In the Shadow of Du Bois*, who suggests that there is no scheme whatsoever that can capture all of black politics.

52. Disch, *Hannah Arendt*, 142.

53. Iton, *In Search of the Black Fantastic*, 16 (emphasis added).

54. Gooding-Williams, *In the Shadow of Du Bois*, 48.

55. Kevin Everod Quashie, *Black Women, Identity, and Cultural Theory: (Un)becoming the Subject* (New Brunswick, NJ: Rutgers University Press, 2004), 5, quoted in Farah Jasmine Griffin, "That the Mothers May Soar and the Daughters May Know Their Names: A Retrospective of Black Feminist Literary Criticism," in S. James, *Still Brave*, 347.

56. Kate Douglass, *Contesting Childhood: Autobiography, Trauma, and Memory* (New Brunswick, NJ: Rutgers University Press, 2010), 12.

57. Rob Nixon, "Literature for Real," *Chronicle of Higher Education*, March 7, 2010.

58. Leigh Gilmore, "American Neoconfessional Memoir, Self-Help, and Redemption on Oprah's Couch," *Biography* 33, no. 4 (Fall 2010).

59. See Calvin Hall, *African American Journalists: Autobiography as Memoir and Manifesto* (Lanham, MD: Scarecrow Press, 2009); Reginald Dwayne Betts, *A Question of Freedom: A Memoir of Learning, Survival, and Coming of Age in Prison* (New York: Avery Trade, 2010); and Asha Bandele, *The Prisoner's Wife* (New York: Scribner's, 1999).

60. For a discussion of the ways contemporary cultural narratives, from memoir and film to magazines and monuments, have used civil-rights cultural memory, see Romano and Raiford, *Civil Rights Movement*.

61. Sidonie Smith, "Performativity, Autobiographical Practice, Resistance," *a/b: Auto/Biography Studies* 10, no. 1 (Spring 1995): 18.

62. Emily M. Hinnov, *Encountering Choran Community: Literary Modernism, Visual Culture, and Political Aesthetics in the Interwar Years* (Selinsgrove, PA: Susquehanna University Press, 2009), 49.

63. Lauren Berlant, guest editor, "Intimacy: A Special Issue," *Critical Inquiry* 24, no. 2 (Winter 1998).

64. Jennifer Fuller, "Debating the Present through the Past: Representations of the Civil Rights Movement in the 1990s," in Romano and Raiford, *Civil Rights Movement*, 168–176.

65. Ibid., 176–177.

66. For discussions of this ad hoc coalition building in the early to mid-1990s, see Aaronette M. White, "Talking Black, Talking Feminist: Gendered Mobilization Processes in a Collective Protest against Rape," in *Still Lifting, Still Climbing: African American Women's Contemporary Activism*, ed. Kimberly Springer (New York: New York University Press, 1999); and Angela Ards, "Sisters Act: Reflections on the Tyson 'Homecoming Flap,'" *Village Voice*, July 25, 1995. The eclectic and at times ad hoc organizing echoes coalitions that formed to demand justice for Recy Taylor in 1944 (and developed eleven years later into the Montgomery Improvement Association); the coalition that formed to support Joan Little in 1970, the inmate who killed her jailer after he sexually assaulted her; the tradition from Harriet Jacobs to nineteenth-century club women who spoke out against the rape of young black girls and women as they challenged lynching (Danielle L. McGuire, prologue to *At the Dark End of the Street: Black Women, Rape, and Resistance—A New History of the Civil Rights Movement from Rosa Parks to the Rise of Black Power* [New York: Knopf, 2010], xvi–xxii).

67. For a discussion of how anti-rape activism and fights against sexual assault have been a central part of freedom struggle, see McGuire, *Dark End of the Street*.

68. Douglass, *Contesting Childhood*, 21.

69. Danielle S. Allen, *Talking to Strangers: Anxieties of Citizenship since "Brown v. Board of Education"* (Chicago: University of Chicago Press, 2004), 37–38.

70. Paula Giddings, "The Last Taboo," in *Still Brave: The Evolution of Black Women's Studies*, ed. Stanlie M. James et al. (New York: Feminist Press, 2009).

71. Gooding-Williams, *In the Shadow of Du Bois*, 211.

72. Nussbaum, *Political Emotions*.

73. Iton, *In Search of the Black Fantastic*, 219. See also Winston James, "The History of Afro-Caribbean Migration to the United States," in *In Motion: The African American Migration Experience*, ed. Howard Dodson and Sylviane Dioufe (Washington, DC: National Geographic, 2004).

74. Perkins, *Autobiography as Activism*, 14.

75. Angela Davis and Kathleen Cleaver, "Rekindling the Flame" (a dialogue moderated by Diane Weathers and Tara Roberts), *Essence*, May 1996, 160, quoted in Perkins, *Autobiography as Activism*, 14.

76. Gillian Rose, *Mourning Becomes the Law: Philosophy and Representation* (Cambridge: Cambridge University Press, 1996).

77. Iton, *In Search of the Black Fantastic*, 226.

78. William Jelani Cobb, *To the Break of Dawn: A Freestyle on the Hip-Hop Aesthetic* (New York: New York University Press, 2007), 130.

79. Powell, *Step into a World*, 10.

80. Leigh Raiford, "Restaging Revolution: Black Power, *Vibe* Magazine, and Photographic Memory," in Romano and Raiford, *Civil Rights Movement*, 242–245. See also Mark Anthony Neal, *Soul Babies: Black Popular Culture and the Post-Soul Aesthetic* (New York: Routledge, 2002).

81. Iton, *In Search of the Black Fantastic*, 289.

82. Gina Dent, "Black Pleasure, Black Joy: An Introduction," in *Black Popular Culture: A Project by Michele Wallace*, ed. Gina Dent (Seattle: Bay Press, 1992), 1–19.

83. Sidonie Smith and Julia Watson, eds., *Reading Autobiography: A Guide for Interpreting Life Narratives* (Minneapolis: University of Minnesota Press, 2010), 193–234.

84. See Michael de Certu, *The Practice of Everyday Life*, trans. Steve Randall (Berkeley: University of California Press, 1984).

Chapter 1
Moving beyond the Strong Black Woman

1. Jonathan Zimmerman, "What Are Schools For?," *New York Review of Books*, October 14, 2010.

2. *Brown* was an amalgam of five elementary school cases filed in separate districts: Charleston, South Carolina; District of Columbia; Richmond, Virginia; Topeka, Kansas; Wilmington, Delaware. For a discussion of the everyday sacrifices required of a robust democracy, see Danielle S. Allen, *Talking to Strangers: Anxieties of Citizenship since "Brown v. Board of Education"* (Chicago: University of Chicago Press, 2004). For a discussion of the "unshared sacrifice" the civil rights laws demand of minorities, see Charles Ogletree, *All Deliberate Speed: Reflections on the First Half Century of "Brown v. Board of Education"* (New York: W. W. Norton, 2004); and Derrick Bell, *Silent Covenants: "Brown v. Board of Education" and the Unfulfilled Hopes for Racial Reform* (New York: Oxford University Press, 2004). For a discussion of the ways *Brown* seemingly has had an impact on almost every aspect of American life except the public schools it sought to redress, see Martha Minow, *In "Brown"'s Wake: Legacies of America's Educational Landmark* (New York: Oxford University Press, 2010).

3. D. Allen, *Talking to Strangers*, 109. See also Danielle Allen, "Ralph Ellison and the Tragicomedy of Citizenship," *Raritan Quarterly* 23, no. 3 (2004).

4. Derrick Bell, *Race, Racism, and American Law*, 2nd ed. (Boston: Little, Brown, 1980), 34. See also Constance Baker Motley, *Equal Justice under Law: An Autobiography* (New York: Farrar, Straus and Giroux, 1998); and Ogletree, *All Deliberate Speed*.

5. Anthony Lewis, "President Sends Troops to Little Rock, Federalizes Arkansas National Guard: Tells Nation He Acted to Avoid Anarchy," in Clayborne Carson et al., comps., *Reporting Civil Rights: Part One, American Journalism, 1941–1963* (New York: Library of America, 2003), 382–385, originally published in *New York Times*, September 25, 1957.

6. David L. Chappell, *A Stone of Hope: Prophetic Religion and the Death of Jim Crow* (Chapel Hill: University of North Carolina Press, 2004). In *Risks of Faith: The Emergence of a Black Theology of Liberation, 1968–1998* (Boston: Beacon Press, 1999), James Cone famously mapped this black prophetic tradition onto the Black Power movement of the late 1960s. For a discussion of nineteenth-century theologians, such as James Theodore Holly and Theophilus Gould Seward, who developed a similar liberationist theology of black redemptive suffering, see Albert J. Raboteau, "Ethiopia Shall Soon Stretch Forth Her Hands: Black Destiny in Nineteenth-Century America," in *African American Religious Thought*, ed. Cornel West and Eddie S. Glaude Jr. (Louisville, KY: Westminster John Knox Press, 2003). And for a discussion of the political activity of clandestine black congregations during slavery, see Raboteau, *Slave Religion: The "Invisible Institution" in the Antebellum South* (New York: Oxford University Press, 1978).

7. Jean Bethke Elshtain, "Political Children," in *Feminist Interpretations of Hannah Arendt*, ed. Bonnie Honig (University Park: Penn State University Press, 1995), 275.

8. Harris-Perry, *Sister Citizen*, 184.

9. Nikhil Pal Singh, introduction to *Black Is a Country: Race and the Unfinished Struggle for Democracy* (Cambridge, MA: Harvard University Press, 2005), 9–10; Kimberlé Crenshaw, "Race, Reform, and Retrenchment," *Harvard Law Review* 101, no. 7 (May 1988): 1331–1387.

10. Alan Freeman, "Antidiscrimination Law: The View from 1989," in *The Politics of Law: A Progressive Critique*, ed. David Kairys, rev. ed. (New York: Pantheon Books, 1990), 121.

11. Examples include the Lifetime series *Any Day Now* (1998–2002); NBC's *I'll Fly Away* (1991–1993); and feature films *Heart of Dixie* (1989), *The Long Walk Home* (1990), *Do the Right Thing* (1989), HBO's *Boycott* (2001), *Ghosts of Mississippi* (1996), and *Malcolm X* (1992).

12. Fuller, "Debating the Present," 168–176.

13. Ibid., 176–177.

14. Melba Beals, *Warriors Don't Cry: A Searing Memoir of the Battle to Integrate Little Rock's Central High* (New York: Washington Square Press, 1994), 155. Subsequent references will be noted parenthetically in the text.

15. Nellie Y. McKay, "The Girls Who Became Women: Childhood Memoirs in the Autobiographies of Harriet Jacobs, Mary Church Terrell and Anne Moody," in *Tradition and the Talents of Women*, ed. Florence Howe (Urbana: University of Illinois Press, 1991).

16. For a discussion of black autobiographies written after the modern civil rights movements with the goal of reviving the radical fervor associated with the period, see Perkins, *Autobiography as Activism*.

17. Zimmerman, "What Are Schools For?"

18. David Margolick, *Elizabeth and Hazel: Two Women of Little Rock* (New Haven, CT: Yale University Press, 2011), 286n2.

19. Linda Christensen, "Warriors Don't Cry: *Brown* Comes to Little Rock," *Rethinking Schools Online* 18, no. 3 (Spring 2004), http://www.rethinkingschools.org/brown/warr183.shtml. See also Linda Christensen, *Reading, Writing, and Rising Up: Teaching about Social Justice and the Power of the Written Word* (Washington, DC: Rethinking Schools, 2000).

20. Eckford quoted in Margolick, *Elizabeth and Hazel*, 188–189. Also e-mail messages to author, July 28 and August 8, 2009.

21. Ted Poston, "The 19-Day Ordeal of Minnie Jean Brown," in Carson et al., *Reporting Civil Rights*.

22. Farah Jasmine Griffin, "Elaine Brown's *A Taste of Power*," *Boston Review: A Political and Literary Forum* 18, no. 2 (March/April 1993), http://bostonreview.net/archives/BR18.2/griffin.html.

23. Ibid.

24. Margolick, *Elizabeth and Hazel*, 126–127, 292n1.

25. Philippe LeJeune, "The Autobiographical Pact," in *On Autobiography*, ed. Paul John Eakin, trans. Katherine Leary (Minneapolis: University of Minnesota Press, 1989). See also S. Smith and Watson, *Reading Autobiography*, 15–19; and Elizabeth W. Bruss, *Autobiographical Acts: The Changing Situation of a Literary Genre* (Baltimore: Johns Hopkins University Press, 1976).

26. Nixon, "Literature for Real." See also Nancy K. Miller, "The Entangled Self: Genre Bondage in the Age of Memoir," *PMLA* 22, no. 2 (March 2007); and Gilmore, "American Neoconfessional."

27. Stepto, *From Behind the Veil*.

28. Sidonie Smith, *Where I'm Bound: Patterns of Slavery and Freedom in Black American Autobiography* (Westport, CT: Greenwood Press, 1974), 8.

29. Miller, "Entangled Self," 541.

30. See V. Smith, *Self-Discovery*; P. Gabrielle Foreman, "Manifest in Signs: The Politics of Sex and Representation in *Incidents in the Life of a Slave Girl*," in *Harriet Jacobs and "Incidents in the Life of a Slave Girl": New Critical Essays*, ed. Deborah M. Garfield and Rafia Zafar (Cambridge: Cambridge University Press, 1996); and Griffin, "Elaine Brown's *A Taste of Power*."

31. Margolick, *Elizabeth and Hazel*, 286n2.

32. Ibid., 148. Other Little Rock Nine memoirs include *The Ernest Green Story* (1993), a made-for-TV movie; the documentary *Little Rock Central High: 50 Years Later* (2007), which focuses on the experience of Minnijean Brown; and Carlotta Walls LaNier's ghostwritten *A Mighty Long Way: My Journey to Justice at Little Rock Central High School* (New York: One World/Ballantine Books, 2009).

33. See Patricia Pace, "All Our Lost Children: Trauma and Testimony in the Performance of Childhood," *Text and Performance Quarterly* 18 (1998): 237–238; Douglass, *Contesting Childhood*; and Robin Bernstein, *Racial Innocence: Performing American Childhood from Slavery to Civil Rights* (New York: New York University Press, 2011).

34. Motley, *Equal Justice*, 106.

35. D. Bell, *Silent Covenants*, 2–3.

36. Lerone Bennett Jr., *What Manner of Man: A Biography of Martin Luther King, Jr.* (Chicago: Johnson, 1964), 72, quoted in Theophus H. Smith, "Exodus," in West and Glaude, *African American Religious Thought*, 319.

37. King, "I See the Promised Land," 203.

38. In addition to Taylor Branch's three-part history, *America in the King Years*, see Singh, introduction to *Black Is a Country*. For a discussion of the central role of King in the normative framing of the civil rights era, see also Charles Payne, *I've Got the Light of Freedom: The Organizing Tradition and the Mississippi Freedom Struggle* (Berkeley: University of California Press, 1995).

39. Kenneth W. Warren, "Ralph Ellison and the Problem of Cultural Authority," *boundary 2* 30, no. 2 (Summer 2003): 167.

40. Ann M. Lane, "Hannah Arendt: Theorist of Distinction(s)," *Political Theory* 25, no. 1 (February 1997): 138.

41. Nicholas D. Katzenbach, Randall L. Kennedy, Patricia J. Williams, and Kevin Kruse, "Brown v. Board of Education, Little Rock, and the Civil Rights Movement" (session 2, "Hannah Arendt and Little Rock: Reflections on the 50th Anniversary of the Desegregation of Central High School," symposium, Princeton University, Princeton, NJ, April 27, 2007).

42. Elshtain, "Political Children," 270.

43. Arendt, *Human Condition*.

44. D. Allen, *Talking to Strangers*, 26.

45. Hannah Arendt, "Reflections on Little Rock," *Dissent* 6, no. 1 (Winter 1959): 55.

46. See Sacvan Bercovitch, *The Puritan Origins of the American Self* (New Haven, CT: Yale University Press, 1975); and Conrad Cherry, ed., *God's New Israel: Religious Interpretations of American Destiny* (Englewood Cliffs, NJ: Prentice-Hall, 1971).

47. See Werner Sollors, *Beyond Ethnicity: Consent and Dissent in American Culture* (New York: Oxford University Press, 1986).

48. See Glaude, *Exodus!*

49. David Walker, *David Walker's Appeal in Four Articles: Together with a Preamble, to the Coloured Citizens of the World, but in Particular, and Very Expressly, to Those of the United States of America* [1829], quoted in Glaude, "Ethiopia Shall Stretch Forth Her Hands unto God," in *In a Shade of Blue*, 67.

50. This verse has a long literary tradition. The first reference in African American letters to this pivotal scripture may well have been in a 1774 letter that Phillis Wheatley

wrote to the Reverend Samuel Hopkins, in which Wheatley invokes the psalm as a
prophecy of African conversion to Christianity:

> Methinks Rev'd Sir, this is the beginning of that happy period foretold by the
> Prophets, when all shall know the Lord from the least to the greatest, and that
> without assistance of human art & eloquence, my heart expanded, with sympa-
> thetic Joy, to see at distant time the thick cloud of ignorance dispersing from the
> face of my benighted Country. Europe and America have long been fed with
> the heavenly provision, and I fear they loathe it, while Africa is perishing with a
> spiritual Famine. O that they could partake of the crumbs, the precious crumbs
> which fall from the table, of these distinguish'd children of the Kingdom. Their
> minds are unprejudiced against the truth therefore tis to be hoped they wou^d
> receive it with their whole heart. I hope that which the divine royal Psalmist says
> by inspiration is now on the point of being accomplish'd, namely, Ethiopia shall
> soon stretch forth her hands Unto God. (William H. Robinson, ed., *Phillis
> Wheatley and Her Writings* [New York: Garland Publishing, 1984], 330.)

51. Raboteau, "'Ethiopia,'" 400. For an interesting analysis of the idea of blacks as
a messianic people, see Wilson Jeremiah Moses, *Black Messiahs and Uncle Toms: Social and
Literary Manipulations of a Religious Myth* (University Park: Pennsylvania State University
Press, 1982).

52. Chappell, *Stone of Hope*.

53. Robert Penn Warren, "Interview with Ralph Ellison," in *Who Speaks for the
Negro?* (New York: Vintage Books/Random House, 1965), 344.

54. Howard Thurman, *Luminous Darkness* (Richmond, IN: Friends United Press,
1976), 47.

55. D. Allen, *Talking to Strangers*, 28.

56. Arendt, "Reflections on Little Rock," 50.

57. D. Allen, *Talking to Strangers*, 50.

58. Stephanie B. Goldberg, "Who's Afraid of Derrick Bell? A Conversation on
Harvard, Storytelling, and the Meaning of Color," *American Bar Association Journal*,
September 1992, 56.

59. Abbey Lincoln, "Who Will Revere the Black Woman?" in *The Black Woman: An
Anthology*, ed. Toni Cade (New York: Mentor/Penguin, 1970), 84.

60. See Farah Jasmine Griffin, "Conflict and Chorus: Reconsidering Toni Cade's
The Black Woman: An Anthology," in *Is It Nation Time? Contemporary Essays on Black Power
and Black Nationalism*, ed. Eddie S. Glaude Jr. (Chicago: University of Chicago Press,
2002).

61. Ogletree, *All Deliberate Speed*, 296–297.

62. D. Bell, *Silent Covenants*, xx.

63. Motley, *Equal Justice under Law*, 84.

64. D. Bell, *Silent Covenants*, 9.

65. Thurman, *Luminous Darkness*, 26.

66. Crenshaw, "Race, Reform, and Retrenchment," 1331.

67. D. Bell, *Silent Covenants*, 9. For a discussion of how questions of equality are better articulated outside the courts, given the Supreme Court's shift from an "equality" to a "liberty" analysis, see Kenji Yoshino, *Covering: The Hidden Assault on Our Civil Rights* (New York: Random House, 2006).

68. Harris-Perry, *Sister Citizen*, 20.

69. Berg, "Trauma and Testimony," 95.

70. P. Gabrielle Foreman, "The Spoken and the Silenced in *Incidents in the Life of a Slave Girl* and *Our Nig*," *Callaloo* 13 (Spring 1990); and Jacqueline Goldsby, "'I Disguised My Hand': Writing Versions of the Truth in Harriet Jacobs's *Incidents in the Life of a Slave Girl* and John Jacobs's 'A True Tale of Slavery,'" in Garfield and Zafar, *Harriet Jacobs and "Incidents in the Life of a Slave Girl."*

71. Darlene Clark Hine, "Rape and the Inner Lives of Black Women in the Middle West: Preliminary Thoughts on the Culture of Dissemblance," *Signs: Journal of Women in Culture and Society* 14 (Summer 1989).

72. D. Allen, "Ralph Ellison," 61.

73. D. Allen, *Talking to Strangers*, 37–38.

74. Douglass, *Contesting Childhood*, 7.

75. Ibid., 21.

76. McGuire, *Dark End of the Street*, xvii.

77. Berg, "Trauma and Testimony."

78. Harris-Perry, *Sister Citizen*, 20.

79. Ibid., 21.

80. Ibid., 22, 109–133.

81. Mary Vermillion, "Reembodying the Self: Representations of Rape in *Incidents in the Life of a Slave Girl* and *I Know Why the Caged Bird Sings*," *Biography* 15, no. 3 (Summer 1992).

82. Harriet Jacobs, *Incidents in the Life of a Slave Girl: Written by Herself*, ed. Jean Fagan Yellin (Cambridge, MA: Harvard University Press, 1987), 56.

83. Maya Angelou, *I Know Why the Caged Bird Sings* (New York: Bantam, 1969), 245.

84. Vermillion, "Reembodying the Self," 255.

85. Margolick, *Elizabeth and Hazel*, 134–135, 120. In many ways *Warriors* does seem to be framed around elements of Elizabeth Eckford's story. In addition to the appropriated walk and friend, the cover art of the abridged edition has a picture of Beals on the steps of Central High in a pose very similar to Eckford's more well-known one: standing statuesque, with a binder held close to her chest. Moreover, according to reports, it was Elizabeth who suffered disproportionately, as she was the most famous and therefore the most targeted. See Margolick, *Elizabeth and Hazel*, 127, 129.

86. K. Warren, "Ralph Ellison," 162, 163.

87. Daisy Bates, *The Long Shadow of Little Rock: A Memoir* (Fayetteville: University of Arkansas Press, 1986), xii.

88. Motley, *Equal Justice*, 84.

Chapter 2
Reclaiming Radical Interdependence

1. Griffin, "That the Mothers May Soar," 343, and "Conflict and Chorus," 113–129. See also Singh, introduction to *Black Is a Country*.

2. Several feminist writers have addressed the way the twin myths of the black male rapist and the promiscuous black woman have motivated ritualistic violence against black men and women through lynching and rape. See Angela Davis, "Racism, Rape, and the Myth of the Black Rapist," in *Women, Race, & Class* (New York: Vintage Books, 1983); Michele Wallace, *Black Macho and the Myth of the Superwoman* (New York: Dial Press, 1978); and Joan Morgan, "strongblackwomen-n-endangeredblackmen: . . . this is not a love story," in *When Chickenheads Come Home to Roost: My Life as a Hip-Hop Feminist* (New York: Simon & Schuster, 1999), 115–140.

3. Humanist Archives, vol. 6, no. 0661, "6.0661 CFP: Black Women in the Academy (1/73)," Humanist Discussion Group, Call for Papers, April 9, 1993. The conference was held at MIT on January 13–15, 1994.

4. See McGuire, *Dark End of the Street*.

5. Griffin, "Conflict and Chorus."

6. Giddings, "Last Taboo." For an anthropological study of the link between the surveillance state, welfare, and domestic abuse, see Dana-Ain Davis, *Battered Black Women and Welfare Reform: Between a Rock and a Hard Place* (Albany: State University of New York Press, 2006).

7. For a discussion of the evolution of antiwelfare rhetoric in the twentieth century, see Adriane Bezusko, "Criminalizing Black Motherhood: How the War on Welfare Was Won," *Souls: A Critical Journal of Black Politics, Culture, and Society* 15, no. 1–2 (2013).

8. For the definitive history of black conservatives in the twentieth century, see Leah Wright Rigueur, *The Loneliness of Black Republicans: Pragmatic Politics and the Pursuit of Power* (Princeton, NJ: Princeton University Press, 2014).

9. Rosemary Bray, *Unafraid of the Dark: A Memoir* (New York: Anchor Books, 1998), 263. Subsequent references will be noted parenthetically in the text.

10. See S. Smith and Watson, *Reading Autobiography*, 286.

11. Lauren Berlant, "Life Writing and Intimate Publics: A Conversation with Lauren Berlant," *Biography* 34, no. 1 (2011).

12. S. Smith and Watson, *Reading Autobiography*, 274–275.

13. Jacquelyn Grant, "Womanist Theology: Black Women's Experience as a Source for Doing Theology, with Special Reference to Christology," in *Black Theology: A Documentary History*, vol. 2, *1980–1992*, ed. James H. Cone and Gayraud S. Wilmore (Maryknoll, NY: Orbis, 1993), 285.

14. S. Smith and Watson, *Reading Autobiography*, 262–263.

15. See Nussbaum, *Political Emotions*.

16. Gilmore, "American Neoconfessional."

17. S. Smith, "Performativity."

18. Ibid., 18.

19. Vincent Harding, *There Is a River: The Black Struggle for Freedom in America* (New York: Mariner Books, 1993).

20. Premilla Nadasen, *Welfare Warriors: The Welfare Rights Movement in the United States* (New York: Routledge, 2005), 1–43.

21. Ibid., 231.

22. Gooding-Williams, *In the Shadow of Du Bois*.

23. Nadasen, *Welfare Warriors*, 19–20, 71–72. See also Premilla Nadasen, "'We Do Whatever Becomes Necessary': Johnnie Tillmon, Welfare Rights, and Black Power," in *Want to Start a Revolution? Radical Women in the Black Freedom Struggle*, ed. Dayo F. Gore, Jeanne Theoharis, and Komozi Woodard (New York: New York University Press, 2009).

24. Nadasen, *Welfare Warriors*, 233–242.

25. Vivian May, "Under-Theorized and Under-Taught: Re-examining Harriet Tubman's Place in Women's Studies," *Meridians: feminism, race, transnationalism* 12, no. 2 (2014): 29.

26. Ibid., 40; Angela Y. Davis, "Reflections on the Black Woman's Role in the Community of Slaves," *Massachusetts Review* 13, no. 1–2 (Winter/Spring 1972): 90, quoted in V. May, "Under-Theorized and Under-Taught," 39–40.

27. See Diana Fuss, "Reading like a Feminist," in *The Essential Difference*, ed. Naomi Schor and Elizabeth Weed (Bloomington: Indiana University Press, 1994), 99.

28. Kathryn Tanner, "The Care That Does Justice: Recent Writings on Feminist Ethics and Theology," *Journal of Religious Ethics* 24, no. 1 (1996): 172–173.

29. Ibid., 175. For a discussion of how privileging an ethics of care reproduces sexist images, particularly about how "the racist and sexist rhetoric of 'welfare mothers' must be made compatible with attention to the racist and *sexist* rhetoric of 'violent criminals' who need to be put in prison," see Mostern, *Black Identity Politics*, 14.

30. Tanner, "Care That Does Justice," 174. For a discussion of the way a private ethic of care is intimately connected to structures in the public sphere, see Susan Okin, *Justice, Gender, and the Family* (New York: Basic Books, 1989).

31. Katie G. Cannon, *Black Womanist Ethics* (Atlanta: Scholars Press, 1988), 4.

32. Rosetta E. Ross, "Religion and Public Life: Early Traditions of Black Religious Women's Activism," *Witnessing and Testifying: Black Women, Religion, and Civil Rights* (Minneapolis: Fortress Press, 2003).

33. See Evelyn Brooks Higginbotham, *Righteous Discontent: The Women's Movement in the Black Baptist Church, 1880–1920* (Cambridge, MA: Harvard University Press, 1993); Carla Peterson, *Doers of the Word: African American Women Speakers and Writers in the North (1830–1880)* (New York: Oxford University Press, 1995); and Kevin Gaines, *Uplifting the Race: Black Leadership, Politics, and Culture in the Twentieth Century* (Chapel Hill: University of North Carolina Press, 1996).

34. [1]When that day comes, the kingdom of Heaven will be like this. There were ten girls, who took their lamps and went out to meet the bridegroom. [2]Five of them

were foolish and five prudent; [3]when the foolish ones took their lamps, they took no oil with them, [4]but the others took flasks of oil with their lamps. [5]As the bridegroom was late in coming they all dozed off to sleep. [6]But at midnight a cry was heard: "Here is the bridegroom! Come out to meet him!" [7]With that the girls all got up and trimmed their lamps. [8]The foolish said to the prudent, "Our lamps are going out; give us some of your oil." [9]"No," they said; "there will never be enough for all of us. You had better go to the shop and buy some for yourselves." [10]While they were away the bridegroom arrived; those who were ready went in with him to the wedding; and the door was shut. [11]And then the other five came back. "Sir, sir," they cried, "open the door for us." [12]But he answered, "I declare, I do not know you." (Matt. 25:1–12 [Revised Standard Version])

35. Margo Culley, ed., *American Women's Autobiography: Fea(s)ts of Memory* (Madison: University of Wisconsin Press, 1992).

36. Perkins, *Autobiography as Activism*, xii.

37. Glaude, *Is It Nation Time?*, 5.

38. Cannon, *Black Womanist Ethics*, 159–178.

39. Eric Gregory, "Augustine and Arendt on Love: New Dimensions in the Religion and Liberalism Debates," *Annual of the Society of Christian Ethics* 21 (2001): 168.

40. Ibid., 155–172. See also Robin D. G. Kelley, *Freedom Dreams: The Black Radical Imagination* (Boston: Beacon Press, 2002).

41. See Gilmore, "American Neoconfessional Memoir."

42. S. Smith and Watson, *Reading Autobiography*, 265, paraphrasing Rita Felski, "On Confession," in *Beyond Feminist Aesthetics: Feminist Literature and Social Change* (Cambridge, MA: Harvard University Press, 1989), 86–121.

43. Gregory, "Augustine and Arendt on Love." See also John von Heyking, *Augustine and Politics as Longing in the World* (Columbia: University of Missouri Press, 2001), as well as "Politics between the Earthly City and the City of God in Christianity" (paper, Cooperation of Church and State Conference, Cardus Centre for Cultural Renewal, Alberta, Calgary, June 9, 2006), 1–16, http://www.cardus.ca/columns/2471/.

44. Cannon, *Black Womanist Ethics*, 163.

45. Clarence E. Hardy III, "Imagine a World: Howard Thurman, Spiritual Perception, and American Calvinism," *The Journal of Religion* 81, no.1 (2001): 96.

46. Glaude, *Is It Nation Time?*, 5. For a discussion of different modalities of agency, see Saba Mahmood, *Politics of Piety: The Islamic Revival and the Feminist Subject* (Princeton, NJ: Princeton University Press, 2004).

47. S. Smith and Watson, *Reading Autobiography*, 266.

48. Frederick Douglass, *Narrative of the Life of Frederick Douglass, an American Slave, Written by Himself* (1846), in *The Classic Slave Narratives*, ed. Henry Louis Gates Jr. (New York: Mentor/New American Library, 1987), 258–259, 271. See also Elaine Brown's *A Taste of Power: A Black Woman's Story* (New York: Anchor Books/Doubleday, 1992), in which she also recounts slavery's lingering effects in describing her constant childhood "night terrors."

49. See Judge J. Waties Waring's dissent, *Briggs v. Elliot*, 98 F. Supp. 529, 538–48 (E.D.S.C. 1951).

50. Thurman, *Luminous Darkness*, 26.

51. Ibid., 24.

52. Hortense Spillers, *Black, White, and in Color: Essays on American Literature and Culture* (Chicago: University of Chicago Press), 390.

53. Howard Thurman, *Deep River: The Negro Spiritual Speaks of Life and Death* (Richmond, IN: Friends United Press, 1975), 52, 48.

54. Thurman, *Luminous Darkness*, 15–16.

55. Howard Thurman, *The Creative Encounter* (Richmond, IN: Friends United Press, 1972), 20, cited in Hardy, "Imagine a World," 89.

56. Mae Gwendolyn Henderson, "Speaking in Tongues: Dialogics, Dialectics, and the Black Woman Writer's Literary Tradition," in *Reading Black, Reading Feminist*, ed. Henry Louis Gates Jr. (New York: Meridian/Penguin, 1990). Also, for a discussion of the ways *Souls of Black Folks* imagines black progress through ideologies of masculinity, see Carby, *Race Men*.

57. Gregory, "Augustine and Arendt on Love," 157. For a similar discussion about the use of "horizontal" and "vertical" metaphors that explicate the relationship between love of God and love of neighbors, see Timothy P. Jackson, *Love Disconsoled: Meditations on Christian Charity* (Cambridge: Cambridge University Press, 1999), 1–31.

58. Gustavo Gutierrez, *The Power of the Poor in History*, trans. Robert R. Barr (Eugene, OR: Wipf and Stock, 2004), 44, 45.

59. Tanner, "The Care That Does Justice," 178.

60. For example, see Joyce M. Bell, *The Black Power Movement and American Social Work* (New York: Columbia University Press, 2014); Glaude, *Is It Nation Time?*; Peniel E. Joseph, *Waiting 'Til the Midnight Hour: A Narrative History of Black Power in America* (New York: Henry Holt, 2006) Peniel E. Joseph, *Stokely: A Life* (New York: Basic Civitas Books, 2014); and Nadasen, *Welfare Warriors*.

61. Martin Luther King Jr., "Where Do We Go From Here?," in *I Have a Dream: Writings and Speeches That Changed the World*, ed. James M. Washington (New York: HarperSanFrancisco, 1990), 172.

62. Pauli Murray, *Pauli Murray: The Autobiography of a Black Activist, Feminist, Lawyer, Priest, and Poet* (Knoxville: University of Tennessee, 1989), 436.

63. Sue Bridwell Beckham, review of *Song in a Weary Throat: An American Pilgrimage*, *Journal of Southern History* 55, no. 2 (May 1989): 354.

64. Christiana Z. Peppard, "Poetry, Ethics, and the Legacy of Pauli Murray," *Journal of the Society of Christian Ethics* 30, no. 1 (Spring/Summer 2010): 29.

65. Murray, *Pauli Murray*, 289.

66. See Frances Beale, "Double Jeopardy: To Be Black and Female," in *The Black Woman: An Anthology*, ed. Toni Cade (New York: Mentor/Penguin, 1970).

67. The students objected to Murray's preference for *Negro* to *black*, which then designated a militant ideology of separatism and newfound cultural pride. In Murray's

reasoning, the capitalized *Negro*, a proper noun, conveyed the dignity afforded other racial groups while more accurately describing a people's physical identity, ranging "from blond Caucasian types to almost pure-black African types." Murray, *Pauli Murray*, 403.

68. See Richard Blackett, review of *Song in a Weary Throat: An American Pilgrimage*, by Pauli Murray, *Georgia Historical Quarterly* 71, no. 4 (Winter 1987); and Suzanne R. Hiatt, "Pauli Murray: May Her Song Be Heard at Last," review of *Song in a Weary Throat: An American Pilgrimage*, by Pauli Murray, *Journal of Feminist Studies in Religion* 4, no. 2 (Fall, 1988).

69. Murray, *Pauli Murray*, 378, quoted in Peppard, "Poetry, Ethics," 23.

70. Lauren Berlant, *The Female Complaint: The Unfinished Business of Sentimentality in American Culture* (Durham, NC: Duke University Press, 2008), viii.

71. Thurman, "Concerning Backgrounds," in *Deep River*, 32. Thurman refers specifically to "Climbin' Jacob's Ladder," a chorus within the parent spiritual, "Keep Your Lamps Trimmed and Burning." See Oral Moses, "What Is a Negro Spiritual?," http://www.thenegrospiritualinc.com/article_what_is_a_negro_spiritual.htm. In "The Sorrow Songs," W. E. B. Du Bois argues that another derivative, "Wrestling Jacob, the day is a-breakin'"—"a paean of hopeful strife"—is one of the "ten master songs" in the African American spiritual canon. Du Bois also notes that the spirituals "express hope in the ultimate justice of things" (386), even considering all empirical evidence to the contrary. Interestingly, this chapter, prefaced by bars from "Wrestling Jacob," ends with a rarely sung chorus, "Let us cheer the weary traveler," reflecting the "incurable optimism" that Thurman describes. W. E. B. Du Bois, *The Souls of Black Folk* (1903), ed. Farah Jasmine Griffin (New York: Barnes & Noble Classics, 2003), 177–188.

72. Berlant, *Female Complaint*, 6.

73. Rosemary Bray, "Illumination" (sermon, Fourth Universalist Society in the City of New York, New York, October 23, 2011).

74. Gutierrez, *The Power of the Poor in History*, 44, 45.

Chapter 3
Honoring the Past to Move Forward

1. June Jordan, *Some of Us Did Not Die: New and Selected Essays of June Jordan* (New York: Basic Civitas Books, 2002), 375.

2. Perhaps one reason for this silence is the desire to avoid asserting "ethnic distinctiveness," which has been used to reinforce notions of black American cultural inferiority. See Jemima Pierre, "Black Immigrants in the United States and the 'Cultural Narratives' of Ethnicity," *Identities: Global Studies in Culture and Power* 11 (2004).

3. Iton, *In Search of the Black Fantastic*, 218–219.

4. See Douglass, *Contesting Childhood*; Pace, "All Our Lost Children," 237–238; and Lisa Hull Reed, "(Re)composing Childhood: Representing the Rhythm of Self in

Postmodern Memoir," *JASAT* (*Journal of the American Studies Association of Texas*) 41 (November 2010). For a discussion of how Romantic, eighteenth-century fictions of childhood innocence figure in the current fascination, see Richard Flynn, "'Infant Sight': Romanticism, Childhood, and Postmodern Poetry," in *Literature and the Child: Romantic Continuations, Postmodern Contestations*, ed. James Holt McGavran (Iowa City: University of Iowa Press, 1999).

5. June Jordan, *Technical Difficulties: African American Notes on the State of the Union* (New York: Vintage Books/Random House, 1992), 18.

6. This is an allusion to 2 Timothy 4:17: "I have fought a good fight, I have finished my course, I have kept the faith."

7. June Jordan, handwritten draft of *Soldier* (with then-working title, "My Childhood") and letter to Harper & Row editor Fran McCullough, 1979, June Jordan Papers, 1936–2002, Arthur and Elizabeth Schlesinger Library on the History of Women in America, Radcliffe Institute for Advanced Study, Harvard University, Cambridge, MA, Box 51.1. See also Felicia R. Lee, "A Feminist Survivor with the Eyes of a Child," *New York Times*, July 4, 2000, where Jordan argues that "childhood is the first, inescapable political situation each of us had to negotiate."

8. June Jordan, *Civil Wars: Observations from the Front Lines of America* (New York: Touchstone, 1995), xxi–xxii.

9. William Boelhower, *Immigrant Autobiography in the United States: Four Versions of the Italian American Self* (Verona, Italy: Essedue, 1982), 29, quoted in Sau-ling Cynthia Wong, "Immigrant Autobiography: Some Questions of Definition and Approach," in *Women, Autobiography, Theory: A Reader*, ed. Sidonie Smith and Julia Watson (Madison: University of Wisconsin Press, 1998), 299.

10. June Jordan, *Soldier: A Poet's Childhood* (New York: Basic Civitas Books, 2000), 39, 66. Subsequent references will be noted parenthetically in the text.

11. See Robert Wuthnow, *American Mythos: Why Our Best Efforts to Be a Better Nation Fall Short* (Princeton, NJ: Princeton University Press, 2006).

12. Jordan, "For My American Family," in *Technical Difficulties*, 5–6.

13. This essay provides many of *Soldier*'s memories. Other stories that appear in both essay and memoir include those in which her father spends hours setting up a still-life photograph of a banana, avocado, and antique Chinese vase in search of beauty; makes irritated calls to municipal offices when the garbage is uncollected; slices coconuts or other tropical fruits with a machete while her mother looks on in "head-shaking dismay," chiding, "'Why now you have to act up like a monkey chaser, eh?'" (Jordan, "For My American Family," 5). See also *Soldier*, 125–128, 149.

14. For instance, the Pharisees represent the hard ground. The twelve disciples, especially Peter, represent the rocky ground. Rich men of high office who know the truth but fail to act, like Herod and Pilate, are considered thorny ground. Most of the women in Mark fall in this fourth category: people who hear "the Word" through faith, which brings them into a new and restored sense of community. For instance, take the faithful women found at the cross or tomb, or those who come for healing. See

Christopher D. Marshall, *Faith as a Theme in Mark's Narrative* (Cambridge: Cambridge University Press, 1989).

15. During the Great Migration of the early twentieth century, the influx of black people in northern cities, such as Chicago, Detroit, New York, and Philadelphia, was accompanied by the rise of sects and cults, whose poor and working-class congregations rejected traditional Christianity in favor of militancy, race superiority, or, as in the case of Father Divine, race neutrality. Wilson Jeremiah Moses, "Chosen Peoples of the Metropolis: Black Muslims, Black Jews, and Others," in West and Glaude, *African American Religious Thought*. See also Juan Williams and Quinton Dixie, "Black Gods in the City," in *This Far by Faith: Stories from the African-American Religious Experience* (New York: Amistad, 2003).

16. See Beryl Satter, "Marcus Garvey, Father Divine, and the Gender Politic of Race Difference and Race Neutrality," in West and Glaude, *African American Religious Thought*, 573, 581.

17. Houston A. Baker Jr., *Blues, Ideology, and Afro-American Literature: A Vernacular Theory* (Chicago: University of Chicago Press, 1984), 224.

18. Ibid., 230. Of course, the myth of progress has been associated with train imagery since the nineteenth century. As James Alan McPherson writes in *Railroad*, nineteenth-century capitalists and "captains of industry" praised the locomotive as a sign of progress, while American writers, such as Herman Melville, Nathaniel Hawthorne, Henry Thoreau, and Emily Dickinson, famously issued more adverse responses. However, "to a third group of people," McPherson writes, "those not bound by the assumptions of either business or classical traditions in art, the shrill whistle might have spoken of new possibilities. These were the backwoodsmen and Africans and recent immigrants." James Alan McPherson and Miller Williams, eds., *Railroad: Trains and Train People in American Culture* (New York: Random House, 1976), 6, quoted in Houston A. Baker Jr., "Belief, Theory, and Blues: Notes for a Post-Structuralist Criticism of Afro-American Literature," in *African American Literary Theory: A Reader*, ed. Winston Napier (New York: New York University Press, 2000), 236.

19. June Jordan, "For My American Family," 8.

20. Charles Olson, *Proprioception* (San Francisco: Four Seasons Foundation, 1965), 2, quoted in Jane Creighton, "Writing War, Writing Memory," in *Still Seeking an Attitude: Critical Reflections on the Work of June Jordan*, ed. Valerie Kinloch and Margret Grebowicz (Lanham, MD: Lexington Books, 2004), 224.

21. See June Jordan, *Living Room: New Poems* (New York: Thunder's Mouth Press, 1985). The essay collection *Moving towards Home: Political Essays* (London: Virago Press, 1989) embodies a similar concept, as do the poems "Moving towards Home," in *Living Room*, 132–142, and "Notes towards Home," in *Directed by Desire: The Collected Poems of June Jordan*, ed. Jan Heller Levi and Sara Miles (Port Townsend, WA: Copper Canyon Press, 2007), 392.

22. Davies, *Black Women*.

23. Audre Lorde, *Zami: A New Spelling of My Name* (Trumansburg, NY: Crossing Press, 1982), 31.

24. Michelle M. Wright, *Becoming Black: Creating Identity in the African Diaspora* (Durham, NC: Duke University Press, 2004), 161.

25. Sharon Patricia Holland, "'Which Me Will Survive': Audre Lorde and the Development of a Black Feminist Ideology," *Critical Matrix* 4 (March 1988): 2–30.

26. Rich, *Directed by Desire*, xxi.

27. See Glaude, *Exodus!*

28. Mostern, *Autobiography and Black Identity Politics*, 24–25. For a discussion of black male fiction writers who also challenge the militant masculinity of the Black Power era, see Roland Murray, *Our Living Manhood: Literature, Black Power, and Masculine Ideology* (Philadelphia: University of Pennsylvania Press, 2006).

29. June Jordan, "Waking Up in the Middle of Some American Dreams," in *Technical Difficulties*, 22.

30. June Jordan, "Black Studies: Bringing Back the Person," in *Moving towards Home*, 21–22. For a similar, humanist view of black social-justice struggles, see Singh, introduction to *Black Is a Country*, 2.

31. S. Smith and Watson, *Reading Autobiography*, 124.

32. June Jordan, "Old Stories: New Lives," in *Moving towards Home*, 81.

33. For a discussion of the development of black children's and young-adult literature since the first publication for black youth, *Joy* (1887), see Dianne Johnson-Feelings, "Children's and Young Adult Literature," in *Oxford Companion to African American Literature*, ed. William Andrews, Frances Smith Foster, and Trudier Harris (New York: Oxford University Press, 1997), 134–136.

34. Richard Flynn, "'Affirmative Acts': Language, Childhood, and Power in June Jordan's Cross-Writing," in Kinloch and Grebowicz, *Still Seeking an Attitude*, 125.

35. Kaavonia Hinton-Johnson, "Taking Children Seriously," in Kinloch and Grebowicz, *Still Seeking an Attitude*, 148–149.

36. Critics applauded the novel's aesthetics and social agenda, naming it a finalist for a National Book Award and awarding Jordan the Prix de Rome in Environmental Design at the American Academy in Rome. African American parents, however, waged fervent campaigns to ban the book for fear that the pedagogical use of Black English would lead to educational disaster.

37. See June Jordan, "Problems of Language in a Democratic State," in *Moving towards Home*, 126–134.

38. June Jordan, "For the Sake of People's Poetry: Walt Whitman and the Rest of Us," in *Passion: New Poems, 1977–1980* (Boston: Beacon Press, 1980), xiii.

39. Quoted in Malcolm Cowley, introduction to Walt Whitman, *Walt Whitman's "Leaves of Grass": The First (1855) Edition* (New York: Viking, 1959), xxix.

40. Jordan, "For the Sake of People's Poetry," xiv, xiii.

41. Ibid., xiv.

42. Ezra Greenspan, ed., *Walt Whitman and the American Reader* (Cambridge: Cambridge University Press, 1990), 110.

43. Whitman, *Walt Whitman's "Leaves of Grass,"* 385–386.

44. June Jordan, "Can I Get a Witness," in *Technical Difficulties*, 219; June Jordan, "Declaration of Independence I Would Just as Soon Not Have," in *Moving towards Home*, 66.

45. Roland Bleiker, "Discourse and Human Agency," *Contemporary Political Theory* 2 (2003): 25–47.

46. S. Smith and Watson, *Reading Autobiography*, 103.

47. Ed Folsom, "Appearing in Print: Illustrations of the Self in *Leaves of Grass*," in *The Cambridge Companion to Walt Whitman*, ed. Ezra Greenspan (Cambridge: Cambridge University Press, 1995).

48. For a discussion of how the values that inspired immigrant striving and success are undermined by realities of life in the United States, see Mary Waters, *Black Identities: West Indian Immigrant Dreams and American Realities* (Cambridge, MA: Harvard University Press, 1999).

49. June Jordan, "The Mountain and the Man Who Was Not God: An Essay on the Life and Ideas of Dr. Martin Luther King, Jr.," in *Technical Difficulties*, 107.

50. June Jordan, "Update on Martin Luther King, Jr., and the Best of My Heart," in *Some of Us*, 44.

51. June Jordan, "South Africa: Bringing It All Back Home," in *Moving towards Home*, 116.

52. June Jordan, "Waiting for a Taxi," in *Technical Difficulties*, 164.

53. Adrienne Rich, foreword to *Directed by Desire: The Collected Poems of June Jordan*, ed. Jan Heller Levi and Sara Miles (Port Townsend, WA: Copper Canyon Press, 2007), xxiii.

54. Creighton, "Writing War, Writing Memory," 253.

55. Margret Grebowicz, "Beyond 'Orientation': On Sex, Poetry, and the Violability of Children," in Kinloch and Grebowicz, *Still Seeking an Attitude*, 168.

56. Jordan, quoted in Tom Terrell, "June Swoon: Reflections of a Poet and Activist as a Young Girl," *Vibe*, September 2000.

57. Adrienne Torf, "Remembering June Jordan," *Women's Review of Books*, October 2002, 15.

58. Jordan's first cousin, Valerie Orridge, who was raised in the Jordan household along with June and is the "Valerie" mentioned throughout *Soldier*, remembers life quite differently. In cooperation with an unauthorized biography, Orridge denies that Mildred Jordan committed suicide or that Granville Jordan beat his daughter. See Valerie Kinloch, *June Jordan: Her Life and Letters* (Westport, CT: Praeger, 2006), 7–29.

59. Barbara Johnson, "My Monster/My Self," *Diacritics* 12, no. 2 (Summer 1982).

60. Jordan, "One Minus One Minus One," in Levi and Miles, *Directed by Desire*, 202.

61. Lee, "A Feminist Survivor."

62. June Jordan, "In Our Hands," in *Moving towards Home*, 174.

63. June Jordan, "Many Rivers to Cross," in *Moving towards Home*, 124–125.

64. Jordan, "In Our Hands," 174.

65. Patricia Hill Collins, "Black Women and Motherhood," in *Black Feminist Thought: Knowledge, Consciousness, and the Politics of Empowerment* (New York: Routledge, 1990), 117.

66. Harris-Perry, *Sister Citizen*, 230.

67. Jordan, *Some of Us*, 374.

68. Perkins, *Autobiography as Activism*, 14.

69. Angela Davis and Kathleen Cleaver, "Rekindling the Flame," a dialogue moderated by Diane Weathers and Tara Roberts, *Essence*, May 1996, 160, quoted in Perkins, *Autobiography as Activism*, 14.

70. There are other similarities: an episodic structure, with individual portraits and descriptions of events; an absent mother; a brutal paternal figure (father for Jordan, grandfather for Gorky); a loving grandmother. And most importantly, "leaving home at 12, self-cultivation through reading and self-reliance by necessity." Jordan writes: "I have always considered Maxim Gorky's *My Childhood* a necessity. It has been to me [indecipherable] universal, authentic, saturated in the mysteries and the violence that I know to be the very soul of my own childhood and perhaps of any childhood." Jordan, handwritten draft of book proposal and letter to Harper & Row, 1979, June Jordan Papers, 1936–2002, Schlesinger Library, Radcliffe Institute, Harvard University, Cambridge, MA, Box 51.1. It is interesting to note that Jordan annually assigned this memoir in literature courses at UC Berkeley.

71. See Gregory Castle, *Reading the Modernist Bildungsroman* (Gainesville: University Press of Florida, 2006); and Jed Espy, *Unseasonable Youth: Modernism, Colonialism, and the Fiction of Development* (New York: Oxford University Press, 2012).

72. Jordan, introduction to *Civil Wars*, xx.

73. Jordan, "Waking Up in the Middle of Some American Dreams," 18.

74. Thulani Davis, "June Jordan, 1936–2002," *Village Voice*, June 25, 2002, quoted in Bobbi Ciriza Houtchens, "A Great Loss; A Treasured Legacy," *English Journal* 92, no. 3 (January 2003).

75. Jordan, *Some of Us*, 79.

Chapter 4
Storytelling as Diasporic Consciousness

1. Boelhower, *Immigrant Autobiography*. For a discussion of how postwar immigrant narratives by non-European writers complicate this model, see Wong, "Immigrant Autobiography."

2. Bharati Mukherjee, "Immigrant Writing: Changing the Contours of a National Literature," *American Literary History* 23 no. 3 (Fall 2011).

3. Edwidge Danticat, "Another Country," in *Create Dangerously: The Immigrant Artist at Work* (Princeton, NJ: Princeton University Press, 2010), 107–113.

4. For a discussion of why Haiti continues to be the poorest country in the Western

hemisphere, see Laurent Dubois, *Haiti: The Aftershocks of History* (New York: Metropolitan Books/Henry Holt, 2012).

5. Danticat, "Another Country," 108.

6. See Glaude, *In a Shade of Blue*; Harris-Perry, *Sister Citizen*; Iton, *In Search of the Black Fantastic*; and Woods, *In the Wake of Katrina*.

7. Glaude, *In a Shade of Blue*, 129.

8. Iton, *In Search of the Black Fantastic*, 285.

9. See Jared Sexton, *Amalgamation Schemes: Antiblackness and the Critique of Multiculturalism* (Minneapolis: University of Minnesota Press, 2008); Frank B. Wilderson III, *Incognegro: A Memoir of Exile and Apartheid* (Cambridge, MA: South End Press, 2008); Frank B. Wilderson III, *Red, White, and Black: Cinema and the Structure of U.S. Antagonisms* (Durham, NC: Duke University Press, 2010); and Sadiya Hartman, *Scenes of Subjection: Terror, Slavery, and Self-Making in Nineteenth-Century America* (New York: Oxford University Press, 1997). Other works that have a similarly pessimistic view of race relations include Derrick Bell, *Faces at the Bottom of the Well: The Permanence of Racism* (New York: Basic Books, 1993); and Kennedy, *Persistence of the Color Line*.

10. Iton, *In Search of the Black Fantastic*, 195.

11. Ibid., 196.

12. Ibid., 257.

13. Ibid., 199.

14. Antje Lindenmeyer, "The Rewriting of Home: Autobiographies by Daughters of Immigrants," *Women's Studies International Forum* 24, no. 3/4 (2001): 424.

15. Iton, *In Search of the Black Fantastic*, 202–203.

16. S. Smith and Watson, *Reading Autobiography*, 282.

17. Wright, *Becoming Black*, 141.

18. Iton, *In Search of the Black Fantastic*, 226. For a discussion of the continuities between slave narratives and contemporary black political autobiographies/memoirs, see Perkins, *Autobiography*.

19. Amy Wilentz, "The Other Side of the Water," *New York Times*, October 8, 2010.

20. Edwidge Danticat, "Create Dangerously: The Immigrant Artist at Work," in *Create Dangerously*, 5.

21. Danticat, "Create Dangerously," 14–15.

22. Quoted in Opal Palmer Adisa, "Up Close and Personal: Edwidge Danticat on Haitian Identity and the Writer's Life," *African American Review* 43, no. 2–3 (Summer/Fall 2009): 349, 352.

23. Quashie, *Black Women*, 5, quoted in Griffin, "That the Mothers May Soar," 337.

24. Disch, *Hannah Arendt*, 142.

25. Ibid., 73.

26. Danticat, reading of *Brother, I'm Dying* (Karibu Books, Washington DC, CSPAN Book TV, September 22, 2007).

27. Danticat, *Brother, I'm Dying* (New York: Knopf, 2007), 186. Subsequent references will be noted parenthetically in the text.

28. Danticat, "Create Dangerously," 7, 12.

29. Ibid., 11.

30. Ibid., 8.

31. Ibid., 19.

32. Jacques Derrida, *The Work of Mourning*, ed. and trans. Pascale-Anne Brault (Chicago: University of Chicago Press, 2003).

33. Mukherjee, "Immigrant Writing," 688. See also Dubois, *Haiti*.

34. John Beverly, "The Margin at the Center: On *Testimonio* (Testimonial Narrative)," in *De/Colonizing the Subject: The Politics of Gender in Women's Autobiography*, ed. Sidonie Smith and Julia Watson (Minneapolis: University of Minnesota Press, 1992), 97, quoted in S. Smith and Watson, *Reading Autobiography*, 282.

35. Lindenmeyer, "Rewriting of Home," 423.

36. Michèle Aina Barale, "Reviews and Responses: *Zami: A New Spelling of My Name* and *Sister Outsider* by Audre Lorde," *Frontiers: A Journal of Women's Studies* 8, no. 1 (1984): 71; and Nellie Y. McKay, "A Painful Growth into Selfhood," *Callaloo* 24 (Spring–Summer 1985).

37. Claudia Tate, ed., *Black Women Writers at Work* (New York: Continuum International, 1984), 115.

38. Martha St. Jean, "Genius: A Talk with Edwidge Danticat," *World Post*, November 23, 2009, http://www.huffingtonpost.com/martha-st-jean/genius-a-talk-with-edwidg_b_295040.html.

39. Danticat, "Create Dangerously," 7.

40. Danticat, "Daughters of Memory," in *Create Dangerously*, 60.

41. Iton, *In Search of the Black Fantastic*, 198.

42. Roseanna L. Dufault, "Edwidge Danticat's Pursuit of Justice in *Brother, I'm Dying*," *Journal of Haitian Studies* 16, no. 1 (2010): 95.

43. Iton, *In Search of the Black Fantastic*, 257.

44. Wright, *Becoming Black*, 141.

45. See also Samantha Pinto, *Difficult Diasporas: The Transnational Feminist Aesthetic of the Black Atlantic* (New York: New York University Press, 2013).

46. Mukherjee, "Immigrant Writing," 691.

47. Wright, *Becoming Black*, 179.

48. Ibid., 2.

Chapter 5
Cultivating Liberatory Joy

Thanks to playwright Eisa Davis for providing a copy of *Angela's Mixtape* expressly for analysis in this book.

1. Iton, *In Search of the Black Fantastic*, 250.

2. Ards, "Organizing the Hip-Hop Generation," 312.

3. Cobb, *To the Break of Dawn*, 130.

4. Gwendolyn Pough, *Check It While I Wreck It: Black Womanhood, Hip-Hop Culture, and the Public Sphere* (Boston: Northeastern University Press, 2004), 104.

5. Eisa Davis, "Sexism and the Art of Feminist Hip-Hop Maintenance," in *To Be Real: Telling the Truth and Changing the Face of Feminism*, ed. Rebecca Walker (New York: Anchor Books, 1995), 137.

6. Griffin, "Conflict and Chorus," 114.

7. Raiford, "Restaging Revolution," 224.

8. Ibid., 223.

9. Angela Davis, "Afro Images: Politics, Fashion, and Nostalgia," in *Picturing Us: African American Identity in Photography*, ed. Deborah Willis (New York: New Press, 1994), 174.

10. Raiford, "Restaging Revoluation," 243.

11. Raiford, "Restaging Revolution," 223.

12. Gina Dent, ed., *Black Popular Culture: A Project by Michele Wallace* (Seattle: Bay Press, 1992), 85–86.

13. Iton, *In Search of the Black Fantastic*, 28, 30-80.

14. Ras Baraka, "Black Youth," 372.

15. Angela Y. Davis, "Black Nationalism: The Sixties and the Nineties," in Dent, *Black Popular Culture*.

16. Ibid., 372.

17. Baraka, "Black Youth," 372. Ulen calls for a re-creation of civil society as well: "What formal structures (as formal as family configurations) do you have in place for us? For your grandchildren? Will you help us rebuild the extended family—the one I remember from my childhood—in our community today?" Eisa Ulen laments the collapse of black civil society and asks for help from elders in re-creating it, with little irony about the fact that those elders created their own institutions. Ulen, "What Happened to Your Generation's Promise of 'Love and Revolution'? A Letter to Angela Davis," in *Step into a World*, 403.

18. Eisa Davis, "Found in Translation: The Emergence of Hip-Hop Theater," in *Total Chaos: The Art and Aesthetics of Hip-Hop*, ed. Jeff Chang (New York: Basic Civitas Books, 2006), 71-72.

19. Marc Bamuthi Joseph et al., "From the Dope Spot to Broadway: A Roundtable on Hip-Hop Theatre, Dance, and Performance," in Chang, *Total Chaos*.

20. Iton, *In Search of the Black Fantastic*, 250.

21. Michael Feingold, "The Decade's Best Theater: From Undervalued Plays and Undervalued Companies, 10 Years of Freewheeling Joy," *Village Voice*, December 22, 2009.

22. Eisa Davis, e-mail to author, February 9, 2015; see http://herbalpertawards.org/artist/2012/eisa-davis and http://www.villagevoice.com/obies/2013.

23. E. Davis, "Found in Translation," 75.

24. Iton, *In Search of the Black Fantastic*, 289.

25. E. Davis, "Found in Translation," 74.

26. Eisa Davis, *Angela's Mixtape*, unpublished screenplay, 2009, in author's possession, 8. Subsequent references will be noted parenthetically in the text.

27. Alexis Soloski, *"Angela's Mixtape* and *Beowulf:* A Thousand Years of Baggage," *Village Voice*, April 15, 2009.

28. E. Davis, "Found in Translation," 74.

29. Morgan, *Chickenheads*, 26. For a discussion of the break as a site of deliberation and debate, see also Chang, *Total Chaos*, 84.

30. E. Davis, "Found in Translation," 73.

31. Powell, introduction, in *Step into a World*, 10.

32. Raiford, "Restaging Revolution," 242–245. See also Neal, *Soul Babies.*

33. Henry Louis Gates Jr. and Nellie Y. McKay, "Adrienne Kennedy," in *The Norton Anthology of African American Literature*, 2nd ed., ed. Henry Louis Gates Jr. and Nellie McKay (New York: W. W. Norton, 2004), 2196.

34. Amiri Baraka, "The Revolutionary Theatre," in Gates and McKay, *Norton Anthology.*

35. Ibid., 1960–61.

36. Amiri Baraka, "Black Art," in Gates and McKay, *Norton Anthology of African American Literature*, 1943–1944.

37. Sandra L. Richards, "Ntozake Shange, 1948–," in *African American Writers: Profiles of Their Lives and Works; From the 1700s to the Present*, ed. Valerie Smith, Lea Baechler, and A. Walton Litz (New York: Scribner's, 1991), 298; Ntozake Shange, *for colored girls who have considered suicide when the rainbow is enuf* (New York: Bantam Books, 1973), 3.

38. Morgan, *Chickenheads*, 18.

39. Ibid., 19.

40. Robert Nemiroff, foreword to *To Be Young, Gifted and Black: An Informal Autobiography*, by Lorraine Hansberry (New York: Signet, 1969), xviii.

41. Lorraine Hansberry, *To Be Young, Gifted and Black: An Informal Autobiography*, adapted by Robert Nemiroff (New York: Signet, 1969), 51–52.

42. Ben Keppel, *The Work of Democracy: Ralph Bunche, Kenneth B. Clark, Lorraine Hansberry, and the Cultural Politics of Race* (Cambridge, MA: Harvard University Press, 1986), 202, quoted in Joy L. Abell, "African/American: Lorraine Hansberry's *Les Blancs* and the American Civil Rights Movement," *African American Review* 35, no. 3 (Fall 2001): 468.

43. Hansberry, *To Be Young*, 51.

44. Nemiroff, foreword to Hansberry, *To Be Young*, xx.

45. Hansberry, *To Be Young*, 5–6.

46. James Baldwin, "An Open Letter to My Sister, Miss Angela Davis," *New York Review of Books*, January 7, 1971.

47. Glaude, *Is It Nation Time?*, 4.

48. Ulen, "What Happened," 401.

49. Ibid.

50. Ibid.

51. Baker, "Critical Memory"; Glaude, *In a Shade of Blue*.

52. Ulen, "What Happened," 402.

53. Morgan, *Chickenheads*, 22.

54. Frantz Fanon, "On National Culture," in *The Wretched of the Earth*, trans. Richard Philcox and ed. Francois Maspero (New York: Grove Press, 2004), 145.

55. Ulen, "What Happened," 402-403.

56. Morgan, *Chickenheads*, 22.

57. E. Davis, "Found in Translation," 76.

58. Daniel T. Politoske and Martin Werner, *Music*, 4th ed. (Englewood Cliffs, NJ: Prentice Hall, 1988), 419.

59. Nussbaum, *Political Emotions*.

60. Eisa Davis, e-mail to author, February 11, 2015.

61. See Bay et al., *Intellectual History*; and Nussbaum, *Political Emotions*.

62. Morgan, *Chickenheads*, 25.

63. Ibid., 26.

64. June Jordan, "The Mountain and the Man Who Was Not God: An Essay on the Life and Ideas of Dr. Martin Luther King, Jr.," in *Technical Difficulties*, 104, 116.

65. Hansberry, *To Be Young*, 116.

66. Iton, *In Search of the Black Fantastic*, 289.

67. Angela Davis, introduction to *Narrative of the Life of Frederick Douglass, an American Slave, Written by Himself: A New Critical Edition* (New York: City Lights, 2009), 30-31.

Epilogue

1. See V. May, "Under-Theorized and Under-Taught"; and Vivian May, *Anna Julia Cooper, Visionary Black Feminist: A Critical Introduction* (New York: Routledge, 2007).

2. Brittney Cooper, "A Response to Ta-Nehisi Coates: Why Black Women Are Overlooked—Again," Salon.com, November 6, 2014, http://www.salon.com/2014/11 /06/black_women_overlooked_again_a_response_to_ta_nehisi_coates_on_ida_b_ wells/.

3. I am indebted to Brittney Cooper and an online Facebook thread she hosted for this discussion, October 8, 2014.

4. Isabel Wilkerson, "The Late Jim Crow," *New York Times*, June 15, 1997.

5. Review, *Library Journal*, July 1996, 126.

6. Lois Elfman, "Author Janet Mock Propels Transgender Conversations in Academia," *Diverse*, April 24, 2014, http://diverseeducation.com/article/63291/.

7. Ibid.

8. Racial distribution of SMU enrollment: Hispanic, 1,081; Asian, 695; Black/ African American, 662; American Indian/Alaska Native, 38; Native Hawaiian/Pacific Islander, 16; two or more races, 242. Minorities as a percentage of total enrollment, 25; minorities as a percentage of undergraduates, 27.5.

9. At least since Allan Bloom's "Closing of the American Mind" twenty-five years ago, critics have complained that colleges and universities are being overtaken and corrupted by liberalism. Alexander E. Hooke, "Academia: Liberal Bastion or Corporate Dream?," *Baltimore Sun*, July 12, 2011.

10. Lane, "Hannah Arendt."

11. Bakari Kitwana, *The Hip Hop Generation: Young Blacks and the Crisis in African-American Culture* (New York: Basic Civitas Books, 2002), xiii.

12. See Charles Johnson, "The End of Black American Narrative"; and K. Warren, *What Was African American Literature?*

13. Steve D'Arcy, "The Rise of the Post-New Left Political Vocabulary," *Public Autonomy Project* (blog), January 27, 2014, http://publicautonomy.org/2014/01/27/the-rise-of-the-post-new-left-political-vocabulary/.

Bibliography

Archives

Digital Collections, Beinecke Rare Book & Manuscript Library, Yale University, New Haven, CT.

June Jordan Papers, 1936–2002, Arthur and Elizabeth Schlesinger Library on the History of Women in America, Radcliffe Institute for Advanced Study, Harvard University, Cambridge, MA.

Hiphop Archive & Research Institute, Hutchins Center for African and African American Research, Harvard University, Cambridge, MA.

Primary Sources

Alexander, Elizabeth. *The Light of the World: A Memoir.* New York: Grand Central, 2015.

Andrews, William L. *Sisters of the Spirit: Three Black Women's Autobiographies of the Nineteenth Century.* Bloomington: Indiana University Press, 1986.

Angelou, Maya. *I Know Why the Caged Bird Sings.* Edited by Joanne Braxton. New York: Oxford University Press, 1991.

Augustine, Bishop of Hippo. *Confessions.* Edited by James J. O'Donnell. New York: Oxford University Press, 1992.

Baldwin, James. "An Open Letter to My Sister, Miss Angela Davis." *New York Review of Books,* January 7, 1971.

Bandele, Asha. *The Prisoner's Wife: A Memoir.* New York: Scribner's, 1999.

Baraka, Amiri. "Black Art." In Gates and McKay, *Norton Anthology of African American Literature,* 1943–1944.

———. *The Dutchman.* In Gates and McKay, *Norton Anthology of African American Literature,* 1946–1960.

———. "The Revolutionary Theatre." In Gates and McKay, *Norton Anthology of African American Literature,* 1960–1963.

Baraka, Ras. "Black Youth Black Art Black Face—An Address." In Powell, *Step into a World*, 371–373.

Baszile, Jennifer. *The Black Girl Next Door: A Memoir*. New York: Simon & Schuster, 2009.

Bates, Daisy. *The Long Shadow of Little Rock: A Memoir*. Fayetteville: University of Arkansas Press, 1986.

Beals, Melba. *Warriors Don't Cry: A Searing Memoir of the Battle to Integrate Little Rock's Central High*. New York: Washington Square Press, 1994.

———. *Warriors Don't Cry: A Searing Memoir of the Battle to Integrate Little Rock's Central High*. Abridged edition. New York: Simon Pulse, 1995.

Betts, Reginald Dwayne. *A Question of Freedom: A Memoir of Survival, Learning, and Coming of Age in Prison*. New York: Avery, 2009.

Bray, Rosemary. "Illumination." Sermon delivered at the Fourth Universalist Society in the City of New York, New York, October 23, 2011.

———. *Unafraid of the Dark: A Memoir*. New York: Anchor Books, 1998.

Brooks, Gwendolyn. *Report from Part One*. Detroit: Broadside Press, 1972.

Brown, Elaine. *A Taste of Power: A Black Woman's Story*. New York: Anchor Books/ Doubleday, 1992.

Brown, Elsa Barkeley, Deborah King, and Barbara Ransby. "African American Women in Defense of Ourselves." *New York Times*, November 17, 1991.

Carey, Lorene. *Black Ice*. New York: Knopf, 1991.

Chambers, Veronica. *Mama's Girl*. New York: Riverhead Books, 1996.

Chin, Staceyann. *The Other Side of Paradise: A Memoir*. New York: Scribner's, 2009.

Common, with Adam Bradley. *One Day It'll All Make Sense: A Memoir*. New York: Atria Books, 2011.

Danticat, Edwidge. *Breath, Eyes, Memory*. New York: Vintage, 1994.

———. *Brother, I'm Dying*. New York: Knopf, 2007.

———. *Create Dangerously: The Immigrant Artist at Work*. Princeton, NJ: Princeton University Press, 2010.

———. *The Dew Breaker*. New York: Vintage, 2004.

———. *The Farming of Bones*. New York: Sohon, 1998.

———. *Krik? Krak!* New York: Vintage, 1996.

———. "Storybook Ending." *O: The Oprah Magazine*, February 2009, 163.

Davis, Angela. *Angela Davis: An Autobiography*. New York: International Publishers, 1974.

Davis, Eisa. *Angela's Mixtape*. Unpublished screenplay, 2009, in author's possession.

———. "Sexism and the Art of Feminist Hip-Hop Maintenance." In *To Be Real: Telling the Truth and Changing the Face of Feminism*, ed. Rebecca Walker, 127–141. New York: Anchor Books, 1995.

Davis, Thulani. *My Confederate Kinfolk: A Twenty-First Century Freedwoman Discovers Her Roots*. New York: Basic Civitas Books, 2006.

Derricotte, Toi. *The Black Notebooks: An Interior Journey*. New York: W. W. Norton, 1997.

Diawara, Manthia. *In Search of Africa*. Cambridge, MA: Harvard University Press, 1996.

Dickerson, Debra J. *An American Story*. New York: Pantheon Books, 2000.

Dillard, Annie. *An American Childhood.* New York: Harper & Row, 1987.

Douglass, Frederick. *Narrative of the Life of Frederick Douglass, an American Slave, Written by Himself.* 1845. Edited by Angela Y. Davis. San Francisco: Open Media Series/City Lights Books, 2010.

Du Bois, W. E. B. *The Souls of Black Folk.* 1903. Edited by Farah Jasmine Griffin. New York: Barnes & Noble Classics, 2003.

Due, Tananarive, and Patricia Stephens Due. *Freedom in the Family: A Mother-Daughter Memoir of the Fight for Civil Rights.* New York: Ballantine Books, 2003.

Ellison, Ralph. "The World and the Jug." In *The Collected Essays of Ralph Ellison,* edited by John F. Callahan, 155–188. New York: Modern Library, 1995.

Equiano, Olaudah. *The Interesting Narrative of the Life of Olaudah Equiano, or Gustavus Vassa, the African, Written by Himself.* 1789. Edited by Vincent Carretta. New York: Penguin Books, 1995.

The Ernest Green Story. TV movie. Directed by Eric Laneuville. Burbank: Walt Disney Television, 1993.

Franklin, Benjamin. *The Autobiography of Benjamin Franklin.* Edited by Leonard W. Lararee et al. New Haven, CT: Yale University Press, 1964.

Free Angela and All Political Prisoners. DVD. Directed by Shola Lynch. New York: Realside Productions, 2012.

Gates, Henry Louis, Jr. *Colored People: A Memoir.* New York: Knopf, 1994.

Haizlip, Shirlee Taylor. *The Sweeter the Juice: A Family Memoir in Black and White.* New York: Simon & Schuster, 1994.

Hansberry, Lorraine. "The Negro Writer and His Roots: Toward a New Romanticism." Speech at the Black Writers' Conference, New York, March 1, 1959.

———. *A Raisin in the Sun.* 1959. Reprint, New York: Vintage Books, 1994.

———. *To Be Young, Gifted and Black: An Informal Autobiography.* Adapted by Robert Nemiroff. New York: Signet, 1969.

Harrison, Kathryn. *The Kiss: A Secret Life.* New York: William Morrow, 1998.

hooks, bell. *Bone Black: Memories of Girlhood.* New York: Henry Holt, 1996.

Hurston, Zora Neale. *Dust Tracks on a Road: An Autobiography.* 2nd ed. Edited by Robert Hemenway. Urbana: University of Illinois Press, 1984.

Jacobs, Harriet. *Incidents in the Life of a Slave Girl, Written by Herself.* Edited by Jean Fagan Yellin. Cambridge, MA: Harvard University Press, 1987.

Jordan, June. *Affirmative Acts: Political Essays.* New York: Anchor Books/Doubleday, 1998.

———. *Civil Wars: Observations from the Front Lines of America.* New York: Touchstone, 1995.

———. *Directed by Desire: The Collected Poems of June Jordan.* Edited by Jan Heller Levi and Sara Miles. Port Townsend, WA: Copper Canyon Press, 2007.

———. *Living Room: New Poems.* New York: Thunder's Mouth Press, 1985.

———. *Moving towards Home: Political Essays.* London: Virago Press, 1989.

———. *On Call: Political Essays.* Boston: South End Press, 1985.

———. *Passion: New Poems, 1977–1980.* Boston: Beacon Press, 1980.

———. *Soldier: A Poet's Childhood.* New York: Basic Civitas Books, 2000.

———. *Some of Us Did Not Die: New and Selected Essays of June Jordan*. New York: Basic Civitas Books, 2002.

———. *Technical Difficulties: African American Notes on the State of the Union*. New York: Vintage Books/Random House, 1992.

Karr, Mary. *The Liar's Club: A Memoir*. New York: Penguin Books, 1995.

Kennedy, Adrienne. *Funnyhouse of the Negro*. 1969. New York: Samuel French, 2011.

———. *People Who Led to My Plays*. New York: Theatre Communications Groups, 1996.

LaNier, Carlotta Walls, with Lisa Frazier Page. *A Mighty Long Way: My Journey to Justice at Little Rock Central High*. New York: Ballantine Books, 2009.

Lee, Chana Kai. *For Freedom's Sake: The Life of Fannie Lou Hamer*. Urbana: University of Illinois Press, 1999.

Little Rock Central High: 50 Years Later. DVD. Directed by Brent Renaud and Craig Renaud. New York: HBO Studios, 2007.

Lorde, Audre. *Sister Outsider: Essays and Speeches*. Trumansburg, NY: Crossing Press, 1984.

———. *Zami: A New Spelling of My Name*. Trumansburg, NY: Crossing Press, 1982.

McCourt, Frank. *Angela's Ashes: A Memoir*. New York: Scribner's, 1996.

McDowell, Deborah E. *Leaving Pipe Shop: Memories of Kin*. New York: Scribner's, 1996.

McMillan, Terri. *Waiting to Exhale*. New York: Viking, 1992.

Moody, Anne. *Coming of Age in Mississippi: An Autobiography*. New York: Laurel/Dell, 1968.

Moore, Wes. *The Other Wes Moore: One Name, Two Fates*. New York: Spiegel and Grau, 2010.

Morgan, Joan. *When Chickenheads Come Home to Roost: My Life as a Hip-Hop Feminist*. New York: Simon & Schuster, 1999.

Motley, Constance Baker. *Equal Justice under Law: An Autobiography*. New York: Farrar, Straus and Giroux, 1998.

Murray, Pauli. *Pauli Murray: The Autobiography of a Black Activist, Feminist, Lawyer, Priest, and Poet*. Knoxville: University of Tennessee Press, 1989. Originally published as *Song in a Weary Throat: An American Pilgrimage*. New York: Harper & Row, 1987.

Obama, Barack. *Dreams from My Father: A Story of Race and Inheritance*. New York: Three Rivers Press, 1995.

Prodigy, with Laura Checkoway. *My Infamous Life: The Autobiography of Mobb Deep's Prodigy*. New York: Simon & Schuster. 2011.

Ransby, Barbara. *Ella Baker and the Black Freedom Movement: A Radical Democratic Vision*. Chapel Hill: University of North Carolina Press, 2002.

———. *Eslanda: The Large and Unconventional Life of Mrs. Paul Robeson*. New Haven, CT: Yale University Press, 2014.

Remnick, David. *The Bridge: The Life and Rise of Barack Obama*. New York: Knopf, 2010.

Rousseau, Jean-Jacques. *Confessions*. Translated by Angela Scholar. New York: Oxford University Press, 2000.

Shakur, Assata. *Assata: An Autobiography*. London: Zed Books, 1987.

Shange, Ntozake. *for colored girls who have considered suicide when the rainbow is enuf*. New York: Bantam Books, 1973.

Staples, Brent. *Parallel Time: Growing Up in Black and White*. New York: Pantheon Books, 1995.

Tarpley, Natasha. *Girl in the Mirror: Three Generations of Black Women in Motion*. Boston: Beacon Press, 1998.

Taulbert, Clifton L. *Once upon a Time When We Were Colored*. Tulsa: Council Oak Books, 1989.

Ulen, Eisa. "What Happened to Your Generation's Promise of 'Love and Revolution'? A Letter to Angela Davis." In Powell, *Step into a World*, 401–403.

Walker, Alice. *In Search of Our Mothers' Gardens: Womanist Prose*. San Diego: Harvest, 1983.

Walker, David. *Walker's Appeal, in Four Articles; Together with a Preamble, to the Colored Citizens of the World, but in particular, and very expressly, to those of the United States of America, written in Boston, state of Massachusetts, September 28, 1829. Third and Last Edition, with additional notes, corrections &*. In *One Continual Cry: David Walker's Appeal to the Colored Citizens of the World, 1829–1830*, edited by Herbert Aptheker. New York: Humanities Press, 1965.

Whitman, Walt. *Walt Whitman's "Leaves of Grass": The First (1855) Edition*. Edited by Malcolm Cowley. New York: Viking, 1959.

Wolfe, George C. *The Colored Museum: A Play*. New York: Grove Press, 1985.

X, Malcolm. *The Autobiography of Malcolm X*. As told to Alex Haley. New York: Ballantine Books, 1964.

Secondary Sources

Abell, Joy L. "African/American: Lorraine Hansberry's *Les Blancs* and the American Civil Rights Movement." *African American Review* 35, no. 3 (Fall 2001): 459–470.

Adisa, Opal Palmer. "Up Close and Personal: Edwidge Danticat on Haitian Identity and the Writer's Life." *African American Review* 43, no. 2/3 (Summer/Fall 2009): 345–355.

"After Brown, What Next? A Conference to Celebrate *In "Brown"'s Wake: Legacies of America's Educational Landmark*." Harvard University, Cambridge, MA, December 4, 2010.

Alexander, Michelle. *The New Jim Crow: Mass Incarceration in the Age of Colorblindness*. New York: New Press, 2010.

Allen, Danielle S. "Ralph Ellison and the Tragicomedy of Citizenship." *Raritan Quarterly* 23, no. 3 (2004): 56–74.

———. *Talking to Strangers: Anxieties of Citizenship since "Brown v. Board of Education."* Chicago: University of Chicago Press, 2004.

Allen, F. "June Jordan, Poetry for the People: A Revolutionary Blueprint." *Library Journal*, December 1995, 115, 120.

Anderson, Benedict. *Imagined Communities: Reflections on the Origin and Spread of Nationalism*. London: Verso Editions, 1983.

Andrews, William L., ed. *African American Autobiography: A Collection of Critical Essays*. Englewood Cliffs, NJ: Prentice Hall, 1993.

———. "African American Autobiography Criticism: Retrospect and Prospect." In Eakin, *American Autobiography*, 195–215.

———. *To Tell a Free Story: The First Century of Afro-American Autobiography, 1760–1865*. Urbana: University of Illinois Press, 1986.

Appiah, Kwame Anthony. "Battling with Du Bois." Review of *In the Shadow of Du Bois: Afro-Modern Political Thought in America*, by Robert Gooding-Williams. *New York Review of Books*, December 22, 2011.

Ards, Angela. "Down with Feminism." Review of *When Chickenheads Come Home to Roost*, by Joan Morgan. *Women's Review of Books* 17, no. 1 (October 1999): 17.

———. "Organizing the Hip-Hop Generation." In Neal and Forman, *That's the Joint*, 311–323.

———. "Sisters Act: Reflections on the Tyson 'Homecoming Flap.'" *Village Voice*, July 25, 1995, 15.

Arendt, Hannah. *The Human Condition*. Chicago: University of Chicago Press, 1958.

———. "Reflections on Little Rock." *Dissent* 6, no. 1 (Winter 1959): 45–55.

———. "A Reply to Critics." *Dissent* 6, no. 2 (Spring 1960): 179–181.

Baker, Houston A., Jr. "Belief, Theory, and Blues: Notes for a Post-Structuralist Criticism of Afro-American Literature." In *African American Literary Theory: A Reader*, edited by Winston Napier, 224–241. New York: New York University Press, 2000.

———. *Blues, Ideology, and Afro-American Literature: A Vernacular Theory*. Chicago: University of Chicago Press, 1984.

———. "Critical Memory and the Black Public Sphere." In *The Black Public Sphere: A Public Culture Book*, edited by the Black Public Sphere Collective, 7–37. Chicago: University of Chicago Press, 1995.

Barale, Michèle Aina. "Reviews and Responses: *Zami: A New Spelling of My Name* and *Sister Outsider* by Audre Lorde." *Frontiers: A Journal of Women's Studies* 8, no. 1 (1984): 71–73.

Bassard, Katherine Clay. "Gender and Genre: Black Women's Autobiography and the Ideology of Literacy." *African American Review* 26 (1992): 119–129.

———. "Spiritual Autobiography." In *African American Writers*, edited by Valerie A. Smith, Lea Baechler, and A. Walton Litz, 2:697–710. New York: Scribner's, 2001.

———. *Spiritual Interrogations: Culture, Gender, and Community in Early African American Women's Writing*. Princeton, NJ: Princeton University Press, 1999.

Bay, Mia. *To Tell the Truth Freely: The Life of Ida B. Wells*. New York: Hill and Wang, 2010.

Bay, Mia, Farah J. Griffin, Martha S. Jones, and Barbara D. Savage, eds. *Toward an Intellectual History of Black Women*. Chapel Hill: University of North Carolina Press, 2015.

Beale, Frances. "Double Jeopardy: To Be Black and Female." In Cade, *Black Woman*, 90–100.

Beckham, Sue Bridwell. Review of *Song in a Weary Throat: An American Pilgrimage*. *Journal of Southern History* 55, no. 2 (May 1989): 353–354.

Bell, Derrick. *Faces at the Bottom of the Well: The Permanence of Racism*. New York: Basic Books, 1993.

———. *Race, Racism, and American Law*. 2nd ed. Boston: Little, Brown, 1980.

———. *Silent Covenants: "Brown v. Board of Education" and the Unfulfilled Hopes for Racial Reform*. Oxford: Oxford University Press, 2004.

Bell, Joyce M. *The Black Power Movement and American Social Work*. New York: Columbia University Press, 2014.

Bell-Scott, Patricia. "'To Write like Never Before': Pauli Murray's Enduring Yearning." *Journal of Women's History* 14, no. 2 (2000): 58–61.

Bennett, Lerone, Jr. *What Manner of Man: A Biography of Martin Luther King, Jr*. Chicago: Johnson, 1964.

Benstock, Shari, ed. *The Private Self: The Theory and Practice of Women's Autobiographical Writings*. Chapel Hill: University of North Carolina Press, 1988.

Bercovitch, Sacvan. *The Puritan Origins of the American Self*. New Haven, CT: Yale University Press, 1975.

Berg, Allison. "Trauma and Testimony in Black Women's Civil Rights Memoirs: *The Montgomery Bus Boycott and the Women Who Started It, Warriors Don't Cry*, and *From the Mississippi Delta*." *Journal of Women's History* 21, no. 3 (Fall 2009): 84–107.

Berlant, Lauren. *The Female Complaint: The Unfinished Business of Sentimentality in American Culture*. Durham, NC: Duke University Press, 2008.

———. "Intimacy: A Special Issue." *Critical Inquiry* 24, no. 2 (Winter 1998): 281–288.

———. "The Intimate Public Sphere." Introduction to *The Queen of America Goes to Washington City: Essays on Sex and Citizenship*, 1–24. Durham, NC: Duke University Press, 1997.

———. "Life Writing and Intimate Publics: A Conversation with Lauren Berlant." *Biography* 34, no. 1 (2011): 180–186.

Bernstein, Robin. *Racial Innocence: Performing American Childhood from Slavery to Civil Rights*. New York: New York University Press, 2011.

Beverly, John. "The Margin at the Center: On *Testimonio* (Testimonial Narrative)." In S. Smith and Watson, *De/Colonizing the Subject*, 91–114.

Bezusko, Adriane. "Criminalizing Black Motherhood: How the War on Welfare Was Won." *Souls: A Critical Journal of Black Politics, Culture, and Society* 15, no. 1–2 (2013): 39–55.

Black Public Sphere Collective, eds. *The Black Public Sphere: A Public Culture Book*. Chicago: University of Chicago Press, 1995.

Blackett, Richard. Review of *Song in a Weary Throat: An American Pilgrimage*, by Pauli Murray. *Georgia Historical Quarterly* 71, no. 4 (Winter 1987): 753–754.

Bleiker, Roland. "Discourse and Human Agency." *Contemporary Political Theory* 2 (2003): 25–47.

Boelhower, William. *Immigrant Autobiography in the United States: Four Versions of the Italian American Self*. Verona, Italy: Essedue, 1982.

Bohman, James. "The Moral Costs of Political Pluralism: The Dilemmas of Difference and Equality in Arendt's 'Reflections on Little Rock.'" In *Hannah Arendt: Twenty Years Later*, edited by Larry May and Jerome Kohn, 54–80. Cambridge, MA: MIT Press, 1997.

Branch, Taylor. *At Canaan's Edge.* Vol. 3 of *America in the King Years, 1965–1968.* New York: Simon & Schuster, 2006.

———. *Parting the Waters.* Vol. 1 of *America in the King Years, 1954–1963.* New York: Simon & Schuster, 1988.

———. *Pillar of Fire.* Vol. 2 of *America in the King Years, 1963–1965.* New York: Simon & Schuster, 1998.

Braxton, Joanne. *Black Women Writing Autobiography: A Tradition within a Tradition.* Philadelphia: Temple University Press, 1989.

Brogan, Jacqueline Vaught. "From Warrior to Womanist: The Development of June Jordan's Poetry." In *Speaking the Other Self: American Women Writers,* edited by Jeanne Campbell Ressman, 198–209. Athens: University of Georgia Press, 1997.

Bruss, Elizabeth W. *Autobiographical Acts: The Changing Situation of a Literary Genre.* Baltimore: John Hopkins University Press, 1976.

Buell, Lawrence. "Autobiography in the American Renaissance." In Eakin, *American Autobiography,* 47–69.

Butler, Judith. *Bodies That Matter: On the Discursive Limits of "Sex."* New York: Routledge, 1993.

———. *Gender Trouble: Feminism and the Subversion of Identity.* New York: Routledge, 1990.

Cade, Toni. *The Black Woman: An Anthology.* New York: Mentor/Penguin, 1970.

Cannon, Katie G. *Black Womanist Ethics.* Atlanta: Scholars Press, 1988.

Carby, Hazel V. *Race Men.* W. E. B. Du Bois Lectures. Cambridge, MA: Harvard University Press, 1998.

———. *Reconstructing Womanhood: The Emergence of the Afro-American Woman Novelist.* New York: Oxford University Press, 1987.

Carretta, Vincent. "Olaudah Equiano or Gustavus Vassa? New Light on an Eighteenth-Century Question of Identity." *Slavery and Abolition* 20, no. 3 (December 1999): 96–105.

Carson, Clayborne. *In Struggle: SNCC and the Black Awakening of the 1960s.* Cambridge, MA: Harvard University Press, 1981.

Carson, Clayborne, David J. Garrow, Bill Kovach, and Carol Polsgrove, comps. *Reporting Civil Rights: Part One, American Journalism 1941–1963.* New York: Library of America, 2003.

Cartwright, Keith. *Sacral Grooves, Limbo Gateways: Travels in Deep Southern Time, Circum-Caribbean Space, Afro-creole Authority.* Athens: University of Georgia Press, 2013.

Casey, Leo. "Citizens in Conversation." *Dissent* 53, no. 4 (Fall 2006): 109–111.

Castle, Gregory. *Reading the Modernist Bildungsroman.* Gainesville: University Press of Florida, 2006.

Certeau, Michel de. *The Practice of Everyday Life.* Translated by Steve Randall. Berkeley: University of California Press, 1984.

Chang, Jeff. *Can't Stop, Won't Stop: A History of the Hip-Hop Generation.* New York: St. Martin's, 2005.

———, ed. *Total Chaos: The Art and Aesthetics of Hip-Hop.* New York: Basic Civitas Books, 2006.

———. *Who We Be: The Colorization of America*. New York: St. Martin's, 2014.

Chappell, David L. *A Stone of Hope: Prophetic Religion and the Death of Jim Crow*. Chapel Hill: University of North Carolina Press, 2004.

Chatterjee, Partha. "Whose Imagined Community?" In *The Nation and Its Fragments: Colonial and Postcolonial Histories*, 3–13. Princeton, NJ: Princeton University Press, 1993.

Cherry, Conrad, ed. *God's New Israel: Religious Interpretations of American Destiny*. Englewood Cliffs, NJ: Prentice-Hall, 1971.

Christensen, Linda. *Reading, Writing, and Rising Up: Teaching about Social Justice and the Power of the Written Word*. Washington, DC: Rethinking Schools, 2000.

———. "Warriors Don't Cry: *Brown* Comes to Little Rock." *Rethinking Schools Online* 18, no. 3 (Spring 2004). http://www.rethinkingschools.org/brown/warr183.shtml.

Clark, Gillian, ed. *Augustine: The Confessions*. Landmarks of World Literature, edited by J. P. Stern. Cambridge: Cambridge University Press, 1993.

Cleaver, Eldridge. *Soul on Ice*. New York: McGraw-Hill, 1968.

Clement, Grace. *Care, Autonomy, and Justice*. Boulder, CO: Westview Press, 1998.

Cobb, William Jelani. *The Substance of Hope: Barack Obama and the Paradox of Progress*. New York: Walker, 2010.

———. *To the Break of Dawn: A Freestyle on the Hip-Hop Aesthetic*. New York: New York University Press, 2007.

Cohen, Cathy J. *The Boundaries of Blackness: AIDS and the Breakdown of Black Politics*. Chicago: University of Chicago Press, 1999.

———. "Deviance as Resistance: A New Research Agenda for the Study of Black Politics." *Du Bois Review* 1, no. 1 (2004): 32–40.

Collins, Patricia Hill. *Black Feminist Thought: Knowledge, Consciousness, and the Politics of Empowerment*. 2nd ed. New York: Routledge, 1990.

———. *Fighting Words: Black Women and the Search for Justice*. Minneapolis: University of Minnesota Press, 1998.

Cone, James. *Risks of Faith: The Emergence of a Black Theology of Liberation, 1968–1998*. Boston: Beacon Press, 1999.

Cooper, Brittney. *Race Women: Gender and the Making of a Black Public Intellectual Tradition*. Forthcoming.

———. "A Response to Ta-Nehisi Coates: Why Black Women Are Overlooked—Again." Salon.com, November 6, 2014. http://www.salon.com/2014/11/06/black_women_overlooked_again_a_response_to_ta_nehisi_coates_on_ida_b_wells/.

Couser, G. Thomas. *Memoir: An Introduction*. Oxford: Oxford University Press, 2012.

Cowley, Malcolm. Introduction to *Walt Whitman's "Leaves of Grass": The First (1855) Edition*, edited by Malcolm Cowley, vii–xxxvii. New York: Viking, 1959.

Creighton, Jane. "Writing War, Writing Memory." In Kinloch and Grebowicz, *Still Seeking an Attitude*, 243–255.

Crenshaw, Kimberlé. "Race, Reform, and Retrenchment." *Harvard Law Review* 101, no. 7 (May 1988): 1331–1387.

Crenshaw, Kimberlé, Neil Gotanta, Gary Peller, and Kendall Thomas, eds. *Critical Race Theory: The Key Writings That Formed the Movement*. New York: New Press, 1995.

Culley, Margo, ed. *American Women's Autobiography: Fea(s)ts of Memory*. Madison: University of Wisconsin Press, 1992.

D'Arcy, Steve. "The Rise of the Post-New Left Political Vocabulary." *Public Autonomy Project* (blog), January 27, 2014. http://publicautonomy.org/2014/01/27/the-rise-of-the-post-new-left-political-vocabulary/.

Davies, Carol Boyce. *Black Women, Writing and Identity: Migrations of the Subject*. New York: Routledge, 1994.

Davis, Angela Y. "Afro Images: Politics, Fashion, and Nostalgia." In *Picturing Us: African American Identity in Photography*, edited by Deborah Willis, 170–179. New York: New Press, 1994.

———. "Black Nationalism: The Sixties and the Nineties." In *Black Popular Culture: A Project by Michele Wallace*, edited by Gina Dent, 317–320. Seattle: Bay Press, 1992.

———. "Black Women and the Academy." *Callaloo* 17, no. 2 (Spring 1994): 422–431.

———. "First Lecture on Liberation." In *Narrative of the Life of Frederick Douglass, an American Slave, Written by Himself: A New Critical Edition*, 45–64. San Francisco: Open Media Series/City Lights Books, 2010.

———. *If They Come in the Morning*. New York: Third Press, 1971.

———. Introduction to *Narrative of the Life of Frederick Douglass, an American Slave, Written by Himself: A New Critical Edition*, 21–40. San Francisco: Open Media Series/City Lights Books, 2010.

———. "Racism, Rape, and the Myth of the Black Rapist." In *Women, Race, & Class*, 172–201. New York: Vintage Books, 1983.

———. "Reflections on the Black Woman's Role in the Community of Slaves. *Massachusetts Review* 13, no. 1–2 (Winter/Spring 1972): 81–100.

Davis, Angela, and Kathleen Cleaver. "Rekindling the Flame," a dialogue moderated by Diane Weathers and Tara Roberts. *Essence*, May 1996, 160.

Davis, Charles T., and Henry Louis Gates Jr., eds. *The Slave's Narrative*. New York: Oxford University Press, 1985.

Davis, Dana-Ain. *Battered Black Women and Welfare Reform: Between a Rock and a Hard Place*. Albany: State University of New York Press, 2006.

Davis, Eisa. "Found in Translation: The Emergence of Hip-Hop Theater." In Chang, *Total Chaos*, 70–77.

———. "Sexism and the Art of Feminist Hip-Hop Maintenance." In *To Be Real: Telling the Truth and Changing the Face of Feminism*, edited by Rebecca Walker, 127–141. New York: Anchor Books, 1995.

Davis, Thulani. "June Jordan, 1936–2002." *Village Voice*, June 25, 2002.

Dawson, Michael C. "A Black Counterpublic? Economic Earthquakes, Racial Agenda(s) and Black Politics." *Public Culture* 7 (1994): 195–223.

———. *Black Visions: The Roots of Contemporary African-American Ideologies*. Chicago: University of Chicago Press, 2003.

de Man, Paul. "Autobiography as De-Facement." *Modern Language Notes* 94, no. 5 (December 1979): 919–30.

Dent, Gina, ed. *Black Popular Culture: A Project by Michele Wallace*. Seattle: Bay Press, 1992.

Derrida, Jacques. *The Work of Mourning*. Edited and translated by Pascale-Anne Brault. Chicago: University of Chicago Press, 2003.

De Veaux, Alexis. "Freedom Fighter." *Women's Review of Books: A Feminist Guide to Good Reading* 20, no. 1 (October 2002): 18.

Disch, Lisa Jane. *Hannah Arendt and the Limits of Philosophy*. Ithaca, NY: Cornell University Press, 1994.

Douglass, Kate. *Contesting Childhood: Autobiography, Trauma, and Memory*. New Brunswick, NJ: Rutgers University Press, 2010.

Dubois, Laurent. *Haiti: The Aftershocks of History*. New York: Metropolitan Books/Henry Holt, 2012.

Dufault, Roseanna L. "Edwidge Danticat's Pursuit of Justice in *Brother, I'm Dying*." In "Re-Conceiving Hispaniola," special issue, *Journal of Haitian Studies* 16, no. 1 (Spring 2010): 95–106.

Eagleton, Terry. *Literary Theory: An Introduction*. Minneapolis: University of Minnesota Press, 1983.

Eakin, Paul John, ed. *American Autobiography: Retrospect and Prospect*. Madison: University of Wisconsin Press, 1991.

———. *How Our Lives Become Stories: Making Selves*. Ithaca, NY: Cornell University Press, 1999.

Elfman, Lois. "Author Janet Mock Propels Transgender Conversations in Academia." *Diverse*, April 24, 2014. http://diverseeducation.com/article/63291/.

Elshtain, Jean Bethke. "Political Children." In *Feminist Interpretations of Hannah Arendt*, edited by Bonnie Honig, 263–284. University Park: Penn State University Press, 1995.

Erickson, Peter. "After Identity: A Conversation with June Jordan and Peter Erickson." *Transition*, no. 63 (1994): 132–149.

———. "State of the Union." *Transition*, no. 59 (1993): 104–109.

Espy, Jed. *Unseasonable Youth: Modernism, Colonialism, and the Fiction of Development*. New York: Oxford University Press, 2012.

Fanon, Frantz. "On National Culture." In *The Wretched of the Earth*, translated by Richard Philcox and edited by Francois Maspero, 145–180. New York: Grove Press, 2004. Originally published in Paris, France, 1961.

Felski, Rita. *Beyond Feminist Aesthetics: Feminist Literature and Social Change*. Cambridge, MA: Harvard University Press, 1989.

Flynn, Richard. "'Affirmative Acts': Language, Childhood, and Power in June Jordan's Cross-Writing." In Kinloch and Grebowicz, *Still Seeking an Attitude*, 119–143.

———. "'Infant Sight': Romanticism, Childhood, and Postmodern Poetry." In *Literature and the Child: Romantic Continuations, Postmodern Contestations*, edited by James Holt McGavran, 105–129. Iowa City: University of Iowa Press, 1999.

Folsom, Ed. "Appearing in Print: Illustrations of the Self in *Leaves of Grass*." In Greenspan, *Cambridge Companion to Whitman*, 135–165.

Foreman, P. Gabrielle. *Activist Sentiments: Reading Black Women in the Nineteenth Century*. Urbana: University of Illinois Press, 2009.

———. "Manifest in Signs: The Politics of Sex and Representation in *Incidents in the Life of a Slave Girl*." In Garfield and Zafar, *Harriet Jacobs and "Incidents in the Life of a Slave Girl": New Critical Essays*, 76–99.

———. "The Spoken and the Silenced in *Incidents in the Life of a Slave Girl* and *Our Nig*." *Callaloo* 13 (Spring 1990): 313–324.

Franklin, V. P. *Living Our Stories, Telling Our Truths: Autobiography and the Making of the African American Intellectual Tradition*. New York: Oxford University Press, 1995.

Fraser, Nancy. "Rethinking the Public Sphere: A Contribution to the Critique of Actually Existing Democracy." *Social Text* 25/26 (1990): 56–80.

———. "Sex, Lies, and the Public Sphere: Some Reflections on the Confirmation of Clarence Thomas." *Critical Inquiry* 18, no. 3 (Spring 1992): 595–612.

———. "What's Critical about Critical Theory? The Case of Habermas and Gender." In special issue on Jürgen Habermas, *New German Critique* 35 (Spring–Summer 1985): 97–131.

Freeman, Alan. "Antidiscrimination Law: The View from 1989." In *The Politics of Law: A Progressive Critique*, edited by David Kairys, 121–150. Rev. ed. New York: Pantheon Books, 1990.

Friedman, Susan Stanford. "Women's Autobiographical Selves: Theory and Practice." In S. Smith and Watson, *Women, Autobiography, Theory*, 72–82.

Fuller, Jennifer. "Debating the Present through the Past: Representations of the Civil Rights Movement in the 1990s." In Romano and Raiford, *Civil Rights Movement in American Memory*, 167–196.

Fuss, Diana. "Reading like a Feminist." In *The Essential Difference*, edited by Naomi Schor and Elizabeth Weed, 98–115. Bloomington: Indiana University Press, 1994.

Gaines, Kevin. "The Historiography of the Struggle for Black Equality since 1945." In *A Companion to Post-1945 America*, edited by Jean-Christophe Agnew and Roy Rosenzweig, 211–234. Malden, MA: Blackwell, 2002.

———. *Uplifting the Race: Black Leadership, Politics, and Culture in the Twentieth Century*. Chapel Hill: University of North Carolina Press, 1996.

Garfield, Deborah M., and Rafia Zafar, eds. *Harriet Jacobs and "Incidents in the Life of a Slave Girl": New Critical Essays*. Cambridge: Cambridge University Press, 1996.

Gates, Henry Louis, Jr. *Figures in Black: Words, Signs, and the "Racial" Self*. New York: Oxford University Press, 1987.

———. "Introduction: Talking Book." In *Pioneers of the Black Atlantic: Five Slave Narratives from the Enlightenment, 1772–1815*, edited by Henry Louis Gates Jr. and William L. Andrews. Washington, DC: Civitas Books, 1998.

———, ed. *Reading Black, Reading Feminist: A Critical Anthology*. New York: Meridian/Penguin, 1990.

Gates, Henry Louis, Jr., and Nellie Y. McKay, eds. *The Norton Anthology of African American Literature*. 2nd ed. New York: W. W. Norton, 2004.

George, Nelson. *Hip Hop America*. New York: Viking Penguin, 1998.

Giddings, Paula. *Ida: A Sword among Lions; Ida B. Wells and the Campaign against Lynching*. New York: Amistad, 2009.

———. "The Last Taboo." In S. James, Foster, and Guy-Sheftall, *Still Brave*, 157–171.

———. *When and Where I Enter: A History of Black Women in America*. New York: William Morrow, 1996.

Gikandi, Simon. "Introduction: Africa, Diaspora, and the Discourses of Modernity." In "Black Atlantic," special issue, *Research in African Literatures* 27, no. 4 (Winter 1996): 1–6.

Gilligan, Carol. *In a Different Voice: Psychological Theory and Women's Development*. Cambridge, MA: Harvard University Press, 1982.

Gilmore, Leigh. "American Neoconfessional Memoir, Self-Help, and Redemption on Oprah's Couch." *Biography* 33, no. 4 (Fall 2010): 657–679.

———. *Autobiographics: A Feminist Theory of Women's Self-Representation*. Ithaca, NY: Cornell University Press, 1994.

———. "Limit-Cases: Trauma, Self-Representation, and the Jurisdictions of Identity." *Biography* 24, no. 1 (Winter 2001): 128–139.

———. *The Limits of Autobiography: Trauma and Testimony*. Ithaca, NY: Cornell University Press, 2001.

Gilroy, Paul. *Against Race: Imagining Political Culture beyond the Color Line*. Cambridge, MA: Harvard University Press, 2001.

———. *The Black Atlantic: Modernity and Double Consciousness*. Cambridge, MA: Harvard University Press, 1993.

———. *Postcolonial Melancholia: The Wellek Library Lectures*. New York: Columbia University, 2006.

Gilyard, Keith. "Kinship and Theory." *American Literary History* 11, no. 1 (Spring 1999): 187–195.

Glaude, Eddie S., Jr. "Black Intellectuals Have Sold Their Souls." *New York Times*, April 10, 2013.

———. *Exodus! Religion, Race, and Nation in Early Nineteenth-Century Black America*. Chicago: University of Chicago Press, 2000.

———. *In a Shade of Blue: Pragmatism and the Politics of Black America*. Chicago: University of Chicago Press, 2007.

———, ed. *Is It Nation Time? Contemporary Essays on Black Power and Black Nationalism*. Chicago: University of Chicago Press, 2002.

Goldberg, Stephanie B. "Who's Afraid of Derrick Bell? A Conversation on Harvard, Storytelling, and the Meaning of Color." *American Bar Association Journal*, September 1992, 56–58.

Goldsby, Jacqueline. "'I Disguised My Hand': Writing Versions of the Truth in Harriet Jacobs's *Incidents in the Life of a Slave Girl* and John Jacobs's 'A True Tale of Slavery.'" In Garfield and Zafar, *Harriet Jacobs and "Incidents in the Life of a Slave Girl,"* 11–43.

Gooding-Williams, Robert. *In the Shadow of Du Bois: Afro-Modern Political Thought in America*. Cambridge, MA: Harvard University Press, 2009.

Gore, Dayo, Jeanne Theoharis, and Komozi Woodard, eds. *Want to Start a Revolution? Radical Women in the Black Freedom Struggle*. New York: New York University Press, 2009.

Grant, Jacquelyn. "Womanist Theology: Black Women's Experience as a Source for Doing Theology, with a Special Reference to Christology." In *Black Theology: A Documentary History*, vol. 2, *1980–1992*, edited by James H. Cone and Gayraud S. Wilmore, 273–289. Maryknoll, NY: Orbis, 1993.

Grebowicz, Margret. "Beyond 'Orientation': On Sex, Poetry, and the Violability of Children." In Kinloch and Grebowicz, *Still Seeking an Attitude*, 157–169.

Greene, Cheryll. "Women Talk: A Conversation with June Jordan and Angela Davis." *Essence*, May 1990, 63.

Greenspan, Ezra, ed. *The Cambridge Companion to Walt Whitman*. Cambridge: Cambridge University Press, 1995.

———, ed. *Walt Whitman and the American Reader*. Cambridge: Cambridge University Press, 1990.

Gregory, Eric. "Augustine and Arendt on Love: New Dimensions in the Religion and Liberalism Debates." *Annual of the Society of Christian Ethics* 21 (2001): 155–172.

Griffin, Farah Jasmine. "Conflict and Chorus: Reconsidering Toni Cade's *The Black Woman: An Anthology*." In Glaude, *Is It Nation Time?*, 113–129.

———. "Elaine Brown's *A Taste of Power*." *Boston Review: A Political and Literary Forum* 18, no. 2 (March/April 1993). http://bostonreview.net/archives/BR18.2/griffin.html.

———. "Introduction." Toward an Intellectual History of Black Women: An International Conference, Columbia University, April 28, 2011.

———. "That the Mothers May Soar and the Daughters May Know Their Names: A Retrospective of Black Literary Criticism." In S. James, Foster, and Guy-Sheftall, *Still Brave*, 336–358.

Gutierrez, Gustavo. *The Power of the Poor in History*. Translated by Robert R. Barr. Eugene, OR: Wipf and Stock, 2004.

Gumbs, Alexis Pauline. "Prophecy in the Present Tense: Harriet, the Combahee Pilgrimmage, and Dreams Coming True." *Meridians: feminism, race, transnationalism* 12, no. 2 (2014): 142–152.

Guy-Sheftal, Beverly, ed. *Words of Fire: An Anthology of African-American Feminist Thought*. New York: New Press, 1995.

Habermas, Jürgen. "Further Reflections on the Public Sphere." In *Habermas and the Public Sphere*, edited by Craig Calhoun, 421–461. Cambridge, MA: MIT Press, 1996.

———. *The Structural Transformation of the Public Sphere: An Inquiry into a Category of Bourgeois Society*. Translated by Thomas Burger. Cambridge, MA: MIT Press, 1991.

Hall, Calvin L. *African American Journalists: Autobiography as Memoir and Manifesto*. Lanham, MD: Scarecrow Press, 2009.

Hall, Jacquelyn Dowd. "The Long Civil Rights Movement and the Political Uses of the Past." *Journal of American History* 91, no. 4 (March 2005): 1233–1263.

Haney, Elly. "Pauli Murray: Acting and Remembering." *Journal of Feminist Studies in Religion* 4, no. 2 (Fall 1988): 75–79.

Harding, Vincent. *There Is a River: The Black Struggle for Freedom in America.* New York: Mariner Books, 1993.

Hardy, Clarence E., III. "Imagine a World: Howard Thurman, Spiritual Perception, and American Calvinism." *Journal of Religion* 81, no. 1 (2001): 78–97.

Harris, Duchess. *Black Feminist Politics from Kennedy to Obama.* New York: Palgrave Macmillan, 2011.

Harris, Fredrick C. *Something Within: Religion in African-American Political Activism.* New York: Oxford University Press, 2001.

Harris-Perry, Melissa V. *Sister Citizen: Shame, Stereotypes, and Black Women in America.* New Haven, CT: Yale University Press, 2011.

Hartman, Saidiya. *Scenes of Subjection: Terror, Slavery, and Self-Making in Nineteenth-Century America.* New York: Oxford University Press, 1997.

Hazard, Lucy Lockwood. *The Frontier in American Literature.* New York: Barnes & Noble, 1941.

Henderson, Mae Gwendolyn. "Speaking in Tongues: Dialogics, Dialectics, and the Black Woman Writer's Literary Tradition." In Gates, *Reading Black, Reading Feminist,* 116–142.

Hiatt, Suzanne R. "Pauli Murray: May Her Song Be Heard at Last." Review of *Song in a Weary Throat: An American Pilgrimage,* by Pauli Murray. *Journal of Feminist Studies in Religion* 4, no. 2 (Fall 1988): 69–73.

Hicks, James L. "We Were Kicked, Beaten." In Carson, Garrow, Kovach, and Polsgrove, *Reporting Civil Rights,* 378–381. Originally published in *New York Amsterdam News,* September 28, 1957.

Higginbotham, Evelyn Brooks. *Righteous Discontent: The Women's Movement in the Black Baptist Church, 1880–1920.* Cambridge, MA: Harvard University Press, 1994.

Hine, Darlene Clark. "Rape and the Inner Lives of Black Women in the Middle West: Preliminary Thoughts on the Culture of Dissemblance." *Signs: Journal of Women in Culture and Society* 14 (Summer 1989): 912–920.

Hine, Darlene Clark, Trica Danielle Keaton, and Stephen Small, eds. *Black Europe and the African Diaspora.* Urbana: University of Illinois Press, 2009.

Hinnov, Emily M. *Encountering Choran Community: Literary Modernism, Visual Culture, and Political Aesthetics in the Interwar Years.* Selinsgrove, PA: Susquehanna University Press, 2009.

Hinton-Johnson, Kaavonia. "Taking Children Seriously." In Kinloch and Grebowicz, *Still Seeking an Attitude,* 145–156.

Hirsch, Marianne. *Family Frames: Photography, Narrative, and Postmemory.* Cambridge, MA: Harvard University Press, 1997.

Hirsch, Marianne, and Valerie Smith, eds. "Feminism and Cultural Memory: An Introduction." *Signs: Journal of Women in Culture and Society* 28, no. 1 (Autumn 2002): 1–19.

Hochschild, Adam. "Haiti's Tragic History." *New York Times,* January 29, 2011.

Holland, Sharon Patricia. "'Which Me Will Survive': Audre Lorde and the Development of a Black Feminist Ideology." *Critical Matrix* 4, no. 1 (March 1988): 2–30.

Honig, Bonnie. *Antigone, Interrupted.* Cambridge: Cambridge University Press, 2013.

———. "Antigone's Two Laws: Greek Tragedy and the Politics of Humanism." *New Literary History* 41, no. 1 (Winter 2010): 1–33.

———, ed. *Feminist Interpretations of Hannah Arendt.* University Park, PA: Pennsylvania State University Press, 1994.

Hooke, Alexander E. "Academia: Liberal Bastion or Corporate Dream?" *Baltimore Sun,* July 12, 2011.

Houtchens, Bobbi Ciriza. "A Great Loss; A Treasured Legacy." *English Journal* 92, no. 3 (January 2003): 144.

Howe, Florence, ed. *Tradition and the Talents of Women.* Urbana: University of Illinois Press, 1991.

Humanist Archives. Vol. 6, no. 0661. "6.0661 CFP: Black Women in the Academy (1/73)." Humanist Discussion Group, Call for Papers, April 9, 1993.

Ice-T., with Douglas Century. *Ice: A Memoir of Gangster Life and Redemption—From South Central to Hollywood.* New York: Ballantine Books, 2011.

Iton, Richard. *In Search of the Black Fantastic: Politics and Popular Culture in the Post–Civil Rights Era.* New York: Oxford University Press, 2008.

Jackson, Timothy P. "The Disconsolation of Theology: Irony, Cruelty, and Putting Charity First." *Journal of Religious Ethics* 20, no. 1 (Spring 1992): 1–35.

———. "Liberalism and Agape: The Priority of Charity to Democracy and Philosophy." *Annual of the Society of Christian Ethics* 13 (1993): 47–72.

———. *Love Disconsoled: Meditations on Christian Charity.* Cambridge: Cambridge University Press, 1999.

———. "Love in a Liberal Society." *Journal of Religious Ethics* 22, no. 1 (Spring 1994): 28–38.

———. "To Bedlam and Part Way Back: John Rawls and Christian Justice." *Faith and Philosophy* 8, no. 4 (October 1991): 423–447.

James, Stanlie M., Frances Smith Foster, and Beverly Guy-Sheftall, eds. *Still Brave: The Evolution of Black Women's Studies.* New York: Feminist Press, 2009.

James, Winston. "The History of Afro-Caribbean Migration to the United States." In *In Motion: The African American Migration Experience,* edited by Howard Dodson and Sylviane Dioufe, 156–169. Washington, DC: National Geographic, 2004.

Jelinik, Estelle C., ed. *Women's Autobiography: Essays in Criticism.* Bloomington: Indiana University Press, 1980.

Jocson, Korina. "'Taking It to the Mic': Pedagogy of June Jordan's Poetry for the People and Partnership with an Urban High School." *English Education* 37 (2005): 132–48.

Johnson, Barbara. "My Monster/My Self." *Diacritics* 12, no. 2 (Summer 1982): 2–10.

Johnson, Charles R. "The End of Black American Narrative." In *Best African American Essays 2010,* ed. Gerald Early, 111–122. New York: Ballantine Books, 2009.

Johnson, Clifton H., ed. *God Struck Me Dead: Voices of Ex-Slaves.* Cleveland: Pilgrim, 1993.

Johnson-Feelings, Dianne. "Children's and Young Adult Literature." In *Oxford Companion to African American Literature*, edited by William Andrews, Frances Smith Foster, and Trudier Harris, 133–140. New York: Oxford University Press, 1997.

Joseph, Marc Bamuthi, Kamilah Forbes, Traci Bartlow, and Javier Reyes. "From the Dope Spot to Broadway: A Roundtable on Hip-Hop Theatre, Dance, and Performance." In Chang, *Total Chaos*, 78–91.

Joseph, Peniel E. *Stokely: A Life*. New York: Basic Civitas Books, 2014.

———. *Waiting 'Til the Midnight Hour: A Narrative History of Black Power in America*. New York: Henry Holt, 2006.

———. "Waiting 'Til the Midnight Hour: Reconceptualizing the Heroic Period of the Civil Rights Movement, 1954–1965." *Souls: A Critical Journal of Black Politics, Culture, and Society* 2 (Spring 2000): 6–17.

Junn, Jane, and Kerry L. Haynie, eds. *New Race Politics in America: Understanding Minority and Immigrant Politics*. Cambridge: Cambridge University Press, 2008.

Katzenbach, Nicholas D., Randall L. Kennedy, Patricia J. Williams, and Kevin Kruse. "Brown v. Board of Education, Little Rock, and the Civil Rights Movement." Session 2, "Hannah Arendt and Little Rock: Reflections on the 50th Anniversary of the Desegregation of Central High School," symposium, Princeton University, Princeton, NJ, April 27, 2007.

Kelley, Robin D. G. *Freedom Dreams: The Black Radical Imagination*. Boston: Beacon Press, 2002.

———. "Stormy Weather: Reconstructing Black (Inter)Nationalism in the Cold War Era." In Glaude, *Is It Nation Time?*, 67–90.

Kennedy, Randall. *The Persistence of the Color Line: Racial Politics and the Obama Presidency*. New York: Pantheon, 2011.

Kent, George E. "Maya Angelou's *I Know Why the Caged Bird Sings* and the Black Autobiographical Tradition." In *African American Autobiography: A Collection of Critical Essays*, edited by William L. Andrews, 162–170. Englewood Cliffs, NJ: Prentice-Hall, 1993.

Keppel, Ben. *The Work of Democracy: Ralph Bunche, Kenneth B. Clark, Lorraine Hansberry, and the Cultural Politics of Race*. Cambridge, MA: Harvard University Press, 1986.

King, Martin Luther, Jr. "I See the Promised Land." In Washington, *I Have a Dream*, 193–203.

———. "Where Do We Go From Here?" In Washington, *I Have a Dream*, 169–179.

Kinloch, Valerie. *June Jordan: Her Life and Letters*. Westport, CT: Praeger, 2006.

Kinloch, Valerie, and Margret Grebowicz, eds. *Still Seeking an Attitude: Critical Reflections on the Work of June Jordan*. Lanham, MD: Lexington Books, 2002.

Kitwana, Bikari. *The Hip Hop Generation: Young Blacks and the Crisis in African-American Culture*. New York: Basic Civitas Books, 2002.

Kloppenberg, James. *Reading Obama: Dreams, Hope, and the American Political Tradition*. Princeton, NJ: Princeton University Press, 2011.

Ladner, Joyce A. "Black Women as Doers: The Social Responsibility of Black Women." *Sage: A Scholarly Journal on Black Women* 6, no. 1 (Summer 1989): 87–88.

Lane, Ann M. "Hannah Arendt: Theorist of Distinction(s)." *Political Theory* 25, no. 1 (February 1997): 137–159.

Larrabee, Mary Jeanne, ed. *An Ethic of Care: Feminist and Interdisciplinary Perspectives.* New York: Routledge, 1993.

Lee, Felicia R. "A Feminist Survivor with the Eyes of a Child." *New York Times*, July 4, 2000.

Lejeune, Philippe. "The Autobiographical Pact." In *On Autobiography*, edited by John Paul Eakin and translated by Katherine Leary, 119–137. Minneapolis: University of Minnesota Press, 1989.

Levenstein, Lisa. *A Movement without Marches: African American Women and the Politics of Poverty in Postwar Philadelphia.* Chapel Hill: University of North Carolina Press, 2009.

Levi, Jan Heller, and Sara Miles, eds. *Directed by Desire: The Collected Poems of June Jordan.* Port Townsend, WA: Copper Canyon Press, 2007.

Lewis, Anthony. "President Sends Troops to Little Rock, Federalizes Arkansas National Guard: Tells Nation He Acted to Avoid Anarchy." In Carson, Garrow, Kovach, and Polsgrove, *Reporting Civil Rights*, 382–385. Originally published in *New York Times*, September 25, 1957.

Li, Stephanie. *Something Akin to Freedom: The Choice of Bondage in Narratives by African American Women.* Albany: State University of New York Press, 2011.

———, ed. "Writing the Presidency." Special issue, *American Literary History* 24, no. 3 (Fall 2012).

Lincoln, Abbey. "Who Will Revere the Black Woman?" In Cade, *Black Woman*, 80–84.

Lindenmeyer, Antje. "The Rewriting of Home: Autobiographies by Daughters of Immigrants." *Women's Studies International Forum* 24, no. 3/4 (2001): 423–432.

Livingston, Myra Cohn. *The Child as Poet: Myth or Reality?* Boston: Horn Book, 1984.

Lubiano, Wahneemo. "Standing in for the State: Black Nationalism and 'Writing' the Black Subject." In Glaude, *Is It Nation Time?*, 156–164.

———, ed. *The House That Race Built.* New York: Pantheon Books, 1997.

Mahmood, Saba. *Politics of Piety: The Islamic Revival and the Feminist Subject.* Princeton, NJ: Princeton University Press, 2004.

Marable, Manning. "Race, Identity, and Political Culture." In *Black Popular Culture: A Project by Michele Wallace*, edited by Gina Dent, 292–302. Seattle: Bay Press, 1992.

———. *Race, Reform and Rebellion: The Second Reconstruction in Black America, 1945–1982.* Jackson: University Press of Mississippi, 1984.

Margolick, David, *Elizabeth and Hazel: Two Women of Little Rock.* New Haven, CT: Yale University Press, 2011.

Marshall, Christopher D. *Faith as a Theme in Mark's Narrative.* Cambridge: Cambridge University Press, 1989.

Mason, Mary G. "The Other Voice: Autobiographies of Women Writers." In S. Smith and Watson, *Women, Autobiography, Theory*, 321–324.

May, Larry, and Jerome Kohn, eds. *Hannah Arendt: Twenty Years Later.* Cambridge, MA: MIT Press, 1997.

May, Vivian. *Anna Julia Cooper, Visionary Black Feminist: A Critical Introduction*. New York: Routledge, 2007.

———. "Under-Theorized and Under-Taught: Re-examining Harriet Tubman's Place in Women's Studies." *Meridians: feminism, race, transnationalism* 12, no. 2 (2014): 28–49.

McAdams, Dan P. *The Redemptive Self: Stories Americans Live By*. New York: Oxford University Press, 2006.

McDowell, Deborah E. "Favorite Son." *Women's Review of Books* 18, no. 2 (November, 2000): 1–3.

———. *Leaving Pipe Shop: Memories of Kin*. New York: Scribner's, 1996.

McGuire, Danielle L. *At the Dark End of the Street: Black Women, Rape, and Resistance—A New History of the Civil Rights Movement from Rosa Parks to the Rise of Black Power*. New York: Knopf, 2010.

McKay, Nellie Y. "The Girls Who Became Women: Childhood Memoirs in the Autobiographies of Harriet Jacobs, Mary Church Terrell and Anne Moody." In Howe, *Tradition and the Talents of Women*, 105–124.

———. "A Painful Growth into Selfhood." *Callaloo* 24 (1985): 491–494.

McPherson, James Alan, and Miller Williams, eds. *Railroad: Trains and Train People in American Culture*. New York: Random House, 1976.

Miller, Nancy K. "The Entangled Self: Genre Bondage in the Age of Memoir." *PMLA* 22, no. 2 (March 2007): 537–548.

———. *Getting Personal: Feminist Occasions and Other Autobiographical Acts*. New York: Routledge, 1991.

Minow, Martha. *In "Brown"'s Wake: Legacies of America's Educational Landmark*. New York: Oxford University Press, 2010.

Mock, Janet. *Redefining Realness: My Path to Womanhood, Identity, Love and So Much More*. New York: Atria, 2014.

Moody, Joycelyn. *Sentimental Confessions: Spiritual Narratives of Nineteenth-Century African American Women*. Athens: University of Georgia Press, 2001.

Morris, Aldon D. *The Origins of the Civil Rights Movement: Black Communities Organizing for Change*. New York: Free Press, 1984.

Morrison, Toni, ed. *Race-ing, Justice, En-gendering Power: Essays on Anita Hill, Clarence Thomas, and the Construction of Social Reality*. New York: Pantheon Books, 1992.

Moses, Oral. "What Is a Negro Spiritual?" n.d. http://www.thenegrospiritualinc.com /article_what_is_a_negro_spiritual.htm.

Moses, Wilson Jeremiah. *Black Messiahs and Uncle Toms: Social and Literary Manipulations of a Religious Myth*. University Park: Pennsylvania State University Press, 1982.

———. "Chosen Peoples of the Metropolis: Black Muslims, Black Jews, and Others." In West and Glaude, *African American Religious Thought*, 534–549.

Mostern, Kenneth. *Autobiography and Black Identity Politics: Racialization in Twentieth-Century America*. Cambridge: Cambridge University Press, 1999.

Mukherjee, Bharati. "Immigrant Writing: Changing the Contours of a National Literature." *American Literary History* 23, no. 3 (Fall 2011): 680–696.

Munro, Martin. *Edwidge Danticat: A Reader's Guide*. Charlottesville: University of Virginia Press, 2010.

Murray, Roland. *Our Living Manhood: Literature, Black Power, and Masculine Ideology*. Philadelphia: University of Pennsylvania Press, 2006.

Nadasen, Premilla. "'We Do Whatever Becomes Necessary': Johnnie Tillmon, Welfare Rights and Black Power." In Gore, Theoharis, and Woodard, *Want to Start a Revolution?*, 317–338.

———. *Welfare Warriors: The Welfare Rights Movement in the United States*. New York: Routledge, 2005.

Napier, Winston. *African American Literary Theory: A Reader*. New York: New York University Press, 2000.

Neal, Mark Anthony. "A History of Black Folk on Twitter." TEDxDuke talk, Duke University, Durham, NC, April 19, 2011.

———. *Soul Babies: Black Popular Culture and the Post-Soul Aesthetic*. New York: Routledge, 2002.

Neal, Mark Anthony, and Murray Forman. *That's the Joint: The Hip Hop Studies Reader*. New York: Routledge, 2004.

Nemiroff, Robert. Foreword to *To Be Young, Gifted and Black: An Informal Autobiography*, by Lorraine Hansberry, xvii–xxiii. New York: Signet, 1969.

Newsom, Carol A., and Sharon H. Ringe, eds. *The Women's Bible Commentary*. Louisville, KY: Westminster John Knox Press, 1992.

Newton, Huey P. *Revolutionary Suicide*. New York: Harcourt Brace Jovanovich, 1973.

Nussbaum, Martha C. *Political Emotions: Why Love Matters for Justice*. Cambridge, MA: Harvard University Press, 2013.

Nygren, Anders. *Agape and Eros*. Translated by Philip Watson. Philadelphia: Westminster Press, 1953.

Ogletree, Charles. *All Deliberate Speed: Reflections on the First Half Century of "Brown v. Board of Education."* New York: W.W. Norton, 2004.

Okin, Susan. *Justice, Gender, and the Family*. New York: Basic Books, 1989.

———. "Reason and Feeling in Thinking about Justice." *Ethics* (January 1989): 229–249.

Olney, James, ed. *Autobiography: Essays Theoretical and Critical*. Princeton, NJ: Princeton University Press, 1980.

———. "'I Was Born': Slave Narratives, Their Status as Autobiography and as Literature." In *The Slave's Narrative*, edited by Charles T. Davis and Henry Louis Gates Jr., 148–170. New York: Oxford University Press, 1985.

Olson, Charles. *Proprioception*. San Francisco: Four Seasons Foundation, 1965.

Pace, Patricia. "All Our Lost Children: Trauma and Testimony in the Performance of Childhood." *Text and Performance Quarterly* 18 (1998): 233–247.

Painter, Nell Irvin. "Hill, Thomas, and the Use of Racial Stereotype." In Morrison, *Race-ing Justice, En-gendering Power*, 200–204.

Patterson, Orlando. *Slavery and Social Death: A Comparative Study*. Cambridge, MA: Harvard University Press, 1985.

Payne, Charles. *I've Got the Light of Freedom: The Organizing Tradition and the Mississippi Freedom Struggle*. Berkeley: University of California Press, 1995.

Peppard, Christiana Z. "Poetry, Ethics, and the Legacy of Pauli Murray." *Journal of the Society of Christian Ethics* 30, no. 1 (Spring/Summer 2010): 21–43.

Perkins, Margo V. *Autobiography as Activism: Three Black Women of the Sixties*. Jackson: University Press of Mississippi, 2000.

Perry, Imani. *Prophets of the Hood: Politics and Poetics of Hip Hop*. Durham, NC: Duke University Press, 2005.

Peterson, Carla. *Doers of the Word: African American Women Speakers and Writers in the North (1830–1880)*. New York: Oxford University Press, 1995.

Pierre, Jemima. "Black Immigrants in the United States and the 'Cultural Narratives' of Ethnicity." *Identities: Global Studies in Culture and Power* 11 (2004): 141–170.

Pinn, Anthony B., ed. *Pauli Murray: Selected Sermons and Writings*. Maryknoll, NY: Orbis Books, 2006.

———. "Religion and 'America's Problem Child': Notes on Pauli Murray's Theological Development." *Journal of Feminist Studies in Religion* 15, no. 1 (Spring 1999): 21–39.

Pinto, Samantha. *Difficult Diasporas: The Transnational Feminist Aesthetic of the Black Atlantic*. New York: New York University Press, 2013.

Piven, Frances Fox, and Richard Cloward. *Poor People's Movements: Why They Succeed and How They Fail*. New York: Vintage, 1978.

Politoske, Daniel T., and Martin Werner. *Music*. 4th ed. Englewood Cliffs, NJ: Prentice Hall, 1988.

Poston, Ted. "The 19-Day Ordeal of Minnie Jean Brown." In Carson, Garrow, Kovach, and Polsgrove, *Reporting Civil Rights*, 396–397. Originally published in *New York Post*, February 9, 1958.

Pough, Gwendolyn. *Check It While I Wreck It: Black Womanhood, Hip-Hop Culture, and the Public Sphere*. Boston: Northeastern University Press, 2004.

Powell, Kevin, ed. *Step into a World: A Global Anthology of the New Black Literature*. New York: Wiley, 2000.

Prosser, Jay. "Life Writing and Intimate Publics: A Conversation with Lauren Berlant." *Biography* 34, no. 1 (Winter 2011): 180–187.

Putnam, Amanda. "Braiding Memories: Resistant Storytelling within Mother-Daughter Communities in Edwidge Danticat's *Krik? Krak!*" *Journal of Haitian Studies* 9, no. 1 (Spring 2003): 52–65.

Quashie, Kevin Everod. *Black Women, Identity, and Cultural Theory: (Un)becoming the Subject*. New Brunswick, NJ: Rutgers University Press, 2004.

Raboteau, Albert J. "'Ethiopia Shall Soon Stretch Forth Her Hands': Black Destiny in Nineteenth-Century America." In West and Glaude, *African American Religious Thought*, 397–413.

———. *A Fire in the Bones*. Boston: Beacon Press, 1995.

———. Introduction to *God Struck Me Dead: Voices of Ex-Slaves*. Edited by Clifton H. Johnson, xix–xxv. Cleveland: Pilgrim, 1993.

——. *Slave Religion: The "Invisible Institution" in the Antebellum South*. New York: Oxford University Press, 1978.

Raboteau, Albert J., and David W. Wills. "Editorial Statement." Working draft, December 1999. https://www3.amherst.edu/~aardoc/Editorial_Statement_12_99.html.

Raiford, Leigh. "Restaging Revolution: Black Power, *Vibe* Magazine, and Photographic Memory." In Romano and Raiford, *Civil Rights Movement in American Memory*, 220–250.

Rampersad, Arnold. "Biography, Autobiography, and Afro-American Culture," *Yale Review* 73, no. 1 (October 1983): 1–16.

——. "Psychology and Afro-American Biography." *Yale Review* 78, no. 1 (1988): 1–18.

Reed, Adolph, Jr. "Black Particularity Reconsidered." In Glaude, *Is It Nation Time?*, 39–66.

Reed, Lisa Hull. "(Re)composing Childhood: Representing the Rhythm of Self in Postmodern Memoir." *JASAT* (*Journal of the American Studies Association of Texas*) 41 (November 2010): 17–21.

Reynolds, David S. "Politics and Poetry: *Leaves of Grass* and the Social Crisis of the 1850s." In Greenspan, *Cambridge Companion to Whitman*, 66–91.

Rich, Adrienne. Foreword to *Directed by Desire: The Collected Poems of June Jordan*, edited by Jan Heller Levi and Sara Miles, xxi–xxviii. Port Townsend, WA: Copper Canyon Press, 2007.

Richards, Sandra L. "Ntozake Shange, 1948–." In *African American Writers: Profiles of Their Lives and Works; From the 1700s to the Present*, edited by Valerie Smith, Lea Baechler, and A. Walton Litz, 295–307. New York: Scribner's, 1991.

Rigueur, Leah Wright. *The Loneliness of Black Republicans: Pragmatic Politics and the Pursuit of Power*. Princeton, NJ: Princeton University Press, 2014.

Robinson, Jo Ann Gibson. *The Montgomery Bus Boycott and the Women Who Started It*. Edited by David J. Garrow. Knoxville: University of Tennessee Press, 1987.

Robinson, William H., ed. *Phillis Wheatley and Her Writings*. New York: Garland, 1984.

Rodriguez, Barbara. *Autobiographical Inscriptions: Form, Personhood, and the American Woman Writer of Color*. New York: Oxford University Press, 1999.

Romano, Renee, and Leigh Raiford, eds. *The Civil Rights Movement in American Memory*. Athens: University of Georgia Press, 2006.

Rose, Gillian. *Love's Work*. New York: New York Review Books Classics, 2011.

——. *Mourning Becomes the Law: Philosophy and Representation*. Cambridge: Cambridge University Press, 1996.

Ross, Rosetta E. "Religion and Public Life: Early Traditions of Black Religious Women's Activism." In *Witnessing and Testifying: Black Women, Religion, and Civil Rights*, 1–30. Minneapolis: Fortress Press, 2003.

Satter, Beryl. "Marcus Garvey, Father Divine, and the Gender Politics of Race Difference and Race Neutrality." In West and Glaude, *African American Religious Thought*, 572–604.

Sexton, Jared. *Amalgamation Schemes: Antiblackness and the Critique of Multiculturalism*. Minneapolis: University of Minnesota Press, 2008.

———. "The Social Life of Social Death: On Afro-Pessimism and Black Optimism." *Tensions* 5 (Fall/Winter 2011): 1–47.

Singh, Nikhil Pal. Introduction to *Black Is a Country: Race and the Unfinished Struggle for Democracy*, 1–14. Cambridge, MA: Harvard University Press, 2005.

Smith, Barbara, Beverly Guy-Sheftall, and Paula Giddings. "What Would Harriet Do? A Legacy of Resistance and Activism." *Meridians: feminism, race, transnationalism* 12, no. 2 (2014): 123–141.

Smith, Sidonie, ed. "Autobiographical Discourse in the Theaters of Politics." Special issue, *Biography* 33, no. 1 (Winter 2010).

———. "Performativity, Autobiographical Practice, and Resistance." *a/b: Auto/Biography Studies* 10, no. 1 (Spring 1995): 17–33.

———. *Where I'm Bound: Patterns of Slavery and Freedom in Black American Autobiography.* Westport, CT: Greenwood Press, 1974.

Smith, Sidonie, and Julia Watson, eds. *De/Colonizing the Subject: The Politics of Gender in Women's Autobiography.* Minneapolis: University of Minnesota Press, 1992.

———. *Reading Autobiography: A Guide for Interpreting Life Narratives.* 2nd ed. Minneapolis: University of Minnesota Press, 2010.

———. *Women, Autobiography, Theory: A Reader.* Madison: University of Wisconsin Press, 1998.

Smith, Theophus H. "Exodus." In West and Glaude, *African American Religious Thought*, 309–337.

Smith, Valerie. "'Loopholes of Retreat': Architecture and Ideology in Harriet Jacobs's *Incidents in the Life of a Slave Girl*." In Gates, *Reading Black, Reading Feminist*, 212–226.

———. *Self-Discovery and Authority in Afro-American Narrative.* Cambridge, MA: Harvard University Press, 1987.

———. "Split Affinities." In *Conflicts in Feminism*, edited by Marianne Hirsch and Evelyn Fox Keller, 271–287. New York: Routledge, 1990.

Sollors, Werner. *Beyond Ethnicity: Consent and Dissent in American Culture.* New York: Oxford University Press, 1986.

Spillers, Hortense. *Black, White, and in Color: Essays on American Literature and Culture.* Chicago: University of Chicago Press, 2003.

Splawn, P. Jane. "New World Consciousness in the Poetry of Ntozake Shange and June Jordan: Two African-American Women's Response to Expansionism in the Third World." *College Language Association Journal* 39, no. 2 (June 1996): 417–432.

Springer, Kimberly, ed. *Still Lifting, Still Climbing: African American Women's Contemporary Activism.* New York: New York University Press, 1999.

Squires, Catherine R. "Rethinking the Black Public Sphere: An Alternative Vocabulary for Multiple Public Spheres." *Communication Theory* 12, no. 4 (November 2002): 446–468.

Steinberg, Stephen. "The Liberal Retreat from Race." In Lubiano, *The House That Race Built*, 13–47.

Stepto, Robert B. *From Behind the Veil: A Study of Afro-American Narrative.* Urbana: University of Illinois Press, 1979.

Stone, Albert E. "Modern American Autobiography: Texts and Transactions." In Eakin, *American Autobiography*, 95–120.

Stover, Johnnie M. "Nineteenth-Century African American Women's Autobiography as Social Discourse: The Example of Harriet Jacobs." *College English* 66, no. 2 (November 2003): 133–154.

———. *Rhetoric and Resistance in Black Women's Autobiography*. Tallahassee: University Press of Florida, 2003.

Sutton, Soraya Sablo, and Sheila Menezes. "In Remembrance of June Jordan, 1963–2002." *Social Justice* 29, no. 4 (2002): 205–206.

Tanner, Kathryn. "The Care That Does Justice: Recent Writings on Feminist Ethics and Theology." *Journal of Religious Ethics* 24, no. 1 (1996): 171–191.

Taylor, Ula. *The Veiled Garvey: The Life and Times of Amy Jacques Garvey*. Chapel Hill: University of North Carolina Press, 2001.

Tate, Claudia, ed. *Black Women Writers at Work*. New York: Continuum, 1984.

Terrell, Tom. "June Swoon: Reflections of a Poet and Activist as a Young Girl." *Vibe*, September 2000, 120.

Thompson, Deborah. "Reversing Blackface Minstrelsy, Improvising Racial Identity: Adrienne Kennedy's *Funnyhouse of a Negro*." *Post Identity* 1, no. 1 (Fall 1997).

Thurman, Howard. *The Creative Encounter*. Richmond, IN: Friends United Press, 1972.

———. *Deep River: The Negro Spiritual Speaks of Life and Death*. Richmond, IN: Friends United Press, 1975.

———. *Jesus and the Disinherited*. Richmond, IN: Friends United Press, 1976.

———. *The Luminous Darkness*. Richmond, IN: Friends United Press, 1989.

———. *A Strange Freedom: The Best of Howard Thurman on Religious Experience and Public Life*. Edited by Walter Earl Fluker and Catherine Tumber. Boston: Beacon Press, 1998.

Torf, Adrienne. "Remembering June Jordan." *Women's Review of Books*, October 2002, 15–19.

Touré. *Who's Afraid of Post-Blackness? What It Means to Be Black Now*. New York: Free Press, 2011.

Tronto, Joan. *Moral Boundaries: A Political Argument for an Ethic of Care*. New York: Routledge, 1994.

Vermillion, Mary. "Reembodying the Self: Representations of Rape in *Incidents in the Life of a Slave Girl* and *I Know Why the Caged Bird Sings*." *Biography* 15, no. 3 (Summer 1992): 243–260.

von Heyking, John. *Augustine and Politics as Longing in the World*. Columbia: University of Missouri Press, 2001.

———. "Politics between the Earthly City and the City of God in Christianity." Paper presented at the Cooperation of Church and State Conference, Cardus Centre for Cultural Renewal, Alberta, Calgary, June 9, 2006. http://www.cardus.ca/columns /2471/.

Walker, Pierre A. "Racial Protest, Identity, Words, and Form in Maya Angelou's *I Know*

Why the Caged Bird Sings." In "Race and Politics: The Experience of African-American Literature," special issue, *College Literature* 22, no. 3 (October 1995): 91–108.

Walker, Rebecca, ed. *To Be Real: Telling the Truth and Changing the Face of Feminism.* New York: Anchor Books, 1995.

Wall, Cheryl A., ed. *Changing Our Own Words: Essays on Criticism, Theory, and Writing by Black Women.* New Brunswick, NJ: Rutgers University Press, 1989.

Wallace, Michele. *Black Macho and the Myth of the Superwoman.* New York: Dial Press, 1978.

Warren, Kenneth W. "Ralph Ellison and the Problem of Cultural Authority." *boundary 2* 30, no. 2 (Summer 2003): 157–174.

———. *What Was African American Literature?* W.E.B. Du Bois Lectures. Cambridge, MA: Harvard University Press, 2012.

Warren, Robert Penn. "Interview with Ralph Ellison." In *Who Speaks for the Negro?*, 325–354. New York: Vintage Books/Random House, 1965.

Washington, James M., ed. *I Have a Dream: Writing and Speeches That Changed the World.* New York: HarperSanFrancisco, 1986.

Waters, Mary. *Black Identities: West Indian Immigrant Dreams and American Realities.* Cambridge, MA: Harvard University Press, 1999.

Werner, Craig. "On the Ends of Afro-American 'Modernist' Autobiography." *Black American Literature Forum* 24, no. 2 (Summer 1990): 203–220.

West, Cornel. "The Paradox of the African American Rebellion." In Glaude, *Is It Nation Time?*, 2–38.

———. *Prophesy Deliverance! An Afro-American Revolutionary Christianity.* Philadelphia: Westminster, 1982.

———. *Race Matters.* Boston: Beacon Press, 1993.

West, Cornel, and Eddie S. Glaude Jr., eds. *African American Religious Thought: An Anthology.* Louisville, KY: Westminster John Knox Press, 2003.

West, Guida. *The National Welfare Rights Organization: The Social Protest of Poor Women.* New York: Praeger, 1981.

White, Aaronette. "Talking Black, Talking Feminist: Gendered Mobilization Processes in a Collective Protest against Rape." In Springer, *Still Lifting, Still Climbing,* 189–218.

White, Deborah Gray, ed. *Telling Histories: Black Women Historians in the Ivory Tower.* Chapel Hill: University of North Carolina Press, 2008.

White, E. Frances. *Dark Continent of Our Bodies: Black Feminism and the Politics of Respectability.* Philadelphia: Temple University Press, 2001.

Wilderson, Frank B., III. *Incognegro: A Memoir of Exile and Apartheid.* Cambridge, MA: South End Press, 2008.

———. *Red, White, and Black: Cinema and the Structure of U.S. Antagonisms.* Durham, NC: Duke University Press, 2010.

Wilkerson, Isabel. "The Late Jim Crow." *New York Times,* June 15, 1997.

Wilkerson, Margaret B. "The Sighted Eyes and Feeling Heart of Lorraine Hansberry." In "Black Theatre," special issue, *Black American Literature Forum* 17, no. 1 (Spring 1983): 8–13.

Williams, Juan, and Quinton Dixie. "Black Gods in the City." In *This Far by Faith: Stories from the African-American Religious Experience*, 171–197. New York: Amistad, 2003.

Winfrey Harris, Tamara. *The Sisters Are Alright: Changing the Broken Narrative of Black Women in America*. Oakland: Berrett-Koehler, 2015.

Wong, Sau-ling Cynthia. "Immigrant Autobiography: Some Questions of Definition and Approach." In S. Smith and Watson, *Women, Autobiography, Theory*, 299–315.

Woods, Clyde, ed. *In the Wake of Katrina: New Paradigms and Social Visions*. Baltimore: Johns Hopkins University Press, 2010.

Wright, Michelle M. *Becoming Black: Creating Identity in the African Diaspora*. Durham, NC: Duke University Press, 2004.

Wuthnow, Robert. *American Mythos: Why Our Best Efforts to Be a Better Nation Fall Short*. Princeton, NJ: Princeton University Press, 2006.

Yoshino, Kenji. *Covering: The Hidden Assault on Our Civil Rights*. New York: Random House, 2006.

———. "The End of Civil Rights? The Supreme Court's Rejection of Identity Politics." James A. Moffett '29 Lecture, Princeton University, Princeton, NJ, April 5, 2007.

Young-Bruehl, *Hannah Arendt: For Love of the World*. New Haven, CT: Yale University Press, 1982.

Index

abolitionism, 7
absence, 22
academia, 56, 79–81
Activist Sentiments (Foreman), 16
adventure-time, 122
aesthetics. *See* Black Aesthetic; care (political emotion); politics
affect: gendering of, 20, 30, 57–58; political emotions and, 8, 16–18, 55, 57–58, 67–78, 98–105, 129, 132–134, 144–152, 154
affirmative action, 58
African Americans: academia and, 56–60, 79–81, 157–162; black counterpublics and, 14–15, 25, 166n41; Black Power movement and, 5, 9, 15, 21–22, 24, 62, 73–75, 79, 102, 128–137, 140–142, 146–147, 151, 170n6; children's literature and, 88–89; church organizations and, 12–14, 36, 39–40; citizenship and, 6, 12–18, 29–36, 48–55, 108–111, 119–125, 160; class politics within, 46–47; cultural prominence of, 15–18, 126–129; diasporic imagination and, 4, 12–13, 19, 22–24, 80–81, 106–129, 156–157; feminist thought and, 3–6, 21–22, 44, 56–60, 153–157; immigrants as, 22–23, 82, 106–125, 156; political traditions of, 10–16, 67–78, 92, 108–109, 126–129; religious tropes and, 12–14, 36–40, 64, 71–72, 86; stereotypes and, 11, 18, 21, 29, 36–38, 48, 50–51, 56–60, 98, 127, 146–147, 153; subject formation and, 5–8, 50, 122–125, 130, 133–134, 151; unity of, 63–64,

92, 166n41. *See also* Black Power movement; civil rights movement; race; racism; slave narratives
agency, 3, 68–72, 80–81, 86, 89–90, 93–94, 122
Aid to Needy Children–Mothers Anonymous, 62
"Ain't Gonna Let Nobody Turn Me Around" (freedom song), 28
Alcott, Louisa May, 75–76
Alexander, Elizabeth, 157
Alexander, Michelle, 14
Ali, Muhammad, 141
alien (term), 82
all deliberate speed, 27
All Deliberate Speed (Ogletree), 45–46
Allen, Danielle, 26, 40, 42, 49
An American Dilemma (Myrdal), 8
American Theatre, 131
Anderson, Benedict, 15
Angela Davis (Davis), 4, 21, 147–148, 155
Angela's Ashes (McCourt), 80
Angela's Mixtape (Davis), 5, 24, 126–152
Angelou, Maya, 18, 26, 48, 51
Anita (Mock), 160
"Another Country" (Danticat), 107
Antigone (Sophocles), 110–114, 116, 120, 122, 160
Antigone, Interrupted (Honig), 111
Ards, Angela, 3
Arendt, Hannah, 19–20, 28, 38–39, 42–44, 51, 158
Aristede, Jean-Bertrand, 112, 116
Arkansas Democrat, 31

217

Wisconsin Studies in Autobiography

WILLIAM L. ANDREWS
Series Editor

My Generation: Collective Autobiography and Identity Politics
John Downton Hazlett

Jumping the Line: The Adventures and Misadventures of an American Radical
William Herrick

Women, Autobiography, Theory: A Reader
Edited by Sidonie Smith and Julia Watson

The Making of a Chicano Militant: Lessons from Cristal
José Angel Gutiérrez

Rosa: The Life of an Italian Immigrant
Marie Hall Ets

Illumination and Night Glare: The Unfinished Autobiography of Carson McCullers
Carson McCullers
Edited with an introduction by Carlos L. Dews

Who Am I? An Autobiography of Emotion, Mind, and Spirit
Yi-Fu Tuan

The Life and Adventures of Henry Bibb: An American Slave
Henry Bibb
With a new introduction by Charles J. Heglar

Diaries of Girls and Women: A Midwestern American Sampler
Edited by Suzanne L. Bunkers

The Autobiographical Documentary in America
Jim Lane

Caribbean Autobiography: Cultural Identity and Self-Representation
Sandra Pouchet Paquet

How I Became a Human Being: A Disabled Man's Quest for Independence
Mark O'Brien, with Gillian Kendall

*Campaigns of Curiosity: Journalistic Adventures of an American Girl in Late
    Victorian London*
Elizabeth L. Banks
Introduction by Mary Suzanne Schriber and Abbey L. Zink

Mark Twain's Own Autobiography: The Chapters from the "North American Review,"
    second edition
Mark Twain
Edited by Michael J. Kiskis

Graphic Subjects: Critical Essays on Autobiography and Graphic Novels
Edited by Michael A. Chaney

A Muslim American Slave: The Life of Omar Ibn Said
Omar Ibn Said
Translated from the Arabic, edited, and with an introduction by Ala Alryyes

Sister: An African American Life in Search of Justice
Sylvia Bell White and Jody LePage

Identity Technologies: Constructing the Self Online
Edited by Anna Poletti and Julie Rak

Masked: The Life of Anna Leonowens, Schoolmistress at the Court of Siam
Alfred Habegger

We Shall Bear Witness: Life Narratives and Human Rights
Edited by Meg Jensen and Margaretta Jolly

Dear World: Contemporary Uses of the Diary
Kylie Cardell

Words of Witness: Black Women's Autobiography in the Post-"Brown" Era
Angela A. Ards

A Mysterious Life and Calling: From Slavery to Ministry in South Carolina
Reverend Mrs. Charlotte S. Riley
Edited with an introduction by Crystal J. Lucky

Made in the USA
Middletown, DE
07 July 2016